RUNNING THROUGH THE WALL

RUNNING THROUGH THE WALL

Personal Encounters with the Ultramarathon

Neal Jamison

BREAKAWAY BOOKS
HALCOTTSVILLE, NEW YORK
2003

ISBN: 1-891369-37-7
ISBN-13: 978-1-891369-37-7
Library of Congress Control Number: 2003102245

Published by Breakaway Books
P.O. Box 24
Halcottsville, NY 12438
(800) 548-4348
www.breakawaybooks.com

Contents

Acknowledgments

I would like to thank the following people for helping an idea become reality:

The ultrarunning community: You are the fellow runner who gave me an electrolyte capsule when I was having problems just 20 miles into the Masochist, or gave me some much-needed words of encouragement as you passed me on the long climb up the mountain. You are the crew that gave a blistered and battered stranger a ride to the next aid station. You are the aid station volunteer who gave a fellow runner your gloves and then stayed well into the cold evening to see the last runner fed and the last crumpled cup cleaned from the trail. You are the woman struggling down the road, who in return for my help gave me a big smile and a thumbs-up at the finish line. Without you, no one would ever run through the wall.

Kara Douglass Thom: It was your collection of essays—*Becoming an Ironman*—that sparked the idea.

My agent, Neil Salkind: Thanks for greeting the idea with excitement and encouragement—and then passing it along.

Garth Battista and Breakaway Books: Thanks for accepting my proposal and continuing to publish some of the best running books in print.

All 40-plus contributors: Thank you for putting up with my incessant e-mails and phone calls asking for more, more, more. I'd especially like to recognize Francesca Conte, David Horton, Clark Zealand, Ian Torrence, and Ed Demoney. My idea for a book like this would likely have withered away without your early enthusiasm and support.

David Horton: Your name appears in many of the essays in this book. And there is a good reason for that. You have introduced many to the sport of ultrarunning. You also head up some of Virginia's best ultra events. Every time I run with you, I walk away with tired legs and a new idea for my next writing project. My wife, after reading all of the essays in the book, told me I needed to name the book after you. Sorry, Horton, but maybe the next one . . .

Don Allison at *UltraRunning Magazine:* Thank you for supporting my endeavor, and for continuing with those of your own.

Everyone on the Ultra List: Thanks for posting those race reports and keeping the sport what it's supposed to be: fun.

Suzanne, my wife: You read, edited, and reread these stories again and again, and found innovative ways to tell me that they still needed work. You also put up with my chronic need to "go check e-mail" (even if I just checked it 20 minutes ago) or "work on the book" when I should have been spending time with you and Evan.

To Evan: May stories like these someday show you that there are no boundaries. Cross the finish line and keep on running.

—NSJ

Foreword

BY DON ALLISON
EDITOR/PUBLISHER, *ULTRARUNNING MAGAZINE*

For the uninitiated, running ultra distances can be difficult to comprehend. Most are aware of 26.2-mile marathons, since they are held in nearly every sizable city, state, and country. Still, the existence of events that go beyond 26.2 miles is surprising to many. The fact is, however, that ultrarunning has been around almost as long as history itself. Man's attempt to cover extremely long distances on foot dates back to the ancient Greeks and beyond.

For most of history, ultra distance running had few organized events. Mostly it consisted of random individual efforts. After a brief surge of popularity in the late 19th century—fueled primarily by wagers on the outcome of indoor 6-day races—the sport slipped back into obscurity. Late in the 20th century, however, ultrarunning began to pick up momentum once again. As it became evident that even those not blessed with great athletic prowess could successfully complete long-distance running adventures, the sport began to take hold. More and more organized ultramarathons grew and flourished, especially those conducted on trails, within viewing distance of nature's splendor. While ultrarunning has not experienced a popularity explosion such as the standard marathon has, it has found its place in the sporting realm.

More than almost any other sporting endeavor, ultra distance running is personal in nature. Perhaps it is the overwhelming magnitude of the task that causes participants to look inward and examine the deep motivations for challenging themselves in this way. Or rather, perhaps it is simply the length of time spent training and on the course that leads to such introspection. As such, behind every participant in every race there is a story. Behind every runner, there is a history that leads them to the starting line of an ultramarathon, and that history colors the drama that plays out over the duration of the event. In *Running Through the Wall: Personal Encounters with the Ultramarathon*, Neal Jamison has assembled 39 stories by over 40 different individuals from over 40 different walks of life. A common thread runs through all of the stories: All of the contributors sought to challenge themselves in this most physical—and mental—of sports. However, each story is as unique as the person telling it is. From first-time ultrarunner and mother-of-three Sophie Speidel to national champions Kevin Setnes and Ann Trason, *Running Through the Wall* presents a full spectrum of experiences.

Embedded within each of these stories is an account of how the contributor came to terms with the inevitable question: "Why?" Why would anyone subject themselves to the pain and discomfort that is an inevitable part of attempting to complete an ultra distance race? Why, when the apparent rewards are so few and the time, effort, and energy required so immense? The answers to these questions are of course determined by individual life experiences and are graphically displayed in *Running Through the Wall*. All of the cornerstone events of life—love, marriage, and friendship, as well as illness, injury, and death—have a profound impact on why ultrarunners take up the challenge of the sport, as shown in each of the 39 stories contained in the book. For some, the obstacles necessary to overcome just to reach the starting line were immense. For others, life events paved the way toward their ultrarunning attempts. For some, ultrarunning provided a necessary escape from tragedy. For others, ultrarunning was an expression of life's goodness.

In addition to learning how each of these ultrarunners answers the eternal question of "why," we also witness how each adventure unfolds. In doing so, we learn that ultimately, it is the sheer challenge that draws us to the sport of ultrarunning. Somewhere within each of these contributors—and within the thousands of others who run ultramarathons—lies a spark of motivation that has ignited the tremendous fire of courage and determination necessary to complete an ultramarathon.

Introduction

NEAL JAMISON

I first took up running in middle school, where I ran the quarter-mile for a track team that, to my recollection, never won a meet. I distinctly remember practice on Wednesdays, when the coach let the milers and cross-country runners have their way with us. I hated those long runs. On more than one occasion I hid in the woods with the shotputters and discus throwers to avoid the pain and suffering. The next time I approached running, I was in college, searching for a way to combat some freshman-year weight gain. This time, however, I tolerated the long runs simply because I knew they would help take off the weight. I discovered road racing as a means of motivating myself to run. 5-kilometer fun runs turned into 10-kilometer fun runs. And before long I was running my first marathon. Like many young runners, I was naive and understood little about proper training, diet, hydration, and so on, and it became painfully obvious when I hit "The Wall" at about 18 miles. Somehow I fought through the pain and finished. But I would never do that again. At least that's what I thought.

Then I moved to Hawaii and met Sandra. I was running at the time, but only short distances in an attempt to stay in shape. Sandra seemed to religiously and effortlessly run 10 miles before breakfast. I, on the other hand, had to force myself to trudge through 2 miles before bedtime. But as we began running together, her dedication and good habits started to rub off on me. I found myself running longer, getting stronger, and training smarter. It was not long before I was running another marathon.

This time, however, I had the proper training and knowledge to get me through "The Wall." I crossed the finish line ready for more—and Sandra was there to help. She talked me into running my first ultra: the Honolulu City Lights 50K—a run that took place in the rain, at night, around a 0.75-mile city block. It might sound monotonous (and in some ways, it was), but with an aid station every 0.75 mile and good crowd support, it turned out to be the perfect first ultra. I was hooked. My second ultra, the Hilo to Volcano 50K, found me crossing the finish line in the top two overall—a phenomenon that had never happened before, and will probably never happen again. Then I took the next logical step and ran my first 50-miler.

Not too long after that 50-mile run, I moved back to Virginia, started a new job and a family, and my running became less of a priority. I still had a love for distance running, but in my mind I just didn't have the time to do it. A couple of years later, I was doing some freelance writing, and an article on trail running led me to the office of ultrarunning guru Dr. David Horton. Before long I was joining him and a few other area ultrarunners on the trails around southwestern Virginia. As we ran, we talked about everything from food to movies to, of course, running. I found out that if you spend enough time running in the woods with an ultrarunner, you *will* hear a great ultrarunning story. It's inevitable. It got me thinking . . .

Around that same time I happened to pick up a copy of Kara Douglass Thom's book, *Becoming an Ironman: Personal Encounters with the Ultimate Endurance Event.* As I read those inspiring stories of first Ironman triathlon experiences, it suddenly occurred to me that there needed to be a similar collection of stories about ultrarunning. After all, it is impossible to run for distances of 50 or 100 miles without coming away with at least one great story to tell! I pitched the idea to a book agent I had worked with in the past. He thought it was a great idea, we presented it to Breakaway Books, and the rest is history. Well almost. Now I had to solicit, compile, edit, and deliver between 30 and 40 personal encounters with the ultramarathon.

My first step was to get in touch with a few runners whom I felt sure would support me. These were the runners I knew personally, those whom I ran with regularly or had run with in the past. With a handful of them on board, I sought out other runners. A vision for the book was already imprinted in my mind, so I personally contacted a few runners whom I felt needed to be a part of this collection in order for it to seem credible or complete. These are the names you will likely recognize as you scan through the table of contents. I also posted a request for submissions to the Internet Ultra List, and the e-mails started rolling in. Before long I was busy with interviews, e-mails, editing, and writing. The book was coming together.

There are some common elements to the stories you are about to read. Sure, there is an inevitable amount of fatigue, blisters, nausea, pain, and despair. It is impossible to downplay or hide that. But there is also a lot of hope, love, self-discovery, friendship, community, selflessness, and, in the end, triumph. And there is also a lot to learn.

These stories will teach you that it is possible to find healing on the trails, whether it be in a Texas park, on a Virginia mountain, or on sacred grounds in an Hawaiian rain forest. They will convince you that even if a mountain or a muddy trail brings you to your knees, all you can do is get up and go at it again. You will see that bonds can form over the course of an ultra—teams grow closer, friends are made, and, sometimes, you find love. Through these stories you will learn that our bodies are capable of going much farther and much harder than our minds can sometimes imagine. But you will also learn that no matter how strong we are, there will come a time to quit.

This book has allowed me to learn from ultrarunners who have been there and seen it all. There are countless lessons among these pages from seasoned veterans like Blake Wood, Suzi Cope, Stan Jensen, and Tim Twietmeyer. But there is also a lot to learn from the younger runners who have a fresh perspective of what it takes to succeed as an ultrarunner. There is a throng of fast, young talent on the rise, and they are represented herein by the likes of Bethany Hunter, Clark Zealand, Krissy Moehl, and Ian Torrence.

Working on this book also allowed me to spend some time with a few of the champions and gurus of our sport. A phone call with Kevin Setnes taught me about the running/walking strategy he employed to control his speed and get him through the 1993 Olander 24-hour race (and earn an American record in the process). David Horton explained in detail how he and Blake Wood became the first Americans to finish the impossible-to-finish Barkley Marathon. I also discussed the popular Western States 100 with two runners who have found much success at its finish line: Ann Trason and Tim Twietmeyer.

Some of my favorite stories, however, are from the names that you will most likely not recognize. These are the runners who finish in the middle or the back of the pack (or even last in more than one case), or "DNF"—do not finish at all. Perhaps I enjoy these because, I too, am just an average ultrarunner. But there is more to it than that. These runners demonstrate that anyone can run an ultra, whether you are a retired marine, a working mother of three, a busy executive, or a member of a popular rock band. All it takes is some dedication, a little training, and the attitude that you can do it. Really, you can.

Feeling Blessed at the Kettle Moraine 100

NAME: BOB METZGER
AGE: 51
RESIDENCE: LAKEVILLE, MINNESOTA
YEARS RUNNING: 13
YEARS RUNNING ULTRAS: 6 1/2

On the Kettle Moraine 100 web site, my name is listed as a "100-mile solo" finisher. That's not the way I see it. Yesterday morning at 10:28 A.M.—28 hours, 28 minutes, and some number of seconds after I started—I crossed the finish line at the Kettle Moraine 100-mile trail run. My training partner and best buddy, Jeff Wold, who planted the "ultra" seed in my mind back in 1995, was at my side, just as he had been since mile 62. My devoted crew, Anna Belu and Kathy Casale, were there waiting and cheering, just as they had been at every crew-accessible aid station along the way. Anna was taking pictures and writing down the numbers. Kathy was wiping a tear from her eye. Race Director Tim Yanacheck came out with a big smile, shook my hand, and handed me my finisher's award. Another friend and occasional training partner, Scott Wagner, smiled at me from the chair into which he had collapsed three minutes earlier. And yet another good buddy and training partner, Larry Pederson, who had paced Scott for those last 38 miles, beamed at me, grinning from ear to ear. Yeah, I'm blessed.

I bought my first pair of running shoes in 1989, and began walking and running to stay in shape. In 1992, I entered the Austin Motorola Marathon as part of a corporate relay team. It was the first race I had ever entered. We had a great time and ran well, but I was totally in awe of the people who were running the whole 26.2 miles. Here I was, doing a 5-mile relay leg, being applauded and cheered on by the soloists I was passing. I was stunned not only by their ability to run a full marathon, but also by their spirit. I told my teammates that one day I would run a marathon. The following year, I ran a half marathon. I had a great first 10 miles, followed by a very tough last 5 kilometers. I hurt for days, and decided that the marathon relay might just be the closest I would get to my 26.2-mile dream.

Layoffs at the company for which I worked threw my training into upheaval. I found my training partners scattered hither and yon, and my life was disrupted in all sorts of ways. I changed jobs, and ran by myself a lot. But my new job was unsatisfying, and my running was unfocused. My marathon training plans were put on hold, but not forgotten. Another change in employment took me to Minnesota on a 6-month contract. Due to the short length of time I would be there, it made no sense for my wife, Chris Markham, and our two sons, Aidan and Ari, to relocate. They stayed behind in Austin, and I vowed to make the best of my time alone and began training for the 1996 Austin Motorola Marathon.

I immediately fell into a bad crowd known as the Dead Runners Society. Upon hearing of my marathon training plans, my new running buddy Jeff advised that I sign up for the Twin Cities Marathon, to be held the first Saturday of October. In a moment of mental weakness, I sent in my entry. I ran some long training runs with my new friends and other folks I met, and had an amazingly strong run at the marathon, finishing in 3:57. Within days, Jeff handed me a Sunmart 50K registration form. Sunmart takes place in Texas, not too far from my home. It coincided nicely with plans to visit my family, so I quickly signed up. Jeff and I ran it, while Chris crewed for us both. The rest is history.

I ran more and more races over the next two years, and got to enjoy seeing Chris and our younger son, Ari, follow in my footsteps. I then ruptured an Achilles tendon in October 2000, and had to work very hard to get back to my pre-injury fitness level. In order to prove to myself that I had achieved that goal, I decided to try something that I had dreamed about since discovering ultrarunning: a 100-mile trail run. The Kettle Moraine 100 was a logical choice, because it is within a day's drive, is on a course with which I am familiar, and is considered a reasonable choice for a first 100 in terms of difficulty.

I stepped up my training in preparation for Kettle Moraine, which included more frequent long runs, more upper-body work in the gym, and more nighttime trail running. I also studied the trail maps, trying to visualize the course. Three weeks before Kettle Moraine, I ran the Ice Age 50, which covers many of the same trails as the Kettle Moraine 100. I was ready to face my dream.

Anna, Kathy, and I left the Twin Cities around 10:00 A.M. on Friday. During the six hours that it took to reach LaGrange, Wisconsin, we talked, listened to music, ate heartily, took turns driving, and had a lot of fun. At about 5:30 that afternoon we checked into the motel and went to packet pickup. I chatted with a runner friend, Christine Crawford, about the warm weather as other familiar faces came and went. I felt very relaxed and ready for my first 100-mile trail run. Other than being a little worried about the heat, I felt confident that I was as trained and ready as I could be.

I slept fitfully that night, apparently more apprehensive about things than I had realized. I woke a number of times, sleeping for about four or five hours total. When the alarm went off at 4:25, I got up immediately to get dressed and eat my breakfast. I didn't feel nervous, but the state of my stomach would indicate otherwise. I ate a peanut butter and banana sandwich on whole wheat bread, a yogurt, and some fresh watermelon. I washed it all down with a pint of orange juice. I tried to be quiet and let my crew get as much sleep as possible. As soon as I was dressed, I stepped outside to check the temperature and look for Jeff. His plan was to arrive around 5:00 A.M. and tumble into one of the beds we would be abandoning. He needed a good day's sleep before assuming pacing duties later that night. Jeff was there, as expected, and within a few minutes my crew and I were headed for the start, and Jeff was sound asleep in the room.

The temperature at the bank in Whitewater was a cool but muggy 56 degrees as we passed by at around 5:15. There wasn't a cloud in the sky, and it was already apparent that the day would heat up quickly. My stomach was feeling queasy, probably a combination of too little sleep, too much breakfast, and nerves. I figured (and hoped) the feeling would pass once I was running. The pre-race atmosphere was low-key, as is typical at a trail ultra. There were lots of hugs, handshakes, and wishes of good luck going around. Anna and Kathy each hugged me right before the start. I think the race director, Tim Yanacheck, issued the start command, but I didn't hear it. At 6:00 sharp, 83 runners headed off into the woods on a 100-mile adventure.

I ran conservatively, drawing on my experience of 30 previous ultras, which included four 24-hour races. As expected, the temperature rose quickly, and I drank steadily from my CamelBak. But unexpectedly, my stomach continued to feel somewhat upset. The smiling faces of Kathy and

Anna at mile 7.5 gave me a huge lift, and the concern on Anna's face (after I spent about five minutes in the Porta-Potti at that aid station) touched me. These two friends had each taken a vacation day and devoted an entire weekend to support me in my 100-mile quest. And Jeff had driven through the night in order to be there to pace me and kick my butt when I slowed. There was no way I could let these people down. I ate some crystallized ginger that I had brought along for battling stomach upset, and headed out on the long stretch to the 31-mile turnaround.

The first 16 miles are well shaded, and the ginger seemed to be doing its job. This part of the course is quite runnable, and I had to force myself to take walking breaks. The ginger had calmed my stomach pretty well, and I was running strong and on pace to easily finish under the 30-hour limit. Shortly after mile 16, however, there are some long stretches of unshaded meadows. The trails are very runnable, but very exposed to the sun. Knowing my usual vulnerability to heat, I became even more diligent about forcing myself to walk periodically, and made an extra effort to keep my water as cold as possible. At the next aid station, I filled my hat with ice, as Kathy and Anna swabbed me down with cold sponges and slathered me with sunblock. I hugged my crew, thanked the volunteers, and was off again into the oven that these meadows had become.

I ran for several hours through this stretch with Phil Oelkers from Illinois. We talked a lot and took turns pulling each other along, making the first enforced cutoff with about an hour to spare. As we returned from the 31-mile turnaround, we discussed our pace, and the dreaded open meadows that lay between us and the next enforced cutoff at mile 62, back at the start/finish area. Around mile 50, after some clouds had mercifully helped us through the meadows, my stomach finally started to feel good, and I picked up the pace a bit. Anna and Kathy had my lights ready for me just when I needed them, and Anna, a scientist by vocation, let me know that I was well ahead of the upcoming 62-mile cutoff. When I got to the 62-mile point, Jeff was ready to begin his role as pacer, and guide me through those last 38 miles. I was 1:25 ahead of the cutoff—it was 10:30 P.M.

Jeff and I have run probably a few thousand miles together since 1995. Perhaps the only person with whom I have run more miles is my wife. She teaches 9th-grade science, and stayed home to wrap up end-of-school stuff, and cheer for our younger son, Ari, who was competing in a 1,600-meter race on Saturday. As Jeff and I headed out into the darkness, he told me that he had just spoken to Chris, and that Ari had run a 4:36, good for a fourth-place medal in his event. That was great news, and got me even more stoked and motivated. We ran through the woods, just as we have so many times before, sharing our love of running and the outdoors. Jeff was wonderful, leading me through the dark, telling me how strong I was, and tripping over all the roots and rocks so I didn't have to. We talked a little, but said so much more. Every once in a while, we turned off our headlamps and enjoyed the silence and the dark of night. We listened wordlessly to the coyotes and frogs, and the other sounds of the night. Every so often, Jeff would tell me how strong I was running, and where we stood in relation to the cutoffs. And at every aid station, Kathy and Anna were there to make sure we were eating and drinking well, that we were staying warm, and to tell us how awesome we looked. It was very dark out there.

A crisp half-moon broke through the clouds about 1:00 A.M. The temperature had fallen, and I felt comfortable for the first time in a while. Virtually all the volunteers and crews, and many other runners, had donned jackets. But Jeff and I were moving very well, and were generating plenty of heat to keep warm. We were almost two full hours ahead of the cutoffs when we hit the 4-mile stretch to the 81-mile turnaround. After stumbling over some roots and rocks, we decided that it was a good time to do some walking. We power-walked most of the way out and back, and were still 1:30 ahead of the final aid station cutoff at mile 85. We turned off our headlamps at 4:59 A.M., and watched a beautiful sunrise from the open meadows along the trail.

We had 15 miles to go, and 6 hours, 15 minutes to get there. And we were still taking frequent running breaks from our awesome walking. All we had to do now was stay strong and avoid doing anything stupid. Our excitement was on the rise, as was Anna's and Kathy's. Their smiles got bigger at each aid station, and even in the daylight, they continued to tell us how good we looked. The volunteers at the 95-mile station had promised pancakes, and they had them ready for us now! I was an hour and a half ahead of the cutoff. The outcome was not in doubt. This was a slam dunk, barring injury or stupidity. I was weary but wide awake and still having fun. And I was hungry. Without a doubt, this was my longest aid station stop of the run. I gobbled down a couple of pancakes with syrup, while Jeff more daringly devoured some breakfast sausage. We headed out well fueled with plenty of time to walk to the finish if we had to.

My stomach problems never completely disappeared, and putting so much food in there all at once had a pretty quick effect on me. For the fourth time, I found a nice quiet spot to squat in the woods. Squatting after 95 miles has all sorts of interesting effects on the body. But I survived, returning quickly to Jeff's side. I shook the cramps out of my quads as we powered up and down the hilly cross-country ski trails that would take us to the finish. The sun was up now, and the temperature was rising, but we were still quite comfortable, albeit weary. It was about this time that we encountered an elderly couple walking together on the trail. They asked if we were participating in the 100-mile race. Jeff replied that I was, and that he was pacing me. The woman then asked me, "What do you do with your mind when you're running a hundred miles?" Without hesitation, I replied, "Ignore it."

The truth is, ultramarathons require far more mental focus than shorter races. We often joke that it requires the absence of a brain, but I think the truth is that much more thought, planning, and focus are needed. A small miscue during an ultra can result in failure, if for no other reason than the extent of time that is involved. Feeling miserable for a few minutes or even an hour during a 10K or a marathon is tolerable. Feeling miserable for half a day or longer is not. Ultrarunning requires more than just physical fitness. It is as much a workout for the mind as for the body.

Jeff and I ran the last mile or so as if we were on fresh legs. A couple of runners passed us, but I could not have cared less. I felt wonderful. As the finish came into sight, I could see Anna and Kathy, and some other friends and spectators as well. They were all cheering and applauding. These were not just casual spectators. These were the folks who had run, crewed for me, crewed for other runners, or otherwise were intimately involved in my day out there. I was truly touched by their wide grins and honest cheers. Anna was snapping photos, Kathy was brushing away a tear, and I was pumping my fist. I finished in 28:28:55, good for 30th place out of 38 finishers, and second among senior masters men. I was more than 1:30 under the 30-hour cutoff, a margin that I had held since Jeff had joined me at the 62-mile point. Tim handed me a lovely little copper kettle as my finisher's award. Anna noticed that it had a little dent in it, and quietly exchanged it. My crew was still working for me. All three of them got big hugs. Jeff, of course, pretended to hate his, but Anna and Kathy each squeezed me tightly and probably kept me from falling down.

I had completed my first attempt at 100 miles on trails, and I was proud. Proud and grateful. I can't offer enough thanks to Jeff, Anna, and Kathy for their help out there. This race taught me that I have wonderful friends, that I am loved. This experience would have been very different had I not had the support of Anna, Kathy, and Jeff, as well as my wife, who was there in spirit.

"100-mile solo" finisher? I don't think so.

Confessions of a Happy Ultra Mommy

NAME: SOPHIE SPEIDEL
AGE: 40
RESIDENCE: CHARLOTTESVILLE, VIRGINIA
YEARS RUNNING: 21
YEARS RUNNING ULTRAS: 2

© Jim Capony

The journey to my first ultra, the 2002 Holiday Lake 50K++, probably began when I was a child. I have fond memories of playing for hours in woods near my childhood home in Princeton, New Jersey. When it was cold and my friends wanted to play inside, I could always be found outside, exploring. As a young teacher, I convinced the school where I was teaching physical education to help finance a nine-day Outward Bound course in western North Carolina. The mental and physical challenge of long-distance hiking around Pisgah National Forest struck a chord within. Despite the pain, I really liked this stuff! I did my first triathlon in 1988, and my first marathon, the Marine Corps Marathon, in 1990. My time at Marine Corps was a respectable 3:40, after a long day of struggling with an IT band injury. I then took a few years away from triathlons and marathons to start my family. My husband, Rusty, and I have three children, ages 11, 9, and 6.

When my youngest child turned 4, I decided that I wanted to improve my fitness and return to racing the sprint triathlons I had given up 10 years prior. My neighbor Susie Burgess, a mother of five, was training for her second Ironman, and she asked me to join her for Tuesday-morning workouts at the pool, in addition to my running and biking workouts. Susie is such a great training partner because she is a mom and understands the demands that family and work can put on a woman. I believe it is important to be around other women who can relate to what I am doing, not women who come up to you at parties (as they have done to me) and ask, "Are you still running like a crazy woman?" I work fulltime as a counselor at an independent school, so I needed to be creative and flexible in scheduling my workouts. I began to get up at 5:00 A.M. in order to be home by 7:00 A.M. to get everyone off to school. I learned to be more organized the night before. I would organize my clothes or pack my gear bag and make the kid's lunches. As I found that I enjoyed the way I felt after early-morning workouts, it became part of my regular routine. I used to try to squeeze in a run in the afternoon, but the morning afforded me more guilt-free time, which, of course, made my training more enjoyable. I started to go to bed earlier (around 9:00 P.M.) and found that I was less interested in staying out late on the weekends. This was fine with the kids, since this led to more "family movie" nights. My husband, who is a former triathlete and runner and now enjoys biking, has been very supportive and understanding of my new lifestyle. We do make time to go out together, but I'd rather spend time with him than go to a huge party. On the weekends, he does breakfast duty while I get in a long run, but I don't have the luxury of training for more than three hours at a time. When I read about other ultrarunners getting in 8-hour runs in the mountains, I am jealous but also grateful that I am able to do what I do. It works for me.

After a season of racing sprint triathlons, I started talking to a colleague and friend, Peter York, about his ultrarunning experiences. Pete is a veteran of the Holiday Lake race as well as the popular JFK 50-miler, and he told me that given my age, experience, and desire for a challenge, "the time was right for an ultra." I laughed at his suggestion, and didn't give it another thought until I read *To the Edge* by Kirk Johnson. In his book, Johnson tells his story of running the Badwater 130-mile race in memory of his late brother. I was particularly taken by his reflections on the "mystery of endurance." I have always been fascinated by adventure stories about ordinary people who have survived the elements and long distances, and *To the Edge* was a prime example. I also read a story about the Hardrock 100 Mile race in *Outside* magazine, and I started entertaining the idea that running an ultra just might be a great new challenge for me. I signed up for the 2001 Richmond Marathon with the idea that it would be good training for the Holiday Lake 50K++ scheduled for February 2002. I told my husband of my plans. He didn't believe me at first ("You want to run how many miles?"), but he has since become my biggest fan. I also told my running friends and mentors, all of whom embraced the idea, supported me unconditionally, ran with me, and helped me all along the way. I don't think I could have trained properly for Holiday Lake without them. The friend-

ships I developed with them is one of the main reasons I want to keep running ultras.

My training for Holiday Lake began in earnest in August as I started
preparing for the Richmond Marathon. In addition to long runs in and
around my hometown, I also included at least three days of swimming and
water running, as well as a weekly spin class at the gym to give my legs a
break and to maintain fitness. I also did one day of speed work on the track.
As the Holiday Lake race approached, I tapered just as I would for a
marathon. I felt rested and ready. I arrived at the race site the night before
and stayed in a small cabin at the park, rooming with three other women.
We were all first-time ultrarunners. I tried to get to bed early, but sleep was
hard to come by. I was excited about the race, and a little nervous.

The alarm went off at 4:50 and I began to prepare for the 6:00 A.M. start.
It was quite cold that morning. I ate Pop-Tarts and drank water and green
tea (what I usually had in training), milled around the lodge with the other
runners, and at the last minute changed from running tights to shorts. It
was a good thing, too, because the temperatures climbed into the 60s later
that day.

When I decided to run the Holiday Lake race, I committed to run the
race slow and easy, just to finish and not worry about time or place. After
all, it was my first ultra. Unfortunately, I have a very strong competitive
streak and before I knew it I had run the first six miles in a too-quick 8:30
pace. But I was feeling good, so I didn't think too much of it. I was running
with a group of guys who were also first-time ultrarunners, and we got into
a great rhythm that was hard to abandon for a slower, more conservative
pace. I also neglected to walk the uphills as I had been advised to do. That
would turn out to be a big mistake! At the first stream crossing, David
Horton (the race director) informed me that I was the second woman,
which of course just got me going even faster. All was well as I entered the
turnaround at mile 16 in 2:25, and then I saw who was behind me: many
more women! A couple of miles later, as fate would have it, my IT band
started to tighten (having never done so in training), and for the rest of the
race I stressed about getting passed and about how to run with a tight IT
band. I walked all the uphills the entire way back to the finish. Another
woman passed me at mile 25 (going uphill!), and that really deflated me. As
the pain in my leg increased, it was all I could do to keep the run/walk pace
going. I had to really dig deep to find the mental fortitude to keep moving.

I had no intentions of quitting, but I did have a few intense conversations with myself on the subject. I think my experience in other sports definitely prepared me for the mental discomfort of the race, and having played and coached team sports helped wash away any notion of stopping. In a national-level lacrosse game, with your team depending on you, you can't stop just because it hurts!

A rush of adrenaline over the last 100 yards helped me cross the finish line in style. I finished in 5:17, the third-place woman. But I was hurting. All I wanted to do was lie down. Finishing that race was the hardest challenge I have ever faced, childbirth (3 times!) included. But I did it, and overall, I enjoyed it. I definitely got what I signed up for! And just like childbirth, the memory of the pain faded quickly and I soon found myself planning my next ultra.

Training for and running my first ultra has allowed me to explore a beautiful world that I otherwise would have never discovered. I have given myself a real gift: the goal to finish an ultra, and the satisfaction of having reached that goal. Life is so much more interesting when we have something to look forward to outside the routine of work and family. Ultrarunning is a sport anyone, at any age can do and enjoy. You don't have to be fast, just willing to set goals and challenge the voice inside that says, *You can't.* You can. Sure, training for an ultra is hard with a young family of 5. It requires flexibility (if my husband has to go out of town, I either take the day off, or get a sitter), communication with my family, a sense of humor, and the realization that it is all for fun. Training and racing are tremendous gifts that I am giving myself and that my family is giving me. I try to never take it for granted. My family has been incredibly supportive because they know this makes me happy, and a happy Sophie is a happy mommy!

Van Trouble at the Umstead 100-Mile Endurance Run

NAME: TIM MORGAN
AGE: 45
RESIDENCE: CLEMMONS, NORTH CAROLINA
YEARS RUNNING: 7
YEARS RUNNING ULTRAS: 5

Photo by World of Color

I was diagnosed with Type 1 (insulin-dependent) diabetes at age 5. My dad taught me from the very beginning that even with my condition, I could do anything anyone else could do. I just had to plan ahead and take the steps necessary to maintain a balance between exercise and eating. I also had to be prepared and have the necessary supplies handy in case my blood sugar got too low (hypoglycemia) or too high (hyperglycemia). I played tennis in high school but after school, I became more sedentary, and as a result, got out of shape and put on some weight.

In 1994, I received a grant from the National Institutes of Health to coordinate a national study to get sedentary people to become more physically active. Although my sedentary lifestyle qualified me for my own study, this did not motivate me to become physically active. What got me started was my sons' interest in running 5K races and trying out for their middle school track teams. In 1996 I took my sons to some open track practice sessions and the following week decided I would try the mile run just for the heck of it. That mile run almost killed me. I decided then and there to get in better shape. I began slowly, walking and running, until I could run 4 miles. As I lost weight and learned to enjoy running, I began running 5K races. These led to 10K, and even 15K races. My first marathon was the Marine Corps Marathon in October 1998. The race was hard and painful, but I was a little disappointed because I thought it would be even harder than it was. The race that year had about 18,000 runners, and it was wall-to-wall people for the first 5 miles. I'm not an elite runner, but I was there to run a race, not attend a crowded party. Afterward, looking for a smaller race, I came across a notice for an event just 20 miles from where I lived, to be run in January

1999, called the North Carolina Fat Ass 50K. No fee, no aid. It sounded perfect, but for a Type 1 diabetic, "no aid" could present a problem.

When I started running I had to learn how to balance my blood sugar by either cutting back on the amount of insulin I took or eating extra before the run to cover the energy expended in the run. It took a little trial and error: Try something, test your blood sugar before and after the run, and adjust from there. As the mileage increased, it was no longer enough to eat before the run, but became important to eat during the run as well. Again by trial and error I figured out how much and when to eat. It's not an exact science and what works one day might not work the next, so it is important for me to check my blood glucose every hour during long runs. In 1999, I was put on an insulin pump, which helped because it gave me more freedom by not having to plan in advance when or how much I was going to eat.

Most ultramarathons have aid stations about every 5 miles with food and drinks, so as long as I carry the blood glucose testing equipment with me and some source of calories in case my blood sugar gets low, things work out well. The only catch is that I have to eat at the aid stations whether I want to or not, even if I'm feeling nauseous. For the Fat Ass 50K, the race director said that even though it was a "no aid" event, he would roam the course, providing aid, but I could not take any chances. The day before the race I drove the course and stashed bottles of energy drink and energy gels every 5 miles. As my dad always said when I was a child, I could do anything, as long as I planned ahead.

There were only 10 runners in that first 50K, and it was great. Everyone was very friendly, offering words of encouragement during the race. The course was hilly and challenging, and when I finished, I felt like I'd really accomplished something. Now that I had finished a tough 50K, 50 miles didn't seem so far out of reach and I signed up to run the 50-mile version of the Umstead Endurance Run in April 1999. I fell in love with trail running while training for Umstead. This newfound love for trails led to my running the Mountain Masochist 50-mile trail run in October 1999. Mountain Masochist was a very tough race that, with 8,000 feet of elevation gain, pushed me to my limits. I dug down deeper the last 10 miles of the race than I ever had before. When I finished I was extremely fatigued and sore, but I felt great satisfaction in having completed such a tough challenge. My next event would be the Umstead 100-mile race in April 2000.

The day before the race, I picked up my two oldest sons (Daniel, 14, and

Brad, 16) from school in our van and proceeded on the 2-hour trip to Raleigh, North Carolina. My plan was for my boys to serve as my crew and pacers. Both are talented runners and I had no concern about them covering the distance, especially at the slow pace I would be going. About 30 miles from the park, the van's transmission began acting up and would not shift into fourth gear. I was still able to travel on the freeway; however, I had to go 15 miles per hour slower than I normally would. This was irritating, but it wasn't going to keep me from getting to the event. A few miles later, the van would not even get into third gear, and our pace was reduced to about 25 miles an hour. We finally arrived at the park, having missed just a couple of minutes of the pre-race briefing.

The night before was fun and anxious. We enjoyed the briefing, and after dinner took a walk down by the lake. I tried to give my sons last-minute instructions on what backup clothes, medical supplies, and lights were in which bag, when to give me what, what to do in case of problems, and tips on what to say or do while pacing. After training for about six months gearing up for this race, I was anxious for it to begin. I tried to put the van out of my mind and convince myself that I could deal with it after the race. Worrying about it now would not help. That night, my sons slept fine. I, on the other hand, tossed and turned all night, looking at the clock to see if it was time to wake up. None of us wanted to get up at 5:00 when the alarm finally went off.

We went to the race headquarters at about 5:30 for breakfast. I checked my blood glucose and it was high, probably from the anxiety caused by the race. I took some insulin to hopefully bring the blood glucose down, but still ate some breakfast to give me the calories I would need for the first 5 miles. We checked out the van, only to find that the transmission was totally gone. Even with a lot of pushing, it would not move an inch. Oh well—we'd have to deal with that later. My sons enjoyed the pre-race gathering of runners, which was like nothing they'd ever seen before. People were putting Vaseline in places they would not have imagined—and then there was the variety of outfits people had on. Some people had on tights, some shorts, some short shorts, some colorful shorts, some old and beat-up shorts, some hats, some camel packs, some waist packs. Nothing like the 5K races the boys were used to where everyone is dressed similarly. Taking it all in, we went down to the lake for the start. The race director said a few words, then gave the start command, and everyone proceeded to walk up a steep hill for the first 200 yards of the race. I was relieved that the event had started. Now I just had to focus on what I was doing and be patient. There was a long way to go. I left the boys to call their mom and deal with the van.

My goal was to start out conservative. The race consists of a 10-mile loop that is repeated 10 times. I wanted to get through the first loop by walking all the uphills and running the flats and downhills smooth and easy. I gave my sons a table with possible lap times so they could know when to expect me at the aid station. My predicted time for the first lap was from 2:00 hours to 2:30, and I thought I was running easy until I came into the finish of the first lap in about 1:40. I was concerned I went out too fast, and my sons were not expecting me yet so they were not there. Toward the end of the second lap, I was still having trouble controlling my speed, and I was starting to feel a hot spot, indicating that a blister was on the way. I warned my boys that I would probably stop at the end of the next lap to have some blister patches put on. While the boys were working on my feet, I drank a meal replacement drink to keep my blood sugar up, and asked Brad what he knew about the van. He told me a tow truck was on its way.

For most of the race I checked my blood glucose levels every hour. Using my insulin pump, I could give myself insulin as needed. Other related stuff I carried in my waist pack and shorts included a glucose meter, a lancet (to stick my finger for drawing blood), extra glucose meter strips, an extra battery for the insulin pump, a backup insulin syringe (in case the pump failed), and extra energy gels in case my blood sugar got too low between aid stations. Talk about planning ahead.

Shortly after starting the third lap, I saw the tow truck coming to our campsite. That was the good news. The bad news was what that meal replacement drink was doing to my stomach. Within a mile of the aid station, I threw up. I kept going, but my stomach was upset and running made it worse. I couldn't run more than a quarter mile without having to walk because of the nausea. I took some Tums, and even tried to eat some apple slices. Nothing helped. Tired of walking, I pushed the running distance farther until I threw up twice, then ran 100 yards and threw up two more times, ran some more and stopped to throw up one last time. Then, after feeling really bad for 5 miles, all of a sudden I felt like a new man, and was able to take off again at a fast pace. While throwing up did make me feel better, I was worried that my blood sugar would drop too low. I forced myself to drink some energy drink and eat some gels. I finished the third lap a little slower mainly due to my stomach problems. The hot spots on my feet felt a little worse so I stopped to have them worked on. My boys were ready for me. They took my shoes and socks off, treated the blisters, and put new socks on. I noticed the van still at the campsite and asked about the tow truck and was told they could not get to it because too many cars were blocking access to it. They would come back later.

As I took off for the fourth lap, the blisters hurt for about a quarter mile and then the patches settled in and my feet began to feel better. The fourth and fifth laps went well. I generally felt okay, but fatigue was setting in. At the halfway point, I was tired, but felt I had more left. I was sure that as long as I could keep walking the uphills and slowly jog on the downhills, I could break 24 hours. I would just have to ignore my body, which was screaming for me to stop and walk.

The rain came at about mile 55, driven by a strong, horizontal wind. I put on a light rain jacket, but within a half-mile the jacket and my shirt underneath were soaked and plastered to my skin by the strong headwinds. I had been listening to a portable radio to distract me from the fatigue. They interrupted the radio program to announce severe thunderstorm warnings for the area and a tornado warning for two nearby counties. We were getting the strong winds of the thunderstorm, and the temperature quickly dropped from the 70s to the 40s. The driving rain had soaked my socks and shoes, and I was concerned what effect this could have on my slightly blistered feet. Most of the other runners I saw on the course were wearing garbage bags. For a newbie like me, it was interesting to see the number of different ways you can wear a garbage bag. As I was running in my rain-soaked jacket, I began to wish that I had a garbage bag instead. But the cold wind and rain motivated me to finish the lap faster and head for shelter. My crew was waiting for me at the end of the loop, and I told them to take everything to the cabin; when I came back from the turnaround in a half mile I would take a break in the cabin. I felt this was no time to be worried about finishing times. I had to get dry, warm, and keep my feet protected. Back at the cabin, I shivered as my boys helped me remove my wet shoes, socks, jacket, and shirt. I worked to get warm while they patched several new blisters that had resulted from running in the soaked shoes. I refueled and dressed warmly for my return to the course. I did not have any waterproof gloves, so Brad gave me his gloves and tied plastic bags around them to keep them dry. About this time, Daniel heard a faint beeping coming from my insulin pump, indicating a problem. I never would have heard it in all the wind and rain. The error message indicated the battery was low. Just my luck, a battery that lasts about six months would pick this day to run out. Fortunately I had a spare, and after a quick change, the pump was okay. That rest stop took 18 minutes, but it was well worth it. When I left the cabin to start the seventh loop, I felt warm, comfortable, and renewed from the rest. That new energy lasted for about half of the seventh loop before it was replaced by an even greater feeling of fatigue.

At the start of the eighth loop I picked up my first pacer, Daniel. We talked about what was happening with the van and when my wife was going to come get us Sunday morning. I told him I was tired but still moving okay. We jokingly compared me to the van: After 30 miles I lost fourth gear and after 50 miles I lost third gear, but I still could walk (first gear) up the hills and could still do a slow jog (second gear) down the hills. During this lap my blood sugar rose a little too high, so I pushed the buttons on my pump to give myself a little more insulin. Daniel helped a lot at the aid stations and provided good companionship. The eighth lap was very good for me. At the start of the ninth loop, I picked up Brad, who would pace me the last 20 miles. We talked about how surprised we were that my times were much better than I predicted and that even if I walked, I could break 22 hours: a time I had only dreamed of. I checked my watch and calculated that even 21 hours was possible, but to break the 20-hour barrier, I would have to run the last two loops in 4 hours and 12 minutes. Was this possible? Was it smart to even try for what might be an unrealistic goal? My last loop had taken 2 hours and 11 minutes. I decided that I would try to maintain or improve my pace, shooting for the 20-hour finish, and would reevaluate my strategy again before the tenth loop.

Brad was a great pacer. We talked about the race and his track season. He pushed me to run the downhills, and reminded me to keep my form smooth and relaxed. His encouragement really helped. I was feeling more tired than ever and my jogging form was getting choppy and rough. Every time he reminded me about my form, my pace seemed to pick up with less energy expended. The ninth lap took 2 hours and 7 minutes. I could still break 20 hours if I could run the last lap in 2:04. I thought I would give it a try. No reason to hold back now. I continued to walk the uphills and ran a little faster (albeit slow) for as long as I could on the downhills. I was feeling even more tired, but had a renewed sense of motivation thanks to Brad and my new 20-hour target. Then, at about mile 93, I noticed a pain in my foot indicative of a bad blister. I tried to continue running, which only confirmed that, yes, I definitely had a painful blister that required attention. I stopped and asked Brad to help me fix the blister. I knew that this stop would make breaking 20 hours totally impossible, but I also knew it was not worth it to push on and really hurt myself. Brad helped me sit down, tended to my new blister, and had me back up and walking after several minutes. We made it to the aid station and stopped for some soup. With just 6 miles to go, we could relax, no longer compelled to push to the extreme for an unrealistic time goal. I still ran as much as I could, and Brad still helped me improve my speed by reminding me to power-walk the uphills and work on form on the downhills. At one point we even jogged strongly past a couple of other runners, which lifted my spirits. We finally crossed the line in 20:06, exhausted, yet amazed and extremely satisfied.

Daniel had a chair ready and waiting for me near the finish line, into which I quickly collapsed. As the pain slowly diminished, a great feeling of accomplishment began to wash over me. All day I had been pushing myself to keep running, keep walking, keep eating, keep drinking, keep enduring toward the finish. Now I could relax, look back, and really appreciate all that I had experienced over the last 20-plus hours. I started the race with the goal of just finishing under the 30-hour cutoff. After 50 miles, with that goal all but achieved, I began calculating and recalculating my time and pace, coming up with new goals that might be possible. First it was my dream goal of 24 hours, then 21 hours, then 20 hours. Talk about motivation! Brad checked with the finish-line official to find out what place I came in. When the official started moving his finger down the list of finishers one by one, I was expecting a long pause, but instead he quickly said, "Sixth place." I almost fell out of my chair! The only race I had ever finished in the top six was a 50K where only six people ran the race.

And in the end, I fared much better than the van. It only took a little pushing and pulling from my crew to get me moving the next morning. The van, on the other hand, required a tow, over $1000 in parts and labor, and a new transmission.

Blisters and Bliss at the Rocky Racoon
100-Mile Trail Run

NAME: BYRON AND JOY CHIKINDA
AGE: HIM—52, HER—42
RESIDENCE: EDMONTON, ALBERTA
YEARS RUNNING: HIM—9; HER—7
YEARS RUNNING ULTRAS: HIM—7;
   HER—6

*Byron and Joy Chikinda have been
running ultras together for over seven
years. They have watched each other
grow in the sport, and they have grown closer along the way. Their teamwork
has pulled them through some challenging runs. Here is one of their stories.*

Byron: I started running to lose weight. One thing led to another and I
found myself running marathons. After running three marathons, it
seemed that the only challenge left was running them faster. Then I read a
story called "Le Grizz" by Don Kardong, about the Le Grizz 50 Miler in
Montana. I just had to try this race. After running my first ultra and meeting the other runners, I knew I had finally found the races I love.
Ultrarunners are very different from other runners. There is an old ultramarathon saying "To finish is to win." Many times I have seen runners stop
and help other runners. You don't see that very often in shorter races.

Joy: I didn't discover I had competitive tendencies until Byron started to
run. Not wanting to be left behind, I started to run too. I ran one marathon,
which felt like giving birth, but somehow I decided that since I could do this
crazy sport, why not go further. Byron was training for the Saskatchewan
50K ultra at the same time as I was training for my first marathon. The training didn't look like much fun, but the event itself looked possible. I ran out
to 12.5K and joined Byron for the last 12.5 (25K total). One of the women
who ran the race told me that I looked pretty strong and that I should have
run the whole race. Motivated by her words, I vowed to take on the next ultra
right beside Byron. I have run almost every race with him since.

After running Le Grizz four times, we decided we were ready to try our first 100 miler. We read good reviews about the Rocky Racoon 100-Mile Trail Run outside Huntsville, Texas. We knew that Rocky Racoon had a very high newbie success rate, and was supposed to be relatively flat. The only problem was that because the race was in February, we would have to train in the winter. It gets pretty cold where we live in Edmonton, Alberta Canada, but we decided to give it a go. Training in December was even more brutal than we feared. We had to split our 6-hour runs into three 2-hour sections because it was –30C (–22F) to –40C (–40F) with the wind chill. We would stop after two hours of running, warm up, dry out our clothes, get dressed again, and head back out. We put up with frozen water bottles, rock-hard energy bars, and frigidly painful bathroom breaks. Not even waist-deep snowdrifts would get between us and our goal.

Byron: We arrived at Rocky Racoon for the weigh-in around noon the day before the run. It was cloudy, windy, and cool. The first sign we saw said, "Please do not harass or feed the alligators." Hang on now. No one said anything about alligators! We came to run 100 miles, not mess with alligators. Besides, how do you "harass" an alligator?

We ate a small breakfast so we could weigh-in as light as possible. Every 20 miles they weigh you. If you lose too much weight, you are forced to stop, and eat and drink until your weight is up again. You never know when a couple of pounds might make a difference. Too much weight loss indicates severe dehydration and can result in disqualification for obvious health reasons.

At the pre-race meal and briefing, Mickey, the race director, mentioned we didn't have to worry about copperheads, rattlesnakes, and water moccasins. They were all hibernating. He also told us that the alligators should be fairly dormant and that all we should encounter are raccoons, armadillos, and coyotes. He cautioned us about the rough conditions of the course, especially the roots, which if we were not careful, could cause us to "kiss Mother Earth."

We spent the night before the event in a hotel in Huntsville, Texas. Joy's nickname is "the love goddess" and we generally sleep very, very well before a race. A good light meal, a sweet snack, a lovely massage, a little love-making, and a good night's sleep make for a great pre-race ritual that has worked for us time and time again.

Joy: We got to the start at about 5:00 the next morning. It was a very cold –4C (24F). We read about the cold temperatures from the year before, and thought, being from Canada, that it would not be so bad. We were wrong. With the high Texas humidity, –4C is very cold. The Rocky Racoon trail is a 20.2-mile loop around Lake Raven, which we would circle five times for a total of 101 miles. (This was supposed to be a 100-mile run, not 101 miles!) We parked the rental car close to the trail and laid out all our extra clothes, food, and gear in the trunk. At the end of each loop we would run by the car and restock, change clothes and shoes, get flashlights or first-aid, and anything else we might need.

The race started promptly at 6:00 A.M. All the runners carried flashlights in the predawn darkness. It was quite a sight to see all those lights moving up the trail. The trail parallels the road into the park for 1.5 miles and then crosses the road into the woods. Though Rocky Racoon is not in the mountains, it is hilly with about 8,000 feet total elevation gain/loss. And if the hills are not enough, it presents another challenge: roots, roots, and more roots. These roots can really get you if you are not paying attention, as we would soon find out.

The runners were really bunched up at the first aid station, and the volunteers were having problems recording everyone's number. The sun was finally rising and we put away our flashlights. After about 1.5 miles of road, we headed back into the woods again. The trail was marked with yellow tape and pie plates spray-painted yellow. Like most trail runs, if you don't pay attention, you might miss these markers and get some "extra running." Mickey had mentioned that they were having a very wet winter, and we quickly saw evidence of that. The trail was quite muddy in places. We watched out for the roots but still hit some that were hidden in the fallen leaves.

Byron: After this part of the course, we went back out to the jeep road for a mile and then arrived at aid station 2–3. The food at this aid station was great. There were sandwiches, soups, all sorts of candies, fruits, cookies, and more. Joy was feeling nauseated at this point so she did not enjoy the food as much as I did. It was getting warm, so we stripped down to just shorts and singlets. We loaded up on water and took off. Upon leaving this aid station, there was a 5-mile "out-and-back trail run" before returning to the same aid station. That is why they call it 2–3. This "out-and-back" is very pretty but also quite rooty. There were also several logs on the trail and a number of muddy sections, which got worse as the runners trudged through them. We met a runner on the trail who had apparently fallen, and was limping and bloody from his knee to his ankle. The roots win again.

Back at aid station 2–3, a volunteer mentioned the forecast for the day was sunny with a high of 20C (68F). To combat the expected warmth, we began to focus on hydrating. Joy also had to stop and tend to some blisters. It was very early in the race to have blisters. I feared it might become a very long day for her, but I didn't want to say anything that might discourage her.

Joy: My feet were not in the best condition at the start of this race. I had been enrolled in a gymnastics class (a mandatory course for my physical education degree), and due to the impact forces from the landings, my feet had taken extra punishment. Unfortunately, this meant that I needed to slice open the toebox of both shoes to relieve the pressure on the first knuckle of the feet. A friendly and resourceful volunteer cut open my shoes with his hunting knife. As I discovered later, this allowed sand into the shoes, and too much movement of the forefoot that later would result in dollar-sized blisters on the inside of each heel. Ah, the joys of ultrarunning!

After the aid station we ran back to the sandy road again and then off into the woods. There were tree stumps and many roots along this part of the course. Despite trying to be careful, we stumbled, hit our toes, fell, and had a tough time with this 5-mile section of the course. Back home where we run, the trees are "neighborly" and keep their roots in the ground where they belong. This is a hilly section, and it became quite swampy. There are several long boardwalks that can make for fast running if you don't mind running on a deck that slopes 15 percent to the right with no handrail. We followed the lake to the fourth aid station (named 174 after the number of its campsite home). We loaded up on water and food, and then headed out. For the next 2.5 miles the course climbs several hills and then descends to aid station 5 and the start/finish line. Our time for the first lap was three hours and 50 minutes. Right on track.

Byron: The second lap was going well, except Joy was getting more bad blisters from running with her shoes loosely laced. We stopped at aid station 2–3 to drain and dress the blisters. I placed duct tape over the dressings to hold them in place. I told Joy that the ultramarathoner's best friend, duct tape, would get her through the race and not to worry about the blistering. This is one of the reasons we stay together: to help and encourage each other. Besides, who needs a radio? I would get to hear nonstop talking for the next 24 hours! Joy loves the aid stations: lots of great food and good conversation. She would have talked with the volunteers all day had I not reminded her that there was a race going on and we were part of it. Off we went.

Joy: Every now and then we would hear a *thump* and a few choice words as another runner tripped over the roots. In the section just before the swamp, Byron was busy talking to another runner and not paying attention when he tripped and "kissed Mother Earth," nearly skewering himself on a broken sapling. Fortunately, he only received a minor laceration, so it was easily disinfected and bandaged at the next aid station. We saw alligator foot prints in the mud in this section. Looks like they were not that dormant after all! We finished this lap a little slower in 4:15, but still right on schedule.

Because sunset and cooler temperatures would arrive before we finished lap 3, we grabbed pants and long-sleeved shirts from the car before heading out. My feet were getting very sore, and I was having another bout of nausea. Byron was beginning to have stomach problems too. There is one thing we have learned about running ultras: If you have a problem, work on it right away before it consumes you. We talked it over, and finally figured out what was causing our stomach problems. We trained with Gatorade, but some of the aid stations were serving Power Ade. A golden rule of racing is that you always eat and drink what you train with. Fortunately Byron had some Gatorade powder in his drop bag at aid station 2–3. For the rest of the race we mixed our own drinks, and before we knew it, our stomach problems were gone.

Blake Wood, the eventual winner, lapped us during the third lap. The man is incredible! He runs a fast pace, smooth, and with a smile on his face. We made room for him to pass and tried to hitch a ride. He just waved and ran on. A few moments later, coming down a hill, a woman tripped on a root and took a terrible fall. She flipped 180 degrees and landed on the back of her head. I have never run an ultramarathon where so many runners have fallen.

Earlier that morning we had left two flashlights at aid station 2–3. They would come in handy now that it was getting darker. And because it was getting cooler as well, we changed into our warmer clothes. My feet were getting worse, but we decided to wait until aid station 5 before working on them. I fell back some, and Byron had to keep waiting for me. Before long he got the hint and slowed down.

Just after dark we heard a very loud splash somewhere ahead. Either someone had fallen into the lake or it was one of those dormant alligators!

A little while later we approached the fourth aid station. It was lit up like a Christmas tree. We had some soup and kept running. We finished our third lap in 4:45.

Byron: I tried to encourage Joy to run faster but the pain on her face told me this was not going to happen. We have run 16 ultramarathons with only one DNF. Our success is attributed to the most important goal of helping each other, even if it means slowing down. The thought of leaving Joy and running ahead is *never* an option. When Joy developed an injury during her first ultra and told me to leave her at an aid station, I did, but for the rest of the race, I felt guilty for leaving her and was worried about her. She got over her injury and even finished the race. But I vowed that day that I would never, ever leave her again. A good finish time is not worth the heartache and worry. We have completed 15 out of 16 ultramarathons, quite success-ful in a sport with such a high DNF rate. By staying together, encouraging each other, helping out through the tough spots, we make a great team. When we started running together we promised each other never to dis-courage or talk negatively to each other. It accomplishes nothing. We use the same approach in our marriage. ultrarunning has added and enhanced our marriage beyond our expectations. The fun and excitement of plan-ning, training, and running ultras together is incredible. We thought we were close before running ultramarathons, but we had no idea how close we could get.

Before starting the fourth lap, we changed into some warmer clothes and worked on Joy's feet. I peeled off all the old bandages and drained the blis-ters. She was in pain but trying to be very cheerful by focusing on what clothes she was going change into for the night running. I mentioned that some of the blisters were very large and deep. Joy responded, "Just drain them and put Compeed bandages on them." Unfortunately, some of the blisters were bigger than the bandages. Thank goodness for duct tape! I told Joy that removing the duct tape after the race would be very painful, but she showed no concern. We spent about 40 minutes at the aid station, but it was time well invested. Joy would never make it to the finish without getting these problems addressed.

I started to tend to my feet, looked up, and was shocked at what I saw. There was Joy standing between two cars naked! "What are you doing?" Joy replied it was a lot easier and faster to strip off all her running clothes and put fresh ones on. Besides it was dark out and there were not many people around. When Joy started to run, she always had tissues to blow her nose. She would never do a nature break in the woods. Instead she would run miles with terrible cramps until she found a gas station or restaurant to use the washroom. But there she was, standing naked in the middle of a 100-mile ultramarathon, in Texas. Running does make you a nature child!

Joy limped out onto the trail in a lot of pain as we started the fourth lap. We had 40 miles to go and she didn't look like she could make it another step. I kept this thought to myself and tried to encourage her to keep going. She pressed on, hoping the toes might eventually go numb. The girl has courage! I wonder how I would act under the same circumstances, with raw feet and swollen toes.

We talked it over and decided to walk the rougher trail sections. Both of us had fallen, hit our toes, and scraped our shins throughout the day. Our ankles and knees were swollen and couldn't take much more abuse. It really is a different course at night. There are glow sticks hung at key parts of the course, but we still needed to pay very close attention. The moon was out, which was a big help, and we both carried flashlights and headlights.

Joy: We draw a lot of strength from supporting each other and I know that without Byron's emotional support and great coaching, I would not have finished Rocky. I got into ultrarunning to enjoy these experiences with Byron, and going solo is the absolute last option for me. After sacrificing 40 precious minutes working on my blistered feet, I was determined to push hard for the last 40 miles of the race. My feet looked and felt raw. As I hobbled out of the aid station, weakly attempting to smile, I could see the concern on Byron's face. I told him that I would give it a go, and that either my feet would feel better by the time we got up the trail, or I would turn around and go back to the start/finish at station 5. Fortunately, the pain in my sore, battered feet slowly dulled as we ran, and I was able to eventually trot at a slow pace.

When we came into aid station 2–3, one woman had to drop out due to a sprained ankle. A volunteer mentioned she was one of the front runners! Even walking, we were still stumbling and tripping. And leaves hid many of those roots.

Byron: I was going up a hill and talking to Joy when I realized that she was not there! I turned around and looked down a long hill. I could see her headlamp swaying back and forth below me. I ran back to rescue her from a "bad spot." She had almost fallen asleep. "I can't go on. I need some sleep!" she mumbled. "Where are you going to sleep," I answered, "in the bushes with the snakes?" I usually carry some caffeine pills, but tonight they were in the car. Then I remembered we had some espresso-flavored energy gel. Joy took some of the caffeinated gel, and within two minutes she was a new woman. In fact, she picked up the pace so much that I had a tough time keeping up with her.

Joy: The noise from the wildlife in the swamp was very loud. It sounded like an outtake from the movie *The Creature from the Black Lagoon*. We could hear coyotes off in the hills. Before long we encountered another runner limping very badly. We asked if he needed help. His running buddy had gone up to aid station 174 to get help. The roots claim yet another runner.

We finished our fourth lap in 6:40. Ouch, I never thought we would be this slow! Oh well, at least we were still making progress. It was getting really cold now. Two runners dropped with hypothermia, and were sitting at aid station 5 wrapped in blankets. They were shivering so violently that volunteers had to hold their cups of coffee for them. I know it was –7C (20F), but it felt more like –20C (7F). We learned to stay away from the fires at the aid station. We were so cold, and the fire was so inviting!

The moon had set and it was very dark. Byron changed batteries in the flashlights. It was a good thing too. My flashlight burned out and shortly after, my headlamp also expired! I attempted to replace the batteries at aid station 2–3, but to no avail. Apparently the bulbs had burned out. So for the next few hours, I had to stay very close to Byron so that I could see. He gave me his flashlight, but when the moon had set, I had a really hard time seeing two feet in front of me.

By the time we got to aid station 1, it was even colder. One runner was looking through his drop bags for more clothes but found none. A female runner handed him a pair of bright pink running tights. What a guy won't do to stay warm!

Byron: We were having a more difficult time finding our way now that it was completely dark. And to make matters worse, someone had removed some of the glow sticks. When we got to aid station 2–3 I had to wake up the volunteers to take down our running numbers. They said that other volunteers did not show up and they were doing a double shift. The volunteers at Rocky Racoon were great. They cooked for us, filled our water bottles, made sandwiches, bandaged feet, and more. Without them there would not be a race. They deserve many thanks.

The 5-mile "out-and-back" was the longest 5 miles of our lives. It went on forever! I heard Joy swear off 100-milers for good more than once. I reminded her to keep a positive mental attitude, and we kept moving.

Joy: I recall thinking *I'm freezing! I can't get my fingers to thaw, and they're bloody painful. My feet hurt, my knees hurt, my back is aching, I'm nauseous, and I'm so tired. I've had it! What was I thinking? I'm so sick of this! No more stinking ultras. I want to go back to the motel and sleep for three days. This stinks!*

Byron, knowing how to really get me going, replied sarcastically, "Okay. That's fine. I'll come home the conquering hero and you can be the doting little wife. No problem. After all, there should only be one ultramarathoner per family, and I don't mind being the special one. It's okay, dear. You can quit now. This just proves that women are the weaker sex . . . " After calling him a few choice names, I laughed and got over my blue period. Byron always knows the right thing to say to me to help me refocus and put things into perspective.

After a long night of cold, dark running, the sun finally started to rise as we neared the finish. It was absolutely beautiful. I was so tired and mentally foggy that it took me a while to realize that it was getting light out. With the new day came new hope that the end was near. Once those precious beams of sunlight began to caress my face, the warmth of the sun melted away my foul mood and rejuvenated my spirits. I was finally able to dispense with my self-indulgence and embrace this new day. We were so close to the finish, victory was ours! We were going to finish this race, and I could return home with my head held high. I had once again faced my personal demons and I had prevailed. Another personal challenge fought and won!

Byron: It was a clear morning and it was a great sight to see the sun rise. This is when we got our second wind and started pushing hard for the finish line. This is my favorite part of any race. With only 10 miles to go the pain and doubts leave your mind. We could feel the excitement of finishing our first 100-mile trail run. There was no way we were going over 26 hours! Joy really dug down deep in those last few miles. I could see the pain in her face but she really wanted it. We ran right through aid station 174. We crossed the finish line holding hands, as we do in all of our races. We finished in 25:52, a little slower than we planned, but we finished! We were 60th out of 94 finishers. There were 134 registered for the race. Looks like the roots took their toll on many. Joy was the 10th woman overall and 4th

in the women's masters division. And she said she would never do another
100-miler? Of course she is planning to do another 100-miler!

Ultramarathons are like life's adventures—if you persevere, you will succeed. You'll never know just how far you can push your body, mind or spirit until you are put to the test. The beauty is, once you have faced and conquered the challenge of running 100 miles, you know that there is nothing
you can't do if you really want to. And after being up for 33 hours, all we
really wanted to do was get some well-deserved rest and start dreaming
about the next race.

Running Because of My Father

NAME: MIKE STRZELECKI
AGE: 39
RESIDENCE: BALTIMORE, MARYLAND
YEARS RUNNING: 12
YEARS RUNNING ULTRAS: 10

I still remember when I first decided to run 50 miles; it was the day I learned my father was dying.

"It's a tumor," revealed my mother by telephone, her quivering voice hinting to its seriousness. Any further details she offered became lost in the vortex of emotions and tears into which I descended. Right then, I inexplicably decided to honor my father by running a 50-mile trail race—an unusual concept being that I was not a runner. As a child, however, I obsessed over the miraculous feats of great explorers like Thor Heyerdahl and Colin Fletcher. And ABC's coverage of the Western States 100-mile trail run showed me that the newest wave of world-class explorers was found on rugged mountain trails participating in extreme endurance events. The next phase of my life was set.

So there I was, nine months and 1,500 training miles later, pacing a fog-veiled parking lot on the Blue Ridge Parkway near Lynchburg, Virginia, battling nerves and 5-in-the-morning autumn chill, awaiting the start of the Mountain Masochist Trail Run. The race course traces a 50-mile scribble northward over high mountains and across narrow valleys, ending at a modest cluster of isolated buildings that calls itself Montebello. Darkness cloaked the scene as runners made last-second preparations and received supportive hugs and encouragement from crew members. My father's cheers would not be heard that day; he had passed away two months prior.

The race began and the cheetahs sprinted off into the darkness. I hung back, plodding with the mountain goats. The metronomic thumping of running shoes served as reminder that 100,000 foot strides lay ahead. "Go out easy," admonished veteran ultrarunners. "Walk the uphills and run the downhills." I nudged my way into a slipstream of other runners moving at my unhurried pace, and emulated their relaxed cadence. Running an ultra-marathon requires reined-in patience, especially early in the race.

My father taught me patience. When I was 4, he took me on my first fishing trip to a farm pond crammed full with bluegills, where he knew I would fill my creel and get hooked on the sport. I left with a stringer full of panfish and a smile wider than the pond, anxious to return another day. The following week, a second fishing expedition ensued. This time, he purposely took me to a particularly unproductive, slow-moving stretch of water where he knew I would have very little luck. As we sat watching the lifeless bobber, my father made a point of diverting my attention to birds flitting around the riparian area and mayflies drifting skyward. We skipped rocks across the water, and identified trees. Eventually, a hefty bass—a whale in my eyes—found its way to my worm, punctuating a wonderful afternoon. That day, my father taught me that patience not only pays rewards, but also opens up new channels of discovery.

Back on the trail, darkness soon broke, and scenic Appalachia opened like a morning flower. From high vantages, mountains of deep gold and russet rolled to the horizon like swells on the ocean. The Mountain Masochist course links one mountaintop to the next. Runners climb a lung-searing 8,040 vertical feet over the 50 miles, like sprinting up the Empire State Building five times. The first significant climb came at mile 6—up 3 miles of wide, deeply rutted trail strewn with fist-sized cobble. The exertion erased the morning chill, and the stones battered my feet. Other punishing climbs followed, assuaged by gentle downhills and lovely crossings of Otter and Cashew Creeks. The crucible climb began at mile 22, near the Lynchburg Reservoir. It was 14 continuous miles of uphill, weaving and winding to the top of Buck Mountain. The 3-hour ascent left my legs aquiver and my spirits squashed. The climb demanded exceptional strength and fortitude.

My father, a teacher by vocation, instilled in me the importance of building a strong body and mind. During my teen years, we passed summers working side by side along the sheer cliffs of a traprock quarry. Using 15-pound sledgehammers, we reduced giant slabs of hard blue rock into building stone. "Crack it along the grain," he'd tell me, encouraging hard swings of the tool. We hand-loaded the broken chunks into the bucket of a front-end loader for weighing. On a good day, we'd chop and hoist 10 tons of payload. The work was brutal and demanding. It left us sweat-drenched and with achy backs. My father made sure I understood that hard work develops strength in body and character.

By mile 30, however, the distance was taking a toll on my body and character. Simple but vital functions became difficult. I forced myself to eat even when my stomach wrenched, and drink Gatorade even when it tasted like bile. I painfully changed socks when too sore to bend over. Forward locomotion was the immediate goal. At mile 34, runners entered a challenging 5-mile loop of single track where the course became more muddy, primitive, and overgrown. I spent precious energy scrambling over rocks and fallen logs. I wore mud splats from falls like Purple Hearts. But through it all, I felt an inextricable connection to the environment through which I was passing. A trail run combines and reduces runner and nature to its most intimate and immediate form. It requires from the runner an abiding respect and admiration for the enveloping natural world.

My father instilled in me a profound love of nature and the unbridled urge to be outdoors. We spent 12 summers together fly fishing the gin-clear waters of Yellowstone Park. On one particularly sunny afternoon, we worked hand-tied flies through riffle water deep into a canyon carved by the Gardiner River. In the water, hefty cutthroat trout were gorging on thick orange salmonflies—a fly fisherman's nirvana. High above us, however, a herd of surefooted bighorn sheep clambered over a talus ledge, kicking scree down the cliff side. My father pulled me away from the feeding trout and led me high onto a nearby ledge where we could spy the maneuvering sheep. We passed the remainder of the day observing one of nature's great theatrical performances. As a youth, I naively thought our quarry was the trout, but on that day I realized it was not. It was nature.

Late in the race, my emotions vacillated like the terrain I crossed. I laughed with other runners, became agitated during spells of soreness and nausea, and sang high praise to the mountains in the midst of adrenaline surges. During the worst stretches, my thighs could conjure up no lift. I was reduced to a shuffle, stumbling over one rock after another. I prayed for steep hills for they would call into action muscles that were fresh, ones that didn't hurt as badly.

Yet the physical pain paled in comparison to emotions surfacing. At mile 45, when I realized that I would complete the race, I broke down and cried.

The finish was simple and understated: some slaps on the back from friends and a handshake from the race director. A few runners milled about in various stages of angst and elation. There was no fanfare. It proved the perfect complement to such a personal and profound experience. I laid down in a field of cool grass to rest my withered legs and watched wispy clouds race by. I recalled my mother's phone call nine months prior, the one that sideswiped my life and brought me to this lonely field for one last outdoor adventure with my dad.

And then I realized: I didn't finish the run to honor my father; I finished it because of my father.

Running With Woofie

NAME: ANTHONY HUMPAGE
AGE: 47
RESIDENCE: SCOTTSDALE, ARIZONA
YEARS RUNNING: 3
YEARS RUNNING ULTRAS: 1 1/2

Photo by Keith Facchino

Team Woofie is named after Anthony's running totem, Woofie, the alpha male brown bear at McNeil River Falls in Alaska. Team Woofie epitomizes strength and endurance, combined with a never - say-die attitude.

The story of my first 100-miler started in the gym on the Monday before the race. I took particular care in my tapering, including adjusting my strength training. Monday would be my last gym day before leaving for Vermont on Wednesday. The back extension machine was occupied, so I decided to do three sets of Good Mornings using an unloaded bar instead. That was a big mistake. On Tuesday morning my hamstrings were screaming loudly. Dismayed, I started a vigorous stretching and icing routine—even stretching during the plane ride to Vermont, much to the amusement of the cabin crew. The improvement in my hamstrings was slow and I was worried sick about them right up to the starting line. Here I was, about to start my first 100-miler, just 16 months after my first marathon. I had come so far in a compressed amount of time, and now something I did the week before in the gym was threatening to do me in.

I was basically sedentary and overweight all my life. I played very few sports at school, as I was teased unmercifully in the changing rooms because I was fat. I would go to school with my kit on underneath my regular clothes so I wouldn't have to change. As a child I also had quite a problem with asthma, which also led me to avoid exercise. By late 1997 I had ballooned up to 275 pounds, which on my frame is a lot. In 1998 I had had enough. I applied myself, completely changed my lifestyle, began weight lifting, and dropped 75 pounds. In 1999 I began running to and from the gym as an adjunct to my weight lifting. In October 1999, I ran in my very first race, a 5K, finishing in 26:03.

At the gym I became acquainted with a gentleman named Noah. He occasionally came to the gym wearing an Ice Age 50-miler T-shirt. We began running together on weekends. Noah told me stories of running and ultras, but even then, long-distance running was completely off my radar screen. It was just not something I thought possible for me.

Eventually, however, I found that I wanted to cover more distance than my running partners and I started venturing out on my own. Bit by bit my mileage increased, until one day I realized that I had run a half marathon. It dawned on me that perhaps even I could run a marathon. I looked into training groups and joined one organized and coached by Ron Cates. I began training for my first marathon, the Desert Classic. On February 18, 2001, I finished the Desert Classic with a sprint finish in 4:48:59.

After the race, Ron and I discussed my running goals. Still intrigued by Noah's tales of ultras, I remember exactly what I said to Ron: "Well, I wouldn't mind trying a 50-miler one day, but not a 100-miler. Those guys are mad. They hallucinate, you know." I also remember Ron's reply very well: "Actually, you'd be good at it. You have the right mental attitude." And that is what one calls a cause set in motion! I set my sights on running a 50-miler within one year, and a 100-miler within two years. Everyone told me I was too ambitious. As it turned out, I ran my first 50-mile race in just over eight months, and my first 100-miler in 16 months.

There is a local race called the Crown King Scramble with both a 50K and a 50-mile component. The race originated, I gather, as a Western States practice run and just got bigger. The course is along the old stage-coach road from Phoenix to Prescott and passes through a great deal of old mining country. Although the 2001 CKS was only a month after my marathon, I decided to enter the 50K and give it a go. I twisted my ankle badly a few weeks before the race, and was so concerned about finishing that I left trekking poles out about halfway. As it turned out, I finished okay, although well back in the pack in 8:17. But the scenery and experience were first-class. Even at this preliminary stage, I was a confirmed ultrarunner.

Fifteen months later I was at a starting line in Vermont, getting ready to do what I once thought impossible: run 100 miles. Only one thing was really bothering me—my hamstrings. I put more care into training and tapering for the VT 100 than for any of my other races. I was also mentally prepared and had a real plan for the race. Prior to going to Vermont I read every online race report I could find. I plotted previous runners' comments on a copy of the race map—for example, where I would encounter long or tough hills. I set a goal of finishing in under 27 hours, and built a spreadsheet with split times and ETAs for each aid station for finishing times of 24, 27, and 30 hours. Thus I would know if I was fast, on target, or slow. I kept one copy, and my wife and crew chief, Paula, had another. We arrived in Vermont a couple of days early and I took the time to walk a couple of the big hills. I didn't want any surprises.

In the month prior to the race I trained myself to run at a slower 11.5- to 12-minute-a-mile pace. I knew that if I went out too fast, the last parts of the race could be miserable. My plan was to conserve my energy and hold to my split schedule.

By the time I got to the start I had my race face on. I might have seemed a bit withdrawn to some; I was just ready to go. I arranged myself toward the back of the pack as a pianist from the porch of a nearby farmhouse was hammering out "Chariots of Fire." This race was going to be two times longer than I had ever run before, so I was about to step into the unknown. I was content, however, that at that particular moment, I was as prepared as I could be. I don't remember a gun, horn, or even a "Go!"; just a cheer from the runners and onlookers and off we went.

The start at Vermont was quite crowded. At about 300 runners, it's a large ultramarathon. I had stationed myself toward the back of the pack to ensure that I would be starting out with a fairly conservative group, as I did not want to be carried along at a pace faster than I really wanted to go. In fact, even at the start I was careful to remind myself that I should keep to my planned pace. As a memory aid, I had written SLOW and DISCIPLINE on my left forearm in red indelible marker. On the right forearm, TWDQ (Team Woofie Doesn't Quit!).

The trails remained pretty crowded for a while. They were muddy too, with some big puddles in places. Although my feet were well taped to guard against blisters, I was careful to keep them dry. They had to carry me for 100 miles, after all. Most of the Vermont surface is run on what I believe are called "carriage roads." These are essentially hard-packed dirt, and make a great running surface. There are a couple of miles of tarmac, hardly worth talking about, and a few miles of single-track trail or foot-path, some of which is on the Appalachian Trail. Living as I do in Arizona, I found the lush greenery and gentle rolling landscape enchant-ing. In many respects it reminded me a lot of my native England. Very little of the course was flat. It seemed we were going up or down most of the time, and the downs were actually harder on my legs than the ups. I was glad I had included a ten-mile weekly hill run in my pre-Vermont training.

I had only one real demon lurking over me before and during the race, and that was asthma. Although I had asthma in my youth, it hadn't really troubled me since my teens. However, in each of the two 50-mile races pre-ceding Vermont, my performance was ruined by major asthmatic episodes, the first of which came on me as a total surprise. Although I finished that race, I was almost brought to my knees, and nearly keeled over a couple of times. It was only sheer bloody-mindedness and Team Woofie spirit that got me to the finish within the cutoffs. At the second fifty-miler, Zane Grey, I was better, but asthma still brought me to a walk for the last 10 miles. At one stage I had completely despaired of even starting Vermont, but work by my pulmonologist *hopefully* had things under control.

My hamstring rehab must have worked, I'm happy to say, and I never once felt like quitting. Paula describes me as "grumpy" at some of the aid station stops, but she knows that's because I was totally dialed in to my goal. I've been in much worse shape, physically and mentally, in shorter races. Perhaps my poise was a result of planning, experience, or Divine intervention. By the time I got to Tracer Brook (55 miles), nearly one hour ahead of my self-imposed time, and having run farther than I ever had before, I knew I *could* finish. By the time I got to the next major aid sta-tion at 60 miles, I knew that, barring an accident, I *would* finish.

One of my highest moments of the whole race came at night, in what I call the Blair Witch woods between Camp 10 Bear aid station and Bill's aid station (miles 68 and 83). The star-decked canopy was just too awe-some to ignore, so I stopped, turned off my flashlight, and just soaked it all in for a few moments. It was very humbling. Coincidentally, these Blair Witch woods were also where I suffered my weakest performance. It was dark, I was on my own, and the footing was a bit rough. I slowed down because I knew I had ample time to finish, and was afraid of falling or injuring myself. I was glad I had run a solo 50-mile night training run back in June, because I was better prepared to face the physiological and psychological downers that you experience alone in the wee hours.

The sign at the Ashley aid station said it was just 1.5 miles to Bill's, but I say "Bull!" I honestly feel it was farther, and my mood became more and more foul with each step. Paula told me later that when she saw my mood at Bill's she had no doubt that I would finish. Bill's, by the way, reminded me of nothing but a battlefield triage unit. It was filled with sorry, blanket-wrapped characters and those who were having various wounds tended. I left as quickly as I could, taking my temper with me on the way to the dreaded climb up Blood Hill.

In the middle of the night, Blood Hill is a long, grinding climb. The course was marked with glow sticks and yellow plates, which generally made path finding easy. However, at one point I encountered a large section without markers. This bothered me immensely at the time and I was very concerned that I had missed a turn. I was only partially consoled by the lights of other runners strung out behind me, and even wondered if I was leading them astray too. Taking a wrong turn would have been a real blow, so it was a huge relief when I finally saw a glow stick up ahead. I was told later that vandals had removed some of the race markers in this section, a recurring problem at the VT 100, I gather.

It wasn't long before I had my first hallucination. I had heard that even experienced ultrarunners suffer these somewhat regularly in 100-milers, so I almost relished the baptism. I would have sworn there was a gate across the road, but it just disappeared as I approached it. My eyes played tricks on me a lot. Several times I thought I was running past buildings, but they were just trees. My most amusing hallucination actually occurred at first light, shortly after leaving the Jenneville aid station (90 miles). I observed a white baby grand piano scuttle crablike across the road. I knew it wasn't real and got quite a laugh out of it. For those who have never had them, I would describe these hallucinations as more like mirages or tricks of the light than I would *real* hallucinations.

Another of my highest moments was perhaps one of my most foolish as well. After leaving Jenneville, I was energized by the light, the certainty that I was going to finish, and was further lifted by passing a group of runners who had passed me earlier. I really turned the wick up, running down out of Jenneville. I was singing Team Woofie songs, very full of myself. I was flying. Well, as much as you can after 90 miles. This downhill blast of speed no doubt led to the mashing of my quads, which made the last few miles of the race quite uncomfortable.

After Densmore Hill (mile 94), on any serious downhill stretch, I was slowed down a lot by my very sore quadriceps. It was only to get worse. I also felt a strange sensation from my left little toe. I sat down to take a look and discovered that the tape I had placed on that toe had come off. This allowed its neighbor toe to rub it so that the whole toe from the knuckle forward had become one big blister. The toenail had lifted off with the skin and was digging into the skin beneath. I rearranged the skin as best I could, put a large gob of Aquaphor on the toe, put my sock back on and continued. After that, the toe felt a bit strange, but was no longer painful.

After South Woodstock I knew I had less than 4 miles to go. And just as well. I had lots of energy left, but my quads just weren't cooperating. I was not consoled by the knowledge that this was probably my own doing, and I gave up quite a bit of time on this section. I was frustrated, but glad to know that I would soon be finished and within the cutoffs. Paula ran out from the finish to meet me, which was a nice touch.

You come on the finish quite suddenly at Vermont. Although my legs were now cheerfully getting their revenge, there was absolutely no way I was going to walk across the finish line. So I gutted it up, managing some form of a shambling run to finish my first 100-miler in 27:45. A bit over my goal, but well within the cutoffs. One additional note about my asthma: I took some preventive medication during the race and breathed freely the whole way. So to any asthmatics that may be reading this I say, "Never give up!"

Knowing from whence I had come—sedentary porker to 100-mile finisher in four years (and first marathon to 100 miles in 16 months)—I had expected to feel completely enthused by my achievement. But instead it felt rather anticlimactic. I went through the voluntary medical line, milled around a little bit, congratulated some other runners who came in after me, then lay down on one of the medical cots and dozed for about an hour. Paula and I had originally planned to stay for the post-race barbecue, but there were no real washing facilities and we were both tired, so we elected to return to our motel.

That night we ate at a local restaurant. I could barely walk, my legs were so stiff. I think the other diners at the restaurant thought I had a disability and looked sympathetically at Paula. I felt like walking around with a sign that said, "It's okay folks. I just ran a hundred miles!" But I got a lot of sympathetic looks from elderly ladies who stopped to hold doors open for me.

It wasn't until the flight back to Phoenix that it finally began to dawn on me what I had accomplished. I cannot believe that I was able to transform myself from where I was in 1997 to where I am today. I keep a copy of the picture Paula took of me crossing the finish line at my office to remind myself that in ultrarunning, as in life, application gets results.

Digging Deep in the Texas Rain

NAME: TRACY BALDYGA
AGE: 32
RESIDENCE: LARAMIE, WYOMING
YEARS RUNNING: 11
YEARS RUNNING ULTRAS: 1

Growing up with asthma, I was led to believe running was off limits for me. My asthma, however, never stopped my love for sports. In high school I participated in track and field, although not as a runner—I threw the discus. After high school, I began running off and on, which, as it turned out, helped my asthma. Along the way I picked up other sports such as rock climbing, fast packing, mountain biking and fencing. I even spent two years as a wildland firefighter. My father is a retired Green Beret and taught me a lot about the outdoors. His stories of mental and physical strength always inspired me to test my limits and still do to this day.

I was out hiking Tahquitz Peak in California's San Jacinto Wilderness with my son in July 2000 when I met an elderly ultrarunner on a 30-mile training run. He waited for us to arrive at the summit, and we sat and talked at great length about running, climbing, and philosophy. I was intrigued as I listened to him talk about the mental aspects of ultrarunning; of really pushing yourself to complete a run no matter how tough things got. This really hit home with me because one year earlier I had tried to take my own life. That was not the first time I had tried to do so either. I have battled very serious depression since 1992. I was diagnosed as bipolar and obsessive-compulsive. Between 1994 and 1999 I was hospitalized eight times for severe depression and twice for manic episodes. I tried various medications, which never seemed to help. I spent months on end not able to leave my house, or sometimes even my bed. When no medications seemed to work there was only doom on the horizon. In early 2000 doctors suggested elec-troconvulsive (shock) therapy. As I sat on that mountaintop I thought to myself about how, at 29 years of age, my life was gone. In just a few short years I had transformed from a straight-A student and athlete to a shell of a person at the end of her road. But I was inspired by my chance meeting that day, and I decided to take up running again. Running allowed me to be alone with my thoughts and gradually I started feeling better about myself. I went back to work and really looked forward to my lunchtime runs. The fog was slowly lifting around me, at least to the point where suicide was no longer in the forefront of my mind. I began to set goals. One of these goals included ultrarunning.

I followed ultras for a while from the sideline. I wanted to participate, but was afraid I wouldn't be fast enough, or strong enough. I feared I wouldn't fit in. While climbing one evening at a local gym, I spoke with a friend, Scott Morgan, about ultras. He had participated in several ultraruns, and talking with him helped dispel my fears. He introduced me to other ultrarunners, and I was on my way. As I got to know more ultrarunners, I found a deep connection with them. I discovered that many of them had been through times of alcoholism, drug addiction, and so on. I found that some were, like me, obsessive-compulsive. Finally there was a group I was a part of, no longer on the periphery staring inside wanting to be "normal." I wasn't someone pretending to be just like everyone else anymore. I felt like I had found a group of like-minded freaks.

My first ultra was the Cuyamaca 50K, and it went pretty well. It was tough in many ways, but enjoyable overall, and I was hooked. My second trail ultra was to be the Sunmart 50-Mile Endurance Run, eight weeks later, in Huntsville, Texas, just outside Houston.

I traveled to Houston two days before the race so I'd have time to get familiar with the course. My asthma is primarily induced by plant allergies, so I wanted to check out the trees and shrubs along the course to make sure they would not cause me any problems. Not knowing the Houston area very well, I got a hotel much too far from Huntsville. That was very inconvenient because I had to wake up so early to get to the start. Coupled with never sleeping well before a race, worrying about all the things that might go wrong, I feared I was in for a tough day at best. I packed all my stuff the night before and reviewed my lists over and over to make sure I had everything. I set my alarm and asked for a wake up call, but still worried all night that my watch would break and the people downstairs would not call. I would doze off, then wake up in a panic and check my watch to see that only 30 minutes had passed. The night seemed endless.

The morning finally came, and I freaked out! The day before, I'd gone out to scout the course and found the weather hot and humid, but overall pleasant. I awoke on race day to hard rain and cold temperatures. I had never seen so much rain falling from the sky, and it only got harder and heavier as I drove to the start. I was upset. I do not do well in the cold and was not at all prepared for this type of weather. For some reason I thought of Texas as hot and arid. Huntsville, however, was like a swamp. There was even a sign entering the park that said to beware of alligators! I just wanted to go home. Would it ever end? This was some sort of sick joke in my mind and not the conditions under which I wanted to run my first 50-miler. How could I finish a 50-mile race if I couldn't even push myself to get out of the car? I was already formulating my DNF excuse.

At the start of the event, I found myself surrounded by a bunch of loons who actually seemed to enjoy the rain! I was shaking from a combination of nerves and cold. I don't even remember hearing anyone say "Start!"— I just remember being in the group of runners as it began to move forward and I was swept along with them into the cold, dark, rainy woods. I wasn't feeling very strong, and I finished the first lap 15 minutes slower than I had planned. I was so worried. I felt like a little ant on the trail, and I didn't understand why I was there and how I would ever finish. I was afraid I would DNF and people would laugh at me. Honestly, time stood still and I just wanted to run away from the course. At this point I truly felt ultras were the worst thing in my life. I was having more self-doubt than I'd ever had before. I was cold, wet, scared, and miserable, but at least I had forgotten about the alligators!

The Sunmart course was a wet and muddy, 12.5-mile loop that we would repeat four times. The beginning of the first loop was enjoyable as it rolled along a single-track trail through woods. But I soon found myself spread out from the other runners, all alone. I could see people every now and then, but the woods still made me feel very alone. As I continued to run, my anxiety began to ease a bit and I became lost in the beauty of this strange new place. There were a lot of roots along the course, and I started to have fun running around and over them. Finally I was back on my journey and things seemed to be going okay. I ran through every puddle enjoying the water and mud splashing on my legs, getting in my shoes and squeezing between my toes. I enjoyed this primal feeling of getting wet and dirty. It was like being a kid again, just enjoying Mother Nature. She was running the show now and I was along for the ride, and what a ride it would be!

After leaving the first aid station I set out on an out-and-back section that went uphill to another aid station. This section of the course was more of a fire road of red-clay earth. It was very strange for me. It was very slick, and I slid back with every step. I saw the top runners go over it like nothing. Their leg strength was totally amazing. They moved across the red clay like gazelles. After the red-clay section I entered the woods again. I really enjoyed this section of the trail on every lap. I always had a surge of energy running through these trees and all the water/mud puddles. Also, my favorite aid station was on this section. They had hot, homemade chicken broth that I looked forward to on every lap. The next wooded section was always the longest for me. I dreaded the footbridges because I didn't have my glasses and I always felt awkward and off balance running across them. Crossing those bridges made me wonder if there really were alligators out there like the sign said. I never did see one. I always knew I was coming along to the next aid station when I saw the American flags along the trail. Being so soon after the events of September 11, my thoughts would turn to all of my military family members, past and present. Seeing the flags gave me a sense of pride and good fortune. I was proud to be an American, and fortunate to have the opportunity to come out here to follow a crazy dream. From that next aid station I would then head into the start/finish area. That part of the trail was very rooty! I paid special attention to that section, as I had a feeling I would still be running after dark. The worst part of the course was an uphill section where the mud was thick and black. I had to walk that section each time. Afterward, the trail became a paved single-track section leading into the parking area where I would turn around and do it all again three more times. It was still raining relentlessly.

As I ran the course, I felt every emotion possible, or so it seemed. I spent a lot of time deep inside myself pondering my past. I thought a great deal about people who had entered my life and what they taught me: the good and the bad, triumphs and tragedies, all the pain and tears and laughter. I didn't think as much about the future. I was just happy to have made it this far. There were times I was overcome with the guilt of the event that had thankfully never transpired: my suicide. The guilt of not having cared for the others who would have been affected. I did think of one thing in the future: Statistics show that if a person attempts suicide once, they will do it again and again. As I ran there in the rain I felt like a statistic. Life was now a slide show in my mind's eye. Snapshots of life just flashed in front of me. All the anger, all the confusion, every moment of weakness. It was like hearing the word *"Why?"* shouted over and over with every flash.

My physical condition was poor at best. I went into the race with tendonitis problems, and by the end of the second lap I had to untie my left shoe due to swelling in my foot. There were times out there when I could not even feel my foot. My anklebones totally disappeared into the swollen tissue. The swelling slowed me down tremendously. My pre-race strategy was to run for 25 minutes and walk for 5, with a goal of finishing in less than 9 1/2 hours. That was no longer possible. I decided to run whenever I felt good and to just keep moving forward whenever I didn't. There were several stretches where I ran for longer than 30 minutes. There were also long walking stretches of 20 minutes or more. Then, as if my foot problems were not enough, at the end of the first lap I had an asthma attack. I was not prepared for the cool temperatures that day and my lungs were having trouble adapting. People kept asking if I was okay because I was coughing so much and having obvious difficulty breathing. I was running off sheer determination now.

I felt I would be justified in quitting when my asthma flared up. In fact, I stopped at the start/finish area after the first lap for about 15 minutes. I knew no one would blame me for quitting, and they would probably even say that I made a good decision. Then I recalled that every time in my life I am faced with fear, I have an asthma attack. If I hear people argue in line at the grocery store, I have an asthma attack. If someone disagrees with me in such a way that I feel stupid, I have an asthma attack. Was this race just another fear? Was I afraid of what I might find in myself out there in those woods? Yes, I was. I was afraid that I would fail. I was afraid that I would DNF because I was too weak or too tired. It's always easier to just quit. Sure, I could quit now, blame my asthma or foot problems, and no one would ever know the truth—that I am afraid of life. Everyone back home already thought I was incredibly brave for even attempting this run. What they didn't know was that on the inside I was so very afraid. I was afraid of this race. I was afraid of living. Everyday I woke up afraid to face the world outside my own bed. I put on that brave, tough-girl exterior because I hoped that if I could convince everyone else that I was strong, then maybe, just maybe, I would believe it too and become that brave girl that others saw.

I sat at that aid station for 15 minutes, pondering the possibilities. I looked at the car keys and the car knowing that I stood alone in my decision. No one there knew me. No one was even paying attention to me. But I knew that if I quit this race that I would continue to be afraid. And in spite of the very good reasons I had for dropping, I would always know the truth. I just sat there and wept. I was a total loser in my eyes at that point. But ironically, battling my negative emotions would now drive me. It was time to put all the viable excuses aside and look inside.

Yes, I have weakness. Yes, I have a lot of irrational fears. But I would beat them. I would finish. So I put away the car keys and walked away from the aid station. And then I ran.

The remainder of the race was very good for me. I cried tears of happiness. For the last few hours I had gone into myself, into a place I didn't want to go. I had to run a 50-mile race to do it, but that's okay. This day was something I had needed for a long time in my life. I reached the last aid station on my last loop and, as I left, was overcome with an emotion that encompassed all emotions. I wept because I knew that I had done so much more than run 50 miles in the Texas rain. My race began years before and could not be measured in miles or hours. I thought of how I was there in the cold, dark, rainy night, running alone on a twisted muddy trail. It was very symbolic. I was in the back of the pack fighting an uphill battle. I was by myself, but I was not alone. My grandfather, dead for several years now, was the one person in my family who never knew of my problems. He was a very loving man and cared for me deeply. My grandmother had never told him about my problems because she knew how much it would hurt him. I was going through another bout with depression when he died, and barely noticed or comprehended his passing. But I felt his presence with me as I left that last aid station. And suddenly I felt I was okay. I wasn't just a statistic. I wasn't just an illness. I realized I am just a person. And like other people, I am strong sometimes and weak at other times. So was that it? Was a 50-mile run all I needed? Maybe. I do think that moments can happen that change the way you think about your life. That was my moment. Out on a trail in Texas in the rain with my grandfather and a bunch of other crazy people just like me.

When that elderly ultrarunner spoke to me on the mountaintop in July 2000, I was taken back. Back to closed steel doors and the days when I could not be trusted to shave my legs without supervision. I hope to never find myself on that journey again. However, the continued journey of self-discovery and self-awareness is one I definitely seek. And I've found it in ultrarunning. I have driven myself to choose life. It may sound strange to anyone who has never seriously wanted to die. When you make up your mind to end your life, finding the strength to live it is nearly insurmountable. I had a lot of people who loved me and supported me. I can recall my aunt crying into my blank face and shouting with anger because she couldn't understand why I wanted to die. But even with caring, loving people on my side, I still had to do it alone. I had to find the strength inside of me. You often hear ultrarunners say, "I had to dig deep" when they talk about running tough races. And that's just what I did. I dug and dug, deeper and deeper. I cried and I shouted and then I found it: that something inside us all. I think of it as a little piece of granite that defines who we are. Granite, steadfast and unbreakable.

For me running ultras is like an exorcism. During every long run and race I think about those years of depression. Sometimes I find tears rolling down my cheeks. The tears are not tears of sadness as they were back then. I cry now because I'm so happy that I chose to dig deep and find the will to live. I am never alone on the trails. I think about a lot of people out there. I see their faces and the love they had for me that I could not see at the time through the fog. Sometimes while running I also think about the people who said that I was just not as tough as other people. That I should just accept the fact that depression was going to destroy my life. I'm so glad they were wrong.

I finished the Sunmart 50-miler in just under 11 hours. I came in 155th out of 193 finishers and even placed 3rd in my age group! I have a picture of me taken at the finish. I look tired, worn, and dirty, but for the first time in a long time, I look content.

Living the Rock-and-Roll (and Running) Lifestyle

NAME: MICHAEL DIMKICH
AGE: 35
RESIDENCE: WOODLAWN HILLS, CA
YEARS RUNNING: 12
YEARS RUNNING ULTRAS: 2 1/2

Ultrarunning has crept up on me. By profession I am a touring musician in a rock band. I used to be a "rock guy" who happened to run, but at some point along the line, I became an ultrarunner who happens to play music for a living. And to think that it all started because I couldn't fit in my *de rigueur* "rock guy" leather pants.

It's the usual 20-something story: I hit an age whereupon the beer, junk food, and general lifestyle associated with being in a band started to take its toll. It was affecting my wardrobe, or, I should say, my ability to fit into it! I was in former Sex Pistols guitarist Steve Jones's band at the time and we were about to do some shows with a band called The Cult and I *really* wanted to wear those leather pants onstage. Something had to give, and it wasn't going to be those pants. I put on a pair of ill-fitting cross-trainers and trudged out the door and down the road a few blocks and it about killed me. I just sat on the curb, attempting not to heave, trying to pull myself together so I could at least walk back to my house. Day after day I went through the same routine until, after a couple of months, I was running 2 miles a day, five days a week. Sure enough, those leather pants fit just fine.

A few years and many miles later, I went on tour with The Cult again. This time I was on board as the second guitarist and along with me came those same, rather battered, leather pants. I generally ran every day as we toured Europe and Scandinavia, now running longer distances. While at home, I sometimes ran with a group based out of a local running shop. Often during the longer runs various members of this group chatted about who was training for or had recently participated in various 100-milers. *One hundred miles?* This was more than I ran over a matter of weeks—and these people were doing it in *one day?* They also seemed to talk quite a bit about math as well. Whenever the topic turned to numbers of any kind, be they mathematical equations or extreme mileage, I just tuned it out. I'd run a number of road marathons and even made the effort to bring my times down, but to say that I had no interest in running 100 miles was an understatement of epic proportions.

Once again, duty called and I was off to tour with The Cult. It had been quite a while since I'd toured "in style," as it were, with a big band, and I leapt headfirst into being a "rock guy" again, putting the "marathon man" on hold. Needless to say, when I got back to the math/ultra group I realized that my fitness had suffered. It was time to get serious about the running again.

As I renewed my running acquaintances and started training in earnest once more, I rediscovered the pleasure running provided me and started entering races again. At this point, music and running crossed paths as a musician friend of mine, Mike from the Goo Goo Dolls, mentioned that he'd done a local 50K not too long ago. I couldn't let another "rock guy" tackle an ultra distance while I just ran marathons. Mike didn't know it at the time but the gauntlet had been laid down. So, imitation being the highest form of flattery, I ran the same 50K (Mike was gone on tour, thank goodness), took it easy, and survived. I did a couple more 50Ks and, at the urging of the math/ultra bunch, took on my first 50-miler: the Avalon Benefit 50. It was during this race that I *really* got a taste of what an ultra is all about as I went out hard like any true road racer would. Big mistake. At mile 44 one of my ultra compatriots passed me like I was standing still (probably because I *was*). I had a major epiphany. *Why am I out here?* Survival instinct took over and I choked down an energy bar, drank a bit, and pulled it together to (mostly) run it in to the finish. I learned my lesson, however, and my next 50-miler went much better. I was hooked.

I was now quite caught up in ultrarunning and, as a result, I paced a friend at the Angeles Crest 100. As I waited for my runner at a dark highway crossing, I was totally spellbound by the sight of a thin line of flashlights moving toward me at the aid station. I was just awestruck by the enormity of what these people were undertaking—and here I was, having never even run holding a flashlight, responsible for getting my runner to the finish line. If she had only known how utterly rookie I was, she probably would have thought twice about using me. She'd gotten a bit dehydrated earlier in the race and had some cramping as a result. In true ultrarunner fashion, however, she gutted it out and made it across the finish line in style. Meanwhile, I felt that what I was doing was so inconsequential. I even felt guilty taking food at the aid stations. My 42 miles of pacing paled in comparison to what she had done. After the race I could no longer say with conviction that I had no interest in running a 100-miler. I had decided then and there that I would run the AC 100 someday, though I relegated it to a far corner of my subconscious like a guilty secret.

Once again, it was time to go to work and on tour I went as my running buddies began their training for the 2001 Angeles Crest 100. On tour we spent plenty of time in the South and, from a runner's perspective, July through August in states like Florida, Texas, and Louisiana is hell on earth. With everyone at home dutifully training, however, I knew that I couldn't slack in spite of the weather. The result was some of the most horrific runs I've ever done.

There's something about traveling on a bus, not unlike flying on an airplane, that just sucks the fluid out of your body. Whenever I woke up on that thing—and it was a top-of-the-line tour bus—I felt like I had a hangover yet I hadn't touched a drop. No matter how plush these buses are, they are still just a steel tube on wheels banging along rutted roads, slamming on their brakes, and having air-conditioning failures. It was like being in a submarine. (Actually, I visited a WWII U-boat on display at the Chicago Museum of Science and Industry, and those guys had more headroom and bunk space than we did!) More often than not I couldn't get a run in until well into the day when it was sure to be at its hottest. This permitted me to reconnoiter our latest stop, and I could always come back with info on the location of the closest Starbucks or record shop. The band thought I was nuts for running like this but at least it was useful! I would run just about anywhere I could, and this included doing stuff like getting a cab in Las Vegas, asking the cabdriver to reset his odometer, and then heading out 12 or 14 miles into the desert on an old road. I'd hand over my fare, hop out, and run back into town, trying all the while to forget the bank clock we'd passed on the drive out whose thermometer read 111 degrees. I figured that it couldn't get much hotter than that at Angeles Crest. I was now training for the race without admitting it to anyone, least of all myself.

It was during this tour that I ran what I consider to be the worst run in the contiguous 48 states. No offense to the citizenry, but it was in Birmingham, Alabama. I ran 14 miles around a massive mall parking lot, cars merging all over the place as I continued along the only suitable running route I could find within 50 miles. When I finished I went up to one of the valet parking attendants at the hotel and asked him if he liked The Cult, to which he replied, "Yeah, they're playing tonight." I said, "I play in the band and will get you some tickets if you'd like, I just need you to drive me around this parking lot so I can get the mileage." He did, and I was able to add another 14 miles to my anal-retentive running log. (Postscript: I did return to Birmingham months later and had a pretty and scenic run through the hills near the university.) Not all of my dealings with concert-goers were so pleasant as it wasn't uncommon that, if I ran near the venue too close to showtime, I would get all sorts of unwanted attention in my running shorts. Hurled beer cans accompanied the hurled insults. All of this from people who had paid good money to see a band in which I played guitar. If they only knew!

As the tour continued, I began to seriously consider doing Angeles Crest. Whenever I was home for a few days or a week at a time, I would head out onto the AC course with my AC-entered friends. The day before the band flew to Japan a bunch of us did the first half of the race as a training run, the farthest I'd run in four or five months. Thank God we were flying first-class as I don't think I could've bent my legs enough to fit into a coach seat! A few weeks later the tour stopped for a month and I got the chance to participate in the Labor Day training weekend during which you run the entire Angeles Crest course over three days. I got wicked blisters, my quads ached like I'd never thought they could, and I was covered in poison oak. Perfect. I was ready.

I wasn't entirely sure that my touring schedule would even allow me to run AC until after I'd already completed the Labor Day training weekend. In retrospect, I think I was almost hoping that I wouldn't be available to run the race, but the completion of the training weekend put me on an inevitable path to the AC 100. So I cleared the decks for my participation in the race: I made it very clear to the band that I would be as unavailable for any last minute rehearsals as any human could be on race weekend. No cell phone with unlimited long distance could reach where I was going. Funny—I was choosing to trudge my way through 100 hot, rugged, and mountainous miles rather than play guitar with a rock-and-roll band. I was about to do what I'd sworn a few years back I'd never do. I was about to run 100 miles through the Angeles National Forest.

Ask my girlfriend—before 50Ks and marathons, I'm a complete nervous wreck. She might use something less diplomatic to describe my usual pre-race state. This time, however, she noted that I was actually *pleasant*! I was just so totally overwhelmed by the task that lay before me that I could be nothing but resigned to my fate. I had no expectations of running a PR, or qualifying for Boston. I just wanted to finish. I had a vague idea of what my finishing time might be if all went well but I knew for sure that, barring a total meltdown, I should be able to beat the 33-hour cutoff. The day and night before the race, spent at the race start in the small town of Wrightwood, was a blur of last-minute preparation and mingling with other race participants. Oh, and Mike from the Goo Goo Dolls was racing too. I wasn't the only running-nerd/musician after all . . .

The race started promptly at 5:00 A.M., a very un-rock-and-roll time by most standards, and I was a bit shocked by the quick pace as we all ran the first half mile along a dark, quiet residential road. The pace and starting route seemed more akin to a road race than a trail race but it certainly lacked the cheering crowds present at any major road marathon. Just the sounds of runners' foot strikes and the odd barking dog. Once we hit the dirt, however, there was no question that I was running anything *but* a road marathon; the trail went practically straight up. A total hiker. Only the most enthusiastic, or uninitiated, attempted to continue running.

The course is a point-to-point along a trail system that vaguely follows, and zigzags across, the Angeles Crest Highway, ultimately dropping down and finishing in Pasadena. Earlier versions of the race finished right at the Rose Bowl until a stint of Guns n' Roses concerts being held there necessitated a change of finish line. I guess rock-and-roll took precedence over ultrarunning *that* weekend. AC is a rugged but beautiful course that tops out at over 9,000 feet, features plenty of great forest scenery, some gnarly climbs, and even gnarlier footing. I was having a blast out on the race course as I followed an ultra veteran's sage words about AC: "If you're not enjoying the scenery, then you're going *too fast!*" Needless to say, I made a point of enjoying the scenery to its fullest. The aid stations were almost a carnival atmosphere as friends and family of many of the runners were there to provide various items of food, drink, and clothing, not to mention moral support, for their runners. As the race progressed I began to find that all of the positive attention paid me by various volunteers and crew reminded me of being sick when you're a child, with people constantly asking "How're you doing? Want some soup?" Great—all the sympathy and nurturing you could ever want without being terminally ill.

The gods of ultrarunning were not, however, going to let me just cruise through AC unpunished as I began to suffer from hot spots, and later blisters of the highest degree, around mile 40. Strange that I could run 52 miles of the course in one go a couple of months prior without a single blister and now I was afflicted well before the halfway point. I was learning all about the unpredictability inherent in 100-milers. After getting some advice regarding my rapidly developing blisters from another runner while between aid stations (this would never happen in the cutthroat world of the road race) I hit the halfway point determined to fix my feet and get back into running a strong race. My crew at this point consisted of my girlfriend Lisa, a veteran utrarunner named Elena, and the runner whom I had paced at AC the previous year, Lora. Elena was an expert at handling blisters and I knew that if anyone could get my feet under control, it would be her. As I sat in a chair and they all attended to me, washing and dressing my horrid feet, I couldn't help but comment that I felt like a Roman emperor with his servants lavishing their attention upon him in all of his royal splendor. It was about then that I was informed that my foot care had been completed and I was to get my butt out of the chair and in gear. Onward and upward.

My feet taken care of with some taping and a change of socks and insoles, I felt reborn and tackled the next leg of the race with newfound zeal, forgetting my friend's advice about "enjoying the scenery." I paid for my exuberance somewhere after mile 60 as my girlfriend Lisa was pacing me and I bonked—hard. I felt somewhat light-headed and it dawned on me that maybe I'd bitten off more than I could chew with this whole 100-mile stuff. It would be a real drag if my race turned into the death march I'd seen befall other runners the previous year. You can drag yourself through the last 30 miles but it ain't pretty, and I wanted to be pretty, in a manner of speaking. As we entered the next aid station I was more than a little worried, until I looked around at all of the other runners in various stages of decay brought about by more than 60 miles of running. While I ate and drank I asked aloud if everyone felt as bad as I did. They all perked up as they confirmed that it was not just me feeling badly. This, along with some calories in my gut, did the trick and we were off toward mile 75.

From mile 75 to the finish I was paced by Lora, the runner I'd paced in 2000, and she talked to me and alternately pushed and pulled the pace to get me over the last major climb, Mount Wilson, which might as well have been Mount Everest at this point in the race. When we hit Sam Merrill aid station, about 13 miles from the finish, it dawned on me, both literally and figuratively, that I was going to finish this thing. Even if I fell and sustained a compound fracture I knew that I could drag my ass in and beat the cut-off. It felt wonderful to ditch the double-bottle waist pack that I had come to detest over the months of training and hours of racing. Just a single hand-held bottle and flashlight all the way in, and if I never saw that waist pack again, so be it. Now it felt like any other Sunday-morning run. At least that's what I was trying to convince my body I was doing, as I would have been out training at this time normally. About 4 miles out from the finish familiar faces started showing up, waiting for those of us from our running group who were in the race. The last mile or two is run on a paved road and my pacer was telling me, "Man, you're flying, we must be doing eight-minute miles." I was just out-of-it enough that I believed her. Just as I approached the finish line, a car full of my training cohorts who had finished earlier were leaving to get some sleep. I will say that it meant a hell of a lot to me that they saw that I was going to finish this thing. I will never forget how great it felt to run those last few hundred feet on a gentle down-hill of soft grass and go under the finish banner. I just sat myself in a chair, simultaneously giddy and uncomprehending that I had just run 100 miles. Just then one of the race directors came over with a finisher's T-shirt and I thought, *Hey, can it get any better than this?*

A matter of days after the Angeles Crest 100 I went on tour again with a newfound sense that none of the things about the touring lifestyle that I had found difficult or irritating would ever bother me again—courtesy of the biggest postrace buzz I've *ever* had! That buzz lasted about one month, after which I was as easily irritated and grumpy as before. Well, not quite. The guys in the band were equally impressed and dumbfounded by my 100-mile saga, though hardly surprised really. When we toured with Aerosmith, one of them mentioned it to their lead singer, Steven Tyler, who used a few expletives in telling me that I was heading for disaster if I kept running ultras. I replied that I know people in their 60s and beyond who are still running strong. Mr. Tyler paused for a moment then said, "Man, *I* know people in their 60s who are still *shooting heroin!*" Well, I guess he had a point. Still, I have every intention of continuing to run as long as my body will permit and have no plans to switch from ultrarunning to shooting heroin.

Until the actual start of the AC 100 I was still unsure if I could, or would, reconcile my life and job as a musician with my life as an ultrarunner. By the time I had completed the race I had, without question, made the transition from the former to the latter. In hindsight, though, I'd made that transition months earlier, somewhere during the miles on a Las Vegas highway or in the parking lot of the Alabama mall. After the Angeles Crest 100 I felt I'd accomplished something much more tangible, more earned, than anything I'd ever done in the fickle ever-changing music business. Success in music is such an unpredictable combination of talent, timing, looks, luck— a myriad of things, most of which you cannot control. In the past it seemed that no matter how hard you tried, how good an album you made, your success was dependent on these unknown factors. Effort and dues paid count for little in music. Running is quite a bit different. If you put in the time and effort, the miles and training, you have a fair shot at achieving your goals. Injuries, blowups, and poor race-day conditions (among other things) are inherent risks, but it's still up to the runner to push through most of that when possible and practicable. It just doesn't work that way in music. I did not finish AC 100 because I was friends with the race director, had the best hair (hardly!), or wore the trendiest shorts (is there such a thing?). I finished because I was motivated to train hard and put in the miles. Wonderfully simple.

A Family Affair

NAME: LISA DEMONEY
AGE: 38
RESIDENCE: OAKLAND, CALIFORNIA
YEAR RUNNING ULTRAS: 6
YEARS PARTICIPATING IN ULTRAS: 23

Ultrarunning has profoundly shaped who I am. My father, Ed Demoney, ran the inaugural Old Dominion 100-miler in 1979. At the time, I was 14 years old and a proud member of his crew, along with my mother and my friend Rick. I'm sure I had no real comprehension of the undertaking, other than that it was inconceivable and sounded slightly crazy. Mostly I was excited about my own part in the adventure—driving down dirt roads in the country, and staying up all night. We had fun defizzing Coke, eating jelly beans, cutting up cantaloupe, trying to figure out what he would want to eat, and cheering him on.

This feat of endurance had never been attempted in our area, so we didn't know what to expect. We'd heard vague rumors of the Western States 100-Mile Endurance Run in California, but little else. There were no books on the subject, no Ultra List or internet websites full of advice, no Powerbars or trail running shoes. Just a bunch of guys going out to test their mettle in the great unknown. I had no idea how this event would shape my life over the years to come.

I'm sure I was oblivious, for the most part, to what my father went through that day. There were times when he didn't think he could continue. At one point we pulled him up from the road, where he lay prone, refusing to budge. Somehow, we convinced him to keep going. I could sense it was a real challenge for him.

He did some things that seemed really odd at the time, like peeing and changing his shorts on the side of the road. (People just didn't do that in public!) I found this unusual behavior highly entertaining and enjoyed seeing a new side of this normally reserved man. In the end, he crossed the finish line hand in hand with Fred Pilon. My father is not a touchy-feely type of guy, but it was obvious that they had come through an epic journey together, and a bond had been formed out there on the dusty trails. They tied for 10th place. I was extremely proud of what he had accomplished.

The only disturbing incident occurred once we returned home after the race. We left on the hour-and-a-half drive immediately after the awards ceremony, and my father's legs cramped badly in the car. When we got home I had to help him out of the car and lift his feet over the doorjamb. That kind of freaked me out. The man who ran 100 miles suddenly couldn't walk. He swore afterward that he would never do it again. My mother and I laughed, knowing even then that he would be back at it. I grabbed my recorder and we got his never-again declaration on tape, which has provided great amusement and teasing for years to come as he continues with ultrarunning and 100-milers.

From that day on, ultrarunning became a core activity in our family, and later became an integral part of my own life. My mother and I have crewed for my father at all types of races across the country—from the Sierras in California to the San Juans in Colorado and the Shenandoahs in Virginia. When he became the race director of Old Dominion from 1985 to 1988, I assisted him in many aspects of race production including some aid stations. Even though I did not begin my own running career until 1997, it was all rubbing off on me. At an impressionable age, I witnessed people doing something that flew in the face of reason. These were not professional athletes or champion marathoners. They were just normal guys, or so I thought. This instilled an anything-is-possible philosophy in me, which continues to guide me in all aspects of my life.

In my younger days, I did not have the discipline required to run ultras, and was content to support my father and his friends from the sidelines. But I always had the goal of running 100 miles and believed I could do it. As we both got older, I realized that it was important to me to share this hobby with my father and time was slipping away.

I had been saying for years that I wanted to run ultras, but had never trained for them. I decided to participate in the California AIDS Ride first, as a way to get started. The AIDS Ride is a fund-raiser, and I figured that if I had to ask people I knew for donations, I'd show up and finish the event. It worked. I rode every inch of the 575-mile course from San Francisco to Los Angeles, California, and collected over $2,700. Several members of the

Virginia Happy Trails Running Club were generous sponsors of my ride.

After that, I began to run. When my dad saw that I was in shape and serious about running, he invited me to join him on an Andes Adventures trip. The first leg of the excursion is a 27.5-mile run on the Inca Trail to Machu Picchu. I had been to Peru with my family as a child, and it has held a special place in our hearts ever since. It seemed the perfect place for my first ultra, so off we went.

The days prior to the run were spent exploring the cities and ancient architecture of Peru, as we acclimated. The night before, we camped next to the ruins of Llactapata ("town on hillside") in tents at 8,400 feet elevation. Although I am not usually bothered by altitude, I developed a case of sleep apnea. Every time I started to doze off, I stopped breathing and woke up gasping for air. I was trying not to disturb my tentmate, and the anxiety was building. I felt extremely claustrophobic. I began to worry about my ability to complete the run on no sleep, which made it even harder to relax.

After my long night's struggle, we were awoken at 3:30 A.M. for breakfast and the start of the run. The weather turned ugly, and it started to rain. I was already unsure of how far I could run. Most of my training had been a combination of hiking and light jogging, and the longest distance I'd covered was 18 miles. Now, with the lack of sleep and the torrential downpour, my fears were compounded. I was confident I could cover the distance, but was unsure about how much of it I could actually run, or how well I would be able to keep pace with my dad.

Once we were running, excitement won out over my fears. It was still dark, so I just concentrated on the little circle of light my headlamp made on the trail before me, not having any idea of the surrounding terrain. I was soaked to the bone, wearing a light windbreaker, a long-sleeved Capilene top, and tights. We had ignored the warning signs and stories of recent storms, assuming the showers would quickly pass. We left our winter gear with the guides who were to meet us at the other end of the trail. This would prove to be a dangerous mistake.

As we gained elevation, I began to get chilled, and the rain turned to snow. We found ourselves in blizzard conditions as we approached the Pass of the Dead Woman, the highest point on the Inca Trail, at 13,779 feet. Several members of our party were wearing only shorts and T-shirts. A few developed hypothermia and were rescued by backpackers who warmed them in their tents with hot liquids. Even with tights and windbreaker, I could not retain my body heat. I was shaking uncontrollably as my body struggled to use its energy resources to simultaneously stay warm and keep moving. I started to panic, as I had during the sleepless night before, and began to doubt my ability to continue. This was the year of El Niño, and the day before we had learned of a party that two weeks earlier had encountered a freak storm, with human and llama casualties. Would we have a similar fate? My father turned around and came back when he saw that I was having trouble. He gently encouraged me to keep moving and told me I would be fine if I just followed in his footsteps. So that's what I did, focusing on one step at a time.

As it turned out, I was mistaken about where we were on the course. I thought that we had much farther to go before we reached the pass. I was relieved and elated when we made it to the top and could see the aid station below. In less than a quarter-mile, the snow turned to rain, and we ran downhill toward the warm coca tea waiting for us at the aid station. Before long, it was hot and sunny and we were having the time of our lives. I wanted to stop and see the ruins and amazing cloud-forest flora along the way, but my father was itching to do some real running and finish in a decent time, so we kept moving. I never felt tired, or had difficulty keeping up after we crossed the divide.

Arriving at the entrance to Machu Picchu, Intipunko ("the gateway to the sun"), was one of the happiest moments of my life. To have survived the dangerous weather, run my first ultra with my father in what I consider to be the holiest and most beautiful place on the planet, all in one day, was the event of a lifetime. It was an epic adventure.

For me, there will always be more to this sport than just the running. Over the decades, the community of ultrarunners has become an extended family. The nature of this society and the unique individuals who comprise it are as important as what they achieve. Veteran ultrarunners welcome newbies, sharing tips and tactics. Elite ultrarunners are frequently seen filling water bottles at aid stations and enjoying the finish-line festivities until the last runner crosses the line.

When I began ultrarunning, I contacted a local race director and inquired about running groups. She graciously welcomed me into the fold. It was only a short time later that I found myself traipsing down the trails of Mount Tamalpais, working aid stations and finish lines at many of the big northern California races with an amazing group of people from all walks of life.

I am now race director of the Montrail/Patagonia American River 50-Mile Endurance Run and manage the start/finish line at Western States. Participating in ultras, whether as a runner, pacer, or volunteer, feeds my soul. We have a terrific community that extends from the shores of the Pacific Ocean to the Atlantic coast, and across the big pond to the continents beyond. Many of my greatest moments have been shared on the trails that we run together. Many of my friends are ultrarunners, and much of my life is scheduled around races and runs.

Ultrarunning has given me a sense that I can achieve the impossible. I confronted many challenges on the Inca Trail in Peru, and I overcame them all. I've since gone on to finish five 50Ks and a 50-miler. I am still pursuing my goal of finishing my first 100-miler. It will happen soon, and I can't wait for Dad to be there to share it with me.

The Toughest 100-Miler East of the Rockies

NAME: ED DEMONEY
AGE: 69
RESIDENCE: ARLINGTON, VIRGINIA
YEARS RUNNING: 30-PLUS
YEARS RUNNING ULTRAS: 24

I participated in football, basketball, and track at Estherville High School, Estherville, Iowa, and even managed to be on the football and basketball teams at Estherville Junior College. Although I was never a quality participant, I did get to play in actual games on a few occasions. As part of the high school track team, our long training runs amounted to no more than 2 miles, as I recall. I wasn't fast enough to run sprints, nor was I suitable for the "long-distance" 1-mile run. I was a high hurdler, and at my relatively short height of 5 foot 9, my lane of the track was usually the one with the most knocked-down hurdles. Thanks to a timely disqualification in the final event of my senior year, I was able to win the fourth place medal (out of five runners). That was the end of my running career until I picked it up again 25 years later in 1973. My goal then was to run every other day and average 1 mile a day for the year. I ran 161 days in all and a total of 379 miles and took great pride in my accomplishment. In 1974 and 1975 I ran 552 and 709 miles, respectively. I found goals kept running interesting. In early 1976 I went to a DC Road Runners Club meeting in search of a new goal for the year. Someone there brought up the subject of a Marine Corps Reserve Marathon scheduled for November 1976. That was it. Now I had a goal, albeit an incredible one, considering I had never run more than 5 miles at any one time.

I entered the first Marine Corps Reserve Marathon with great apprehension. I had few long training runs and only two 20-milers. But I felt prepared. The marathon went well, and I finished in 3:24:35. As I crossed the finish line, one of my mentors congratulated me and informed me that I had qualified for Boston, which had a qualifying time of 3:30 in those days. Although finishing that first marathon was a very positive experience, I was not all that interested in doing another. My wife Rosalie, however, encouraged me to go ahead and do Boston to get it out of my system. So I took her advice, and continued training. I ran the Shamrock Marathon in March and Boston on Patriot's Day. Rosalie's plan to get it out of my system backfired, because by this time I was really into running. We went to Estherville in August to visit relatives, and I decided to do the Omaha Marathon while there. I finished with a time of 3:27:31, which was good enough for eighth place in the masters division and a kiss from Miss Nebraska.

One of the interesting developments during this time was the reaction of my colleagues at the Federal Reserve Board to my marathon running. A number of us ran at lunchtime, and everyone was rather skeptical when I announced my plans to run that first Marine Corps Reserve Marathon. My finishing, however, completely changed their attitude. The group of potential marathoners expanded greatly, and continued growing as I continued finishing marathons.

In early 1979 I heard about a meeting to discuss an Old Dominion 100 Mile Run. I went to the meeting where Dr. Don Richardson discussed the upcoming event. Most of those there had run a marathon, and about half had run 50 miles. Only a couple had run 100 miles, the Western States Endurance Run. The Old Dominion 100 Mile Ride was an established horseback event, starting and ending at Morven Park in Leesburg, VA. Some of the eastern riders had participated in the Tevis Cup, a 100 mile ride on the Western States Trail, and decided it would be neat to have runners join the endurance riders in the Old Dominion. The idea of running 100 miles was incomprehensible, but I decided to run it anyway. About the only ultrarunner I had any knowledge of at the time was Ed Ayres, publisher of *Running Times*. Ed was a competitive runner, and had won the JFK 50-miler in 1977 with a time of 6:04. I called him for advice. I wasn't doing any really long runs, but I had completed a few marathons, and I ran a 50K fun run in March, before the first OD on the second weekend in June. That first 100-miler was a successful struggle shared by my crew, which consisted of Rosalie, our daughter Lisa, and her friend and classmate Rick. Doing 100-mile runs was definitely part of the unknown for everyone involved in the race, and it was a real breakthrough for me. My body took a beating, but I accomplished my mission. I ran across the meadows filled with wildflow-ers. I ran up and down the mountains. I ran from darkness into daytime, through the heat of the day, and back into the coolness of evening and the obscurity of nighttime. Despite the pain that followed, the result was enjoy-ment and self-esteem that grew greater as time passed by. My 1979 OD time of 22:18:34 stands as my 100-mile PR.

Ultrarunning provides the flavor in my life. It has given me the oppor-tunity for adventure and escape. Not being a very talented runner, I've proven that ordinary runners are capable of extraordinary achievements. There have been times when ultrarunning helped me to cope with life's stressful moments, maintaining my sanity. At other times my running expe-riences have been rapturous, such as runs in the San Juan Mountains of Colorado, the Andes of South America, and even our aging mountains in Virginia. I am fortunate to have been able to tread unknown, mysterious trails when ultrarunning was in its infancy, running the first Old Dominion 100 Mile Endurance Run. Finishing Rocky Racoon in 2000 was especially rewarding because it meant I had run 100-milers in each of four consecu-tive decades.

Through my role as race director over the years, I've known many ath-letes and watched them through good and bad, knowing and unknowing, fast and slow, fresh and exhausted. It has been a pleasure to watch other ultrarunners develop—some into truly amazing athletes. Also rewarding have been the friendships and shared hardships along the way. Ultrarunning has also helped in maintaining good family relations although my wife has not always shared my joy in ultrarunning. Nevertheless, she has been very supportive. Our daughter Lisa is also an ultrarunner, and a race director as well. Lisa and I shared a remarkable and near life-threatening experience in 1997 while running the Inca Trail to Machu Picchu. It was her first ultra!

Perhaps as much as anything the sport has given me the opportunity to enjoy God's creation. I am always thankful for the opportunity to run on mountain trails, and I find solace, excitement, and joy in observing our out-door world. I am eternally grateful to be running, especially at my age, when so many others are unable to participate in any recreational activities.

As my life has changed, so has the sport of ultrarunning, and I've been there just about every step of the way. Being there led me into my role as the race director for the first Massanutten Mountain Trail 100-miler, run in

1995. Those first MMT runners suffered through an early-morning thunderstorm, which got severe in some sections of the course, but everything went reasonably well and a new, slow, tough ultra was created in Virginia. The Massanutten Mountain Trails 100 Mile Run perfectly defines today's ultrarunning. It is a trail run designed for enjoyment, not speed. It's on mountain trails amid remarkable and memorable scenery. There is a sense of comradeship among the competitors. It is a low-key adventure run in its purest form: the ultrarunner against the mountains. The time limit of 36 hours, while a true test for some, is definitely manageable by even the slow, trained, and determined ultrarunner. The event stands out in my mind as comparable to the 100-mile trail runs in the West such as Angeles Crest, Western States, and Wasatch Front. It is not only a challenging event, it also gives runners some insight into what the old, established western 100-milers are all about. It is a qualifier for Hardrock and other difficult 100-milers. Earning the symbolic MMT 100 finisher's buckle is a real achievement.

As the race director of this tough event, it seemed only reasonable for me to run the second MMT 100 in 1996. I needed to prove that I could not only design a tough trail 100-miler, but finish the course as well. The week before the event I ran the beginning and ending parts of the MMT. I think it is important to visualize the finish of a 100-miler in advance of the event. The Thursday prior to the race involved much preparation and "race directing." In the evening we anxiously awaited the arrival of our three Japanese guests. The anxiety grew when their arrival was delayed. It was nearly midnight by the time they arrived. We drove to the Skyline Ranch Resort, race headquarters, on Friday morning. We had arranged for a cabin at the resort for the Japanese party, and the rest of us stayed at a motel in nearby Front Royal. I had enlisted Chris Scott to take over my role as race director while I ran. Chris stepped in on Friday and encouraged me to forget about race director duties and concentrate on being a runner. It sounded good to me. I attended the race briefing and dinner, and mingled with the other runners.

We woke up early on Saturday and drove to the start from our Front Royal motel. There was a breakfast for the runners at the start area, and I indulged in juice, bagel, Danish, and coffee. I need food before I run. I was nervous, but had every expectation of finishing. The only question was, how long would it take?

Light rain fell as Chris gave the start command promptly at 5:00 A.M., launching 72 eager runners down the road and toward the Massanutten Mountain East Trailhead. Gary Knipling and I started out running together as we had at Vermont in 1992, Gary's first 100-miler. A much faster runner, Gary wanted to go out with me at the start in large part to make sure he didn't go out too fast. It was my belief, however, that I needed to run the first part of the MMT 100 fairly aggressively or I would find it difficult to beat the cutoff times later in the race. In other words, a strong start was necessary to assure finishing, and running with Gary helped me to start fast. We reached the 8.7-mile Shawl Gap Trailhead aid station at 6:48 A.M. (just ahead of my 7:00 A.M. goal) along with another 15 runners who arrived about the same time. It was wet, but we were having fun and I was on my way.

The MMT 100 is a loop course, mostly on the Massanutten Mountain trails in the George Washington National Forest. Some sections include country or forest service roads. It is rugged terrain, roughly 80 percent trail and 20 percent road, including about 4 miles on asphalt. The MMT 100 is definitely challenging due to the rocks and roots that abound throughout the course. The rocky trails, with short but steep ascents and descents, make it slow going in contrast to other 100-milers.

I was ahead of schedule and continued to do well through the first parts of the course. Gary was running strong, and he would sometimes go ahead of the three or four of us running together and stop to take our picture. When we hit a 3.7-mile road section going into the Habron Gap aid station (24.3 miles), Gary and another stronger runner ran ahead. I, on the other hand, began slowing down and fell off my planned schedule. I wanted to be at the Visitor Center aid station (47.7 miles) by about 5:00 P.M. and was 30 minutes over that time. I also wanted to complete the southern section of the course before it got dark and missed that by at least 30 minutes as well. That's about when things started to get rough.

The most frequently asked question among runners after the event was "Where were you when the storm hit?" An hour or so after darkness fell, the MMT 100 became ravaged by torrential downpours. Thunderstorms came in waves with what must have been at least 50-mile-per-hour wind gusts. Aid stations were devastated by the wind, with tarps blown down and tables overturned. I was lucky when the storm hit. It was about 9:00 P.M. and I had just reached the US 211 East aid station, about 30 minutes behind schedule. Due to my tardiness, I was anxious to leave the aid station as quickly as I could. Fortunately, Rosalie had a much clearer picture of the elements to come and got me into the car just before the storm came up surprisingly fast. Everyone ran for cover, and we enjoyed the shelter of our car while the rain poured. I had managed to get a change of clothes out of the trunk of the car and got into them for the miles ahead. Unfortunately, the car trunk door never got closed and all of its contents were soaked from the hard rain. No doubt Rosalie saved my race right then and there. I would have been in terrible shape had I left the aid station prematurely and been caught by the storm. Other runners were not so lucky. Many were out there on the trail, some in shorts and T-shirts. Several runners' races came to an abrupt end due to the chilling and demoralizing storm. Of the 72 entrants that year, only 37 finished, including 6 in under 24 hours. I'm sure there would have been several more finishers had it not been for the weather.

The storm passed and I continued into the night. It was a long, slow night during which I walked a lot and watched other runners pass me by. When daylight came I was still walking. Two runners (Leo Flynn and Rich Lacey) caught up with me and somehow motivated me to start running again. We stayed fairly close together after Woodstock Gap (82.5 miles). Rich was having a tough time, and Leo stayed with Rich in order to keep him going. It's not uncommon in ultrarunning to see one runner sacrifice his or her finishing time in order to help another runner through a bad spot. That's exactly what was happening here. The three of us ran together for the next 6 miles, arriving at Powells Fort (88.4 miles) at about 10:30 in the morning. Leo remarked that he couldn't run downhills anymore due to soreness in his legs. I was having the opposite problem. I couldn't run uphills, but downhills had become my strength. Before long, both Leo and I began feeling better, resulting in a little friendly competition. I was using the downhills to put some distance between us, and he used the uphills to close the gap again. Between Powells Fort and Elizabeth Furnace (95.8 miles), I pulled ahead of Leo and Rich by about 12 minutes, thanks to a 4-mile downhill.

By getting Rich to Elizabeth Furnace and on his way to the finish line Leo figured he had done enough and really set out to catch me. There was one long climb, one long downhill and then less than a mile to go to the finish line. I was slow going uphill, and Leo caught and passed me. On the next downhill, I was able to pass him again, and I tried valiantly to put as much distance between us as possible. I knew I had to be well ahead when we hit the bottom because it was mostly flat the rest of the way in. By this time Leo and I were racing. I mean we were both running hard, and Leo had miraculously regained his downhill running skills. There were three stream crossings on the trail before we came to the road leading to the finish. The usual procedure was to proceed cautiously through the streams. But Leo and I would have none of that. Neither of us slowed down for the streams, which were knee-deep or higher from all the rain. I heard him behind me splashing through a stream as I ran as hard as I could to stay in front of him. As we neared the end of the trail, it was obvious that Leo was catching up with me, which he finally did with less than a mile to go. He was definitely the stronger runner, so I let him go without putting up another challenge. There was no real desire on my part to try to stay with him. In fact, part of me wanted him to go ahead so I could enjoy the finish by myself.

Leo was soon out of sight, and I was left alone with my thoughts. I took it easy, jogging and walking, until I got to the grassy field at the finish area. Tired as I was, I was determined to finish in style and enjoy the last run to the finish line. As I ran, the grim determination that had scarred my face for the last 30 hours vanished, and was replaced by a big smile. The last 200 yards gave me the opportunity to savor my accomplishment, think back about all the preparation, and reflect on everything that had occurred during all those hours on the course. I could taste the finish, and it felt great knowing I had proved I could finish my course, my race. I hadn't created something I couldn't do myself. It was truly pleasing to be greeted at the finish line with a handshake from Chris Scott. It was also quite pleasing to finally be able to sit down, relax, and rejoice. I was the 33rd of 37 finishers (72 starters) with a time of 33:58. I am proud of my finish. I feel it gives me great credibility as the MMT 100 race director to have earned the finisher's buckle for the toughest 100-mile trail run east of the Rockies.

Massanutten Mountain Trails 100 Miler:
A Triumph of Desire over Reason

NAME: KEITH KNIPLING
AGE: 27
RESIDENCE: CHICAGO, ILLINOIS
YEARS RUNNING: 5
YEARS RUNNING ULTRAS: 4

They say you always remember your first time . . . first 100, that is. Mine was the 1999 Massanutten Mountain Trails 100 in the Shenandoah Valley of Virginia. The MMT, known appropriately as "the toughest 100 east of the Rockies," is a difficult 100-mile run over the trails of Massanutten Mountain in the George Washington National Forest of Virginia.

I guess it all began in the summer of 1998 when, after earning my B.S. in materials engineering from Virginia Tech, I through-hiked the Appalachian Trail from Maine to Georgia. I completed the 2,160-mile journey on December 15, 1998. Following my through-hike, I enjoyed an unprecedented level of fitness. After all, over the previous five and a half months I had put in nearly 2,200 base miles. If ever there was a time to try running ultras, now was it.

The notion of running ultramarathon distances was not new to me. My father, Gary, had been running ultras since the late 1980s and had finished three 100s prior to 1999. Furthermore, I had firsthand experience by pacing him at two of these 100-milers. I was particularly familiar with the MMT, having paced the last 18 miles for my dad and uncle, Ronald, when they ran MMT together in 1997.

So a little over two weeks after kissing the bronze plaque on Georgia's Springer Mountain, I ran my first ultra: the annual New Year's "Redeye" Fat Ass hosted by the Virginia Happy Trails Running Club (VHTRC). With my newfound fitness, I expected it to be easy, but I was sorely mistaken. About two-thirds into the run my hamstrings knotted up, reducing my stride to a labored shuffle. I finished the Fat Ass, but the suffering I endured in doing so certainly changed my perception of ultras. As is the case with most ultrarunners, however, the pain of that experience steadily faded with time, and within a few months I was back for more.

My next ultra, the Bull Run Run 50-miler, was April 17, 1999. As with the Fat Ass, I was still enjoying the residual fitness from my through-hike and felt like I should capitalize on it. In the time between January and April, I doubt I ran 75 miles. Despite this, I finished Bull Run strong, in just over 10:30. In contrast to the Fat Ass, Bull Run seemed relatively easy. I had so much fun that over the last few miles of the race I began to contemplate running the upcoming MMT. Without hesitation, on the Monday following Bull Run I sent my check and application to Ed Demoney. MMT was May 8, less than three weeks away.

It's probably a good thing I didn't hesitate in sending that application, because a few days following Bull Run I noticed pain in both knees, particularly after walking down stairs. I figured that this was normal wear and tear—after all, I had just run 50 miles—and I merely wrote it off, fully expecting it to clear up in a matter of days. Days and weeks went by, however, with no noticeable improvement. In the interim between Bull Run and MMT I tried to run on half a dozen occasions. Without exception, the pain in my knees flared up within the first few minutes of activity. The Thursday evening before Massanutten I called home to touch base with Dad about the weekend. I called on the pretense of discussing logistics—where and when we would meet, and so on. But mostly I called to tell him that I would not be running the MMT. I still planned on coming up for the race, with the intention of volunteering or crewing for him. He was obviously regretful and told me to play it by ear. And by the end of our conversation, he had talked me into packing my running shoes. I would attempt the MMT, but I would be lucky to make it to the first aid station, considering that just two days prior I wasn't able to run a mile.

At 4:45 on race morning, the call was made and 101 runners gathered in the cool stillness of the predawn air. Final well wishes were exchanged, a few last pictures snapped, and then a reverent hush fell over the crowd. Ed Demoney stood before us, gave the runners final instructions, and offered a few last words of encouragement. He then asked us to bow our heads and commenced with reading the Blessing, an MMT tradition.

I approached my first 100 with the same reverence and humility as I had when hiking the AT. Indeed, positioned there at the start in pensive meditation, listening to Ed was eerily reminiscent of 10 months previous, when I started my through-hike. Standing on the summit of Mount Katahdin, watching the cairns of white blazes fade south into the mist, I did not simply declare then and there that I was going to through-hike the AT. Rather, I resolved to walk with unwavering tenacity and, with a bit of divine favor, hoped that would be enough to get to Georgia. Standing before the enormous undertaking of running 100 miles, I was similarly humbled by the task's magnitude and austerity. I was surrounded by people who were about to voluntarily subject themselves to severe discomfort, sleep deprivation, and overall physical trauma. If history were any indication, fully one-third of these people would not finish. As my first 100, the odds of me finishing were considerably less, never mind the fact that I had not been able to run a single mile in the previous three weeks. With those thoughts weighing on my mind, Ed said "Amen," and then we were off.

In ultras, I generally avoid committing to running with other people, and there was an implicit understanding between Dad and me that we would not necessarily run MMT together. Always the humble one, my dad jokingly insisted that I take off at the start and not wait for him. I didn't tell him this, but this was indeed my intent. With two prior MMT finishes, I was certain Dad would finish. I was also certain that, assuming I didn't drop, he would eventually catch me and, if things worked out just right, we might be able to finish together.

I did make it to the first aid station at the Massanutten Mountain East Trailhead with no hint of discomfort in my knees. That was a major accomplishment, considering it was the farthest I'd run since Bull Run. Of course I had only gone 2.4 miles, and there was still a long way to go. At the trailhead, runners filed onto the single-track and began the ascent of Massanutten Mountain. The miles went by relatively uneventfully and with each mile under my feet my confidence grew. Instead of wondering when I would drop, my thoughts shifted to when I might finish. Maybe things would be okay after all? Then, crossing Peach Orchard Gap near Duncan Knob (mile 37), I detected a faint yet eerily familiar twinge in my right knee. Ordinarily I probably would not have paid much attention to this minor irritation—running through pain is a natural process for ultra-runners. However, under the circumstances, a lump welled up in my throat. The pain was not acute, but it was noticeable. From this point it was a long descent into Gap Creek aid station that I tried to run as gently and conservatively as possible, realizing that downhills were the worst thing for my knee now.

Between Gap Creek and the Visitor Center aid station (mile 47.3), things pretty much stayed the same. I ran strong on the uphills, but the descents were becoming increasingly difficult. It is a short, but tough, 2-mile climb from the Visitor Center to Bird Knob. This isolated aid station is the southernmost point on the MMT and, situated at mile 49.5, may be considered the true midpoint of the race. Near the top of this climb runners are treated to a well-earned view of the Shenandoah Valley to the west. While many runners protest this rocky scramble, I rather enjoyed this climb. If nothing else, it was a nice excuse to walk, and the respite felt good for my knees. Furthermore, the encouragement of all the runners ahead of me descending from the aid station elevated me to the top.

Of course, what goes up must come down, and the rocky steep descent off Bird Knob ravaged my precarious knees to the point that, by the time I reached the bottom, my gait had been reduced to a gingerly hobble down the rocks. I passed a number of familiar faces on this out-and-back section, but naturally I was most interested in where Dad was. Finally I met him about halfway down. He could see that I was suffering and I could see that he was looking good. Although this was the last out-and-back on the course, I knew I'd be seeing him again.

I had completed the first half of the MMT in just over 13:30 and, with the liberal 36-hour cutoff for completing the race, I still considered myself to be in good stead for a finish. I reached the next aid station, Route 211 East (mile 53.7), right at 8:00 P.M. I had left my first drop bag here. Since I had expected to get here just before dark, this was the logical place to leave my lights and warm clothes for the night section. Indeed, I was not far off my originally anticipated pace. For the first time since starting the run 15 hours ago, I sat down and proceeded to rummage through my drop bag. I had been in the aid station only a couple of minutes when I heard a familiar voice. I looked up to see Dad. When I had last seen him about an hour previously, I enjoyed a 20-minute advantage over him. Seeing him now here with me was bittersweet. Of course I was glad he had caught up, but to have done so in the short span of 4 miles was evidence of just how precipitously my pace had slowed. I wasted no time and gathered my things, grabbed a final bite to eat, and left the aid station before Dad had a chance to sit down. I left without him, not intending to be antisocial, but rather because I suddenly realized that I had little time to spare. Heading up the trail, I started crunching numbers in my head. The good news was that, having run 54 miles, I was more than halfway done. Furthermore, I had covered this distance in 15 hours, which left 21 hours to finish the run. With my decrepit knees and approaching darkness, however, running was no longer an option. Covering 46 miles in 21 hours seemed simple enough (a mere 2.2 miles per hour). Somewhere in my gut, however, emerged the realization that this might be a struggle to the bitter end. Little did I know how prophetic this inkling would prove to be.

Darkness settled in on the forest, and soon my world was reduced to the white circle of trail illuminated by my headlamp. The cool of the night was an anticipated relief from the heat and humidity we had been subjected to most of the day. I could only power-walk now and within half a mile from the aid station Dad caught me. I, somewhat apologetically, explained that I could no longer run—I would have to walk this one in. I was truly regretful in a sense, because it would have been nice to be able to run with him to the finish. Just as I had left him at the start, I fully expected him to go on without me now. In order to entice him to stay with me however, I really began to pick up the pace. Indeed, I could see he was struggling to keep up on the climbs and, from a pure conditioning standpoint, I realized that I was feeling better than he was. We were only a couple of miles from the next aid station, Scothorn, when my dad asked to take a break. This was very uncharacteristic of him, especially within such close proximity to aid. Because I was feeling so good, and because we were so close to Scothorn aid station, I was reluctant to stop.

In hindsight, I probably should have kept moving since I had little time to spare. Furthermore, by virtue of the fact that he was still able to run, when Dad inevitably did come around, it would take little time for him to catch me. For some reason, though, I acquiesced. We found a campsite at a trail intersection and just sat there. We didn't say much. He was busy tending to some chafing problems he was having, and I was preoccupied by the minutes ticking away in my head. Perhaps, subconsciously, I was offering up a concession. I knew that I was going to walk this in, and so I figured that, if I stayed with him now, maybe he would stay with me the rest of the way. We sat there for about 10 minutes or so, then pushed on to the aid station.

As planned, my uncle Ronald was waiting for us at Scothorn aid station when we arrived at 10:20 P.M. A veteran of the MMT, he had come up to accompany one or both of us on a couple of night segments. The fact that Dad and I were running together now was a convenient coincidence. Even though my race had unraveled and I could no longer run, I felt that, in a sense, things were really coming together. And I was really looking forward to running these next sections with my dad and uncle.

Having Ronald with us was rejuvenating, but I struggled over the next few miles to keep up with them. Eventually we came to a county road, and on the faster surface Dad and Ronald pulled ahead of me. With him up ahead, I noticed that Dad was moving about as awkwardly and gingerly as I was. When we had stopped three hours earlier, he was complaining of chafing, an inevitable reality in ultras, and Dad was particularly prone to chafing in his crotch.

My dad looked like he was hurting, but two-thirds into a 100 everyone hurts. We continued on the road for a couple of miles, and occasionally Dad and Ronald would stop and take short breaks before continuing on. I was a few hundred yards back and usually, while they were stopped, I could catch up. But once we started again they would invariably move on ahead. We yo-yo'd like this several times as we trudged on up the road, and finally Ronald stopped and allowed me to catch up. When I got up to him, Ronald told me Dad was going to drop. This caught me completely off guard. If anyone was going drop, it should've been me—about 20 miles back! What business did he have dropping?

A short time later, Dad stopped and Ronald and I caught up. The searing pain on his face was unmistakable, and it was evident he was pretty torn up. *Hamburger* was the word he used to describe his crotch. Though less evident, I could also see he was torn up emotionally and in hindsight, I think Ronald had stopped for me because Dad didn't want to tell me face to face he was dropping. For the past mile or so, for as long as we had been on this road, vehicles periodically passed us. Since it was now past midnight, this procession was presumably runners' crews heading to the aid station ahead. We waved down the next car, my dad got inside, and, as the car drove away, his race was done.

Within 10 minutes Ronald and I arrived at the next aid station. Dad was there and helped get me hot soup and filled my bottles, and I really regretted now that he had gotten in that car. Surely he would have no trouble maintaining the pace I anticipated for the remainder of the run, and it would have been great to finish my first 100 with him. However, what was done was done. Ronald offered to stay with Dad and help him change and get back to Skyline, but Dad insisted that Ronald stay with me through the next section to Edinburg Gap, where Ronald's car was.

In a sense, it was sheer good fortune that my dad decided to drop where he had. The year 1999 was the debut of the now infamous "Short Mountain" section. MMT was always known for its rocks, but Short Mountain gave the race a new level of notoriety. For nearly four and a half miserable hours Ronald and I tediously picked our way through the night across the 8-mile heap of rocks that is Short Mountain. I entered this section still able to walk, but Short Mountain put an end to that. I now could hardly bend my knees.

Edinburg Gap is a major aid station and it is here that, for many people, the race is decided. Situated the distance of one marathon from the finish, most people who leave Edinburg intend to finish. Of course, many runners choose not to leave. When Ronald and I arrived, there were a handful of runners here—some on their feet and some in cots. It was now 5:15 A.M., and I had crossed the 24-hour threshold. Despite the fact that it taken me 4:21 to cover the previous 8.2-mile section over the infamous Short Mountain—a hard-earned 1.8 miles per hour average—I was still comforted by the 2-hour cushion I enjoyed over the cutoff.

Dad had gotten a ride from the previous aid station, and was sleeping in the back of a van when we rolled in. I bid Ronald farewell and thanked him for his help, and took off. I later found out that after I left Edinburg Gap my uncle Ronald confided to my dad that, with the way I was now walking, there was no way I would finish.

I left Edinburg witnessing my second sunrise on this run. Most ultra-runners dread dawn—the hours from 4:00 to 6:00 A.M.—primarily because this is when fatigue sets in. Almost on cue, during the climb out of Edinburg Gap I began to be overcome by exhaustion. It was almost as if someone had pulled the plug and I felt the energy in my body slowly, but steadily, drain out. I did not feel particularly sick or queasy. On the contrary, I fell into a rather pleasant detachment from my body.

The stretch between Edinburg Gap and the next aid station, Woodstock Tower, is a long 8.2 miles. I was told that, after having traversed Short Mountain, the rest of the course would be quite runnable. Indeed, most of this section consisted of beautiful, gently graded, moss-covered trail. It would have been fun to run this, but at the moment it seemed such a pleasant thought just to lie on the moss and do nothing. I was now alone in the woods, certainly among the last few runners still on the course, and with no one around to dissuade me otherwise, the temptation to take a short nap was difficult to resist . . .

Abruptly, I awoke and found myself standing on a trail in the woods. I quickly collected myself and realized that I was somewhere around 75 miles into a 100-mile race. I looked at my watch and, immediately, a lump welled up in my throat. I was now convinced that I had no chance of finishing this race. I didn't know how long I was out. I didn't even know which way was which—it all looked the same. I figured that either way would take me somewhere, and since I was now beyond the cutoff, where I chose to drop was of little consequence. I presumed that the way I was facing was the way I should go, and so I shuffled down the trail in that direction.

Woodstock Tower aid station is named after an old fire tower situated approximately a half-mile before the station. The abandoned fire tower is now open to the public, and is a popular destination for its stunning views. I knew the tower was readily visible from the trail, and, assuming I was headed in the right direction, this would be my landmark. After a little more than an hour of fairly vigorous walking I thought I could make out the silhouette of the fire tower up in the trees to the left. I considered this a little peculiar, as I was expecting the tower to be on my right. However, as I neared the structure, I could clearly see a young couple up on the platform, and as I got even closer I could hear them talking. I knew now that I would be in the aid station any minute.

I continued down the trail for 15 minutes, and began to wonder where the aid station was. Another 15 minutes went by, and another, and still no sign of a road, spur, or anything indicative of an aid station. Nearly an hour after passing the tower, I became convinced that I had strayed off course. I should have arrived at the aid station over an hour ago. The green ribbons used to mark the course seemed few and far between, and now I even wondered if they were real. Whenever I saw one I would walk up to it and let it run through my fingers, making sure I was not hallucinating those as well. Utter confusion racked my befuddled mind and, with no other logical alternative, I figured as long as I kept walking, I'd end up somewhere.

Nearly an hour after I "saw" the fire tower, I looked off to my right and saw the real Woodstock Tower. A few minutes later I loped into the aid station, fully expecting to be pulled for having missed the cutoff. Dad was there waiting for me, all cleaned up now and in "civilian" clothes. From Edinburg, he had gotten a ride with Ronald back to Skyline and had showered and changed. This was fortuitous because, since he had driven his car here, I now had a convenient ride back to the start. As I approached he was amazingly upbeat and congratulatory. "You mean, I'm not late?" I asked. "Nah, you're doing great," was his response. It was 8:51 A.M., and I was still nearly two hours ahead of the cutoff.

Those previous 8.2 miles had been an emotional struggle, teetering precariously on the verge of reality and delusion. The fire tower, the couple, their voices, even my nap—I had hallucinated it all! For the better part of three hours I had been roaming around alone in the woods in a delusional daze. Sitting there in the aid station, I was just glad to be somewhere familiar. Indeed, this *was* familiar. Two years ago I had paced Dad and Ronald in from this very spot. The realization that I was now on familiar ground, and still very much in the race, breathed new life into my poor feet. For the first time, the end seemed tangible. Granted, I was still 18 miles from the finish, but there were only two more aid stations which, in my beleaguered mind, sounded close.

The next 5.6-mile section to Powells Fort seemed longer than I recalled. I suppose everything feels long after having run 88 miles. I was in Powells Fort aid station only a couple of minutes before a group runners came sauntering in. First was Bill Wandel, followed in close succession by James Moore and Matt Mahoney. It was a relief to know I was not the only one out here—these were the first runners I had seen in the last six hours since Edinburg Gap. The four of us were certainly now the last runners on the course.

I was taken aback by how much this throng seemed to be enjoying themselves. They were cracking jokes, smiling, and just glad to be out in the woods running. They didn't seem concerned in the least. These guys were experienced 100-milers. Maybe they knew something I didn't. I asked Bill, "Do you think we'll make it?" Surprised by my concern, he said we were in great shape, citing the fact that we were still ahead of the cutoff by an hour and a half. But for me, that was the problem. My 2-hour cushion at Woodstock Tower had now slipped to an hour and a half. As I had been for the last 40 miles, I was losing precious time to the cutoffs.

As we left the aid station I tried to stay with Bill and James—if not for their company then for their guidance. Both of these runners were MMT veterans and I wanted to be with someone who knew the course, realizing full well that an errant turn now would certainly cost me the race. Despite my efforts, however, Bill and James were moving at a pace I could not match, and once again I found myself alone in the woods.

It must have been 1:00 P.M. when I crested the western ridge of Massunetten Mountain. From here I could look east across Fort Valley and to the opposite ridge. I was now looking at the last climb of the race, and the finish was just on the other side, finally within sight. Having run this section before, I knew the descent into Elizabeth Furnace was on a gradual, beautifully switchbacked trail that wound in and around the undulations in the ridge as it made its way down into the valley. The surface is unusually smooth (for MMT) and I hoped to make good time into the next aid station.

I had forgotten just how long this descent was, and after about half an hour of "running," my knees screamed in protest. That was a fast half hour—I may have even broken 3 miles per hour, but now the aching was just too much and I was reduced to hobbling down the trail as before. Before long, Matt, whom I had passed on the climb a couple of miles back, ran by me. "Any idea how far to the Elizabeth Furnace?" I asked before he got too far away. He consulted his map and, as he continued down out of sight, replied, "Probably a mile and a half." A mile and a half! I felt a swelling bubble of anguish burst from somewhere deep inside. I wanted to sit there and cry, but crying seemed to take too much effort right now. Throughout the race I had set intermediate goals to get to the next aid station before the cutoff. In actuality what I had done was repeatedly delude myself into more and more suffering. I was tired. I was tired of the deception. I no longer cared about when I finished. Assuming I could get out of Elizabeth Furnace before the cutoff, what happened after that was of little concern—even if I finished over 36 hours, there would be nothing that could detract from the fact that I had run 100 miles. Indeed, part of me hoped to finished over 36:00—if nothing else than as affirmation that I had not done all this for a mere pewter belt buckle. Of course, I had to get there first.

I knew what lay ahead from the Elizabeth Furnace aid station—in fact, I could see it. Of the 5.3 miles to the finish, the first 2 miles were a steep climb out of the valley, the next 2 miles were an even steeper descent off Massanutten Mountain, and then the remainder of the race was relatively flat to the finish at Skyline Resort. I arrived at Elizabeth Furnace to discover my 90-minute cushion now reduced to a mere 39 minutes. However, I had made the cutoff and, for the first time in the race, I was confident that I was going to run 100 miles. The only question that remained was whether it would officially count.

I had two and a half hours left until the 36-hour cutoff. I asked the aid station worker how far it was to the finish and, as expected, she indicated 5.3 miles. I ran the math over and over in my head and I didn't like the result. I had to average better than 2 miles per hour, which, considering the big climb and descent before me, seemed utterly impossible. The volunteer then informed me that Ian Torrence, who had won the race over 14 hours ago, had done this section in 1:13. "No sweat," she said.

I sat there on the bench bent over, my elbows resting on my knees, trying to digest an orange slice. I looked down at my poor feet, somehow trying to comprehend the fact that they had carried me 95 miles. I then gazed at the tall ridge before me and, exasperated, my head dropped back toward my feet. I was beyond exhaustion and I wondered how I was going to muster the energy to get up the climb. Suddenly, with the final mountain of the race before me, I felt as humble and insignificant as I had 33 hours ago, standing at the start line listening to Ed read the prayer. And in this brief poignant moment, it occurred to me just how far, and how long, I had come. I stood up, grabbed my bottles, and made my way toward whatever destiny awaited.

It was as if my motor were running on fumes as I ascended—at any moment I felt like I could collapse and pass out right in the middle of the trail, as I had thought I had done back before Woodstock Tower. I continually tried to rev myself up by rubbing my eyes and talking to myself. To any observer, I surely looked insane. Eventually I topped out on the ridge in the saddle of Shawl Gap. From here it was, at last, all downhill. My watch read 3:30 P.M. I had made it up the climb in good time—now my knees had to survive the descent. That, however, was easier said than done. My knees vehemently protested, and wanted nothing more than just to sit and rest. Although I had made good time on this section thus far, I did not think I could spare the time to afford them this luxury.

As things flattened out I was able to hobble less and walk more. Finally, at nearly 4:45 P.M., I approached the edge of a field and across the clearing could make out Skyline Ranch Resort—and the finish line. I popped out into the field and somehow, somewhere, found the impetus to begin running. (In hindsight, I wish I had waited because this was a long field and once I started, I couldn't stop!) About halfway across the expanse, I could hear applause and cheering erupting from the finish line. Half a minute later I found myself crossing the finish line. I was the 60th and final finisher at the 1999 MMT. I finished in 35:44:02, a mere 16 minutes under the cutoff.

Reaching the end of a 100 is supposed to trigger a surge of intense elation. Against long odds, through physical suffering and mental anguish, I found myself here, standing in a field, with no more miles to run. It would be nice to say it was the happiest moment of my life and that I was overwhelmed with euphoria, but that would be a gross exaggeration, for at the time only two thoughts lumbered through my exhausted mind. The first was a dazed realization of *Isn't this strange? You really have done it, after all.* The second was the realization that I would never have to run 100 miles again.

Certainly MMT was a defining moment for me as an ultrarunner. Before MMT, I was an amateur runner at best. Getting through MMT confirmed my stature as a runner and an ultrarunner. And though I vowed *Never again*, I came back to MMT the following year and improved my time by nearly five hours. The following year I used my two MMT finishes as a qualifier for Hardrock. And just this year, 2002, I finished the MMT in eighth place in 26:39—better than 10 hours faster than when I first did it in 1999.

More significantly, though, the 1999 MMT taught me that running 100 miles is a draining process. In the process of completely exhausting myself, I connect with an inner part of me ordinarily veiled by the everyday distractions of life. During that short time spent on a trail in the mountains, my life is reduced to its simplest terms. Most ultrarunners are people who find goodness and joy in difficult times, who see beyond the misery to the beauty of nature, and who truly realize the elemental and important aspects of life. Going for a run always clears my head, but running 100 miles distills my soul.

Reverse Psychology at the Western States 100

NAME: SCOTT MILLS
AGE: 50
RESIDENCE: ALEXANDRIA, VIRGINIA
YEARS RUNNING: 23
YEARS RUNNING ULTRAS: 21

I grew up in northern New Jersey and although I was athletic in high school, I hated running. I was a pretty good soccer player and because the competition was not too tough, I was offered a scholarship to play at the Air Force Academy. I took the deployment to the Air Force Academy in Colorado Springs and played soccer there for four years. After graduating in 1973 I played soccer in the city leagues for a while, but my body was getting beat up so I decided to quit. As soon as I quit my weight skyrocketed from 160 to almost 195. I'm 5 foot 10, and 35 extra pounds is a lot of weight. I didn't feel good. A friend of mine asked me to start running with him. Recalling how much I had hated running in my high school and college days, I was unenthusiastic to say the least. Reluctantly, however, I went along. I didn't really enjoy it very much, but it was much-needed exercise, so I stuck with it. Soon thereafter I was reassigned to Sacramento, CA, where I met my wife-to-be, Jean. She was a runner, and my infatuation with her convinced me that running was okay after all.

Jean and I trained for and ran a 5K race together. Then we moved up to a 10K race, and about six months later we thought that maybe a half marathon would be fun. It was. A year later I decided to go for it all and began training for the Lake Tahoe Marathon. I'll never forget that run. I hit the halfway point in an hour and a half, which is pretty respectable. Then I died a thousand deaths and was the last finisher, in 5:30. But I didn't let the pain of the hard marathon dissuade me. By now the extra weight had come off, I felt better, and I was really enjoying running.

One day I saw a few runners coming down the trail behind my house and asked them what they were doing. They told me they were running in the American River 50-mile race. I was captivated, first of all by the fact that there was a 50-mile race, and second that it literally ran through my backyard! I set my sights on that race, started training immediately, and ran the AR 50 in 1981. My legs were so beat up that I couldn't walk for three weeks. But I finished it. Sure my time was slow, probably over 12 hours, but for me it was all about finishing. I was very happy, and ready for more.

About that time, a friend of mine who had also run the 50-miler told me about a 100-miler up in the Sierras called the Western States 100. That planted the seed, and it wasn't long before I signed up. I trained hard and completed my first Western States in 1982 in about 21:30. I was completely hooked and in love with ultrarunning.

Ultrarunning is different from shorter-distance running in several ways. Perhaps the biggest difference between an ultra and a shorter distance race is the mind-set you must adopt. The mental attitude that I try to take to each race is one where the goal is going the distance and finishing. That often means working with other runners instead of competing against them. In ultras I am competing against the distance and myself rather than against my fellow runners. One of the things I like about ultrarunning is how many people finish together. You don't see that in marathons or shorter distances. Another big difference is the mental toughness required. There are mental aspects that make an ultrarunner different than a shorter-distance runner. You must be able to realize that no matter how bad you feel, it is probably not going to get worse, and in most cases it will get better if you can mentally regroup and just keep going.

By 1997, I had run about twenty 100-mile ultras, and I was beginning to feel like I had it down. I had again qualified for the Western States 100 that year, and Jean and I went out about a week before to "vacation" with some friends. We drove up to Lake Tahoe the day before the race and spent the night there in a cabin. I never sleep well the night before a race. Typically I'm so wired that I'm lucky to get two or three hours of rest. That's been the way for me throughout the years. The most important night of sleep for me is two nights before. Jean usually doesn't sleep well either because of my tossing and turning. Our strategy for the last 10 years is to make sure we have separate beds. That way I can toss and turn all over the place, and she can still get a good night's sleep.

The next morning was a typical 100-miler morning for me. I was in good shape that year, so I planned to start out a little harder than usual. I got up about an hour before the start, took a quick shower and drank a couple of cans of high-calorie meal replacement drink. I also had some bananas and a cup of coffee. Then I started going through my ritual of getting ready for the start: putting Vaseline on my feet, getting dressed, and so on. I woke Jean about 30 minutes before the start. She just needed a few minutes to take a quick shower and get me to the start to drop me off. As soon as the gun went off, she headed back to the hotel to pick up the bags and begin the long drive up to the first aid station. At Western States that is about a 70-mile drive.

I believe CREW stands for "Cranky Runners, Endless Waiting," and over the years, Jean is the best crew I've ever had. I used to lose my temper some with her when I was younger. But as I've matured, I've started to appreciate more the sacrifices that she makes. I am more positive now. There have been times where I've snapped at her. I'd like to think that was the miles talking, not me. She has seen it all, and nothing really bothers her. She is very good at cleaning me up and taking care of my wet and dirty clothes as I head on down the trail. She's had a lot of practice at this, and she really has it down to a routine. She keeps a checklist so nothing gets overlooked. She's just great! When I come into an aid station, I'm not thinking about all the different things that I need. She has all my stuff laid out: clean socks, fresh shoes, Vaseline, some aspirin, two cans of meal replacement, refilled water bottles, and on and on. She massages me and puts sunblock all over me. It can get extremely hot at Western States so she keeps an ice chest stocked with cold towels to put over my head and shoulders to cool me down. Then she begins asking me questions: Do you need Vaseline? Do you need socks? Do you want to carry any extra food? How many gel packets do you want? How many salt tablets? Are you having any problems with this or that? She's almost like a pit crew at an automobile race. She's really efficient and gets me in and out of most of the aid stations quickly, and without forgetting something important. I may have more than 20 miles to run before I see her again, and that is a significant amount of time to be without something I need.

At this point, Jean had crewed me in about 20 other 100-mile races, and I don't think I had every really considered quitting during a race. I had been in pain and suffered some before, just like most other long-distance runners. We all have ups and downs, aches and pains, blisters and doubts. But in my mind I've never really thought to myself, *I'm going to quit.* Rather I've just pushed through to the next aid station, where I can see Jean, regroup, get restocked, and just keep going. But at this particular event in 1997 I went out a little too hard, trying to run faster than I had in the past. It was a hotter day too. There's such a fine line between trying to gear it up a notch and putting yourself in jeopardy later on. I think I pushed a little beyond that line, and for the first time ever, I really thought I could not do it. I was physically a wreck. Every step I took hurt my feet so much. I had blisters the size of silver dollars on both of my heels and my forefeet. My legs were also hurting due to the fact that I was running differently to protect my feet. It was getting bad. I was worried that I might fall down and not be able to get going again. I just didn't know if I could do 9 more miles. I needed to get to that next aid station. I needed Jean and her sympathy, encouragement, and help. I had plenty of time to stay at that aid station and still get to the finish under 24 hours and I knew Jean could make it better, no matter how long it took. When I saw her with only 9 miles to go I expected her to tell me to regroup and go on like she had done so many times before. I kind of envisioned sitting down and whining and crying, knowing that Jean would take care of me and encourage me to press on. That's what I wanted. That's what I needed. I walked into the aid station with tears rolling down my cheeks, looked at her, and said, "I've never felt this bad. What am I going to do?"

She looked me in the eyes and very matter-of-factly said, "It's obvious. Just quit!"

I had come into the aid station expecting her (wanting her) to tell me to pull it together, to push on, to keep going. But instead she told me to quit? When she said that it just struck the wrong chord with me. It was not what I expected her to say. I don't think it was reverse psychology: She meant it. She knew I had nothing to prove. I did not take it that way, however. I got mad at the thought that after I had run 91 miles, she would just let me quit. She was only saying what anyone with half a brain would say. "If you feel terrible, just quit!" But her words really took me by surprise. Adrenaline is an amazing thing. I was pretty short with her. "Like hell I'm going to quit!" I jumped up, grabbed my bottles, and started running.

I took off so fast that I left my pacer, Jerry, back at the aid station where he was still filling his own bottles. Jerry approached Jean, not knowing where I was at that moment, and told her that he was really worried about me. In all the years he had paced me at Western States, this was the worst shape he had ever seen me in. Then he asked her, "By the way, where is Scott now?" Jean replied, "Well, Jerry, he took off down the trail and he was moving fast, so you need to quit wasting time here and go catch him!" So Jerry took off and about five minutes later caught up to me. He asked, "What in the heck did Jean do or say to get you going?" I told him, "She told me to quit! Can you believe that she would say such a thing?" He just started laughing. I felt better physically, but it was due to the adrenaline surge and desire overcoming the physical pain. The mind can and often does limit your performance. Sometimes all it takes is someone to help turn those negative thoughts around.

I started moving pretty well. Before I stormed out of the aid station, Jean had given me some Advil to help take the edge off my feet. After about half an hour, the Advil combined with my being ticked off at her, and I was able to run pretty well the rest of the way in. It was my slowest time ever for that section of the course, but it still got me in faster than I ever thought possible considering how I had been feeling just a few miles back at the aid station. I was so excited as I approached the finish line. I felt simply ecstatic. I crossed the finish line in 22:40 and promptly hugged Jean and gave her a big kiss. She was just smiling and laughing. I think that in her own mind she knew that I was not going to quit.

Jean would have accepted it if I had quit. In fact, she would have thought that was the smart thing to do. However, never having quit a race, I would not have accepted it as well. To me, ultrarunning is about finishing, no matter how fast. I would rather have crawled in on my hands and knees than quit at that aid station with just 9 miles to go. Jean supports me and is proud of what I do, but her perspective is that it is just a sport. It's not life or death. She knows that ultrarunning is important to me, yet she maintains a healthy perspective of where it all fits into other aspects of life.

Ultrarunning is a very selfish sport in many ways. Ultrarunners spend a lot of time away from their families, training and traveling to races. And even if a runner's family or spouse tags along, it's still all about the runner. They are there for the runner. They are in the car driving around to aid stations. They are up all night, waiting and worrying. In many ways, the easy part is the running. Over the years Jean has been just phenomenal. One of the things I love so much about her is that she has given so much of her time and energy to come to all these races. I've done several runs that were

30- to 40-hour ordeals: all night for two days! That's a lot of work. Jean has been there for every one of my 100-milers. It is no coincidence that many of our vacations have been scheduled around ultra distance races in different parts of the country. It is not to say that we haven't done things that she wants to do, but the pendulum is heavily on my side. I don't make it up to her by buying her a special gift or taking her on a cruise, but she doesn't need that. I like to think I make up to her in the way that we live our lives and how we treat one another with respect and love.

I've never won a race, but I've also never had a DNF, and that is thanks to Jean and her support, loyalty, and unselfish attitude. Ultrarunning has shown me that man's physical and mental strength is well beyond the limits that most people think possible, and, at least in my case, man cannot do it alone. There are not enough years left in my life to ever repay her for all the things she's done for me. But that does not mean I won't keep trying.

Ultrarunning's Last Great Race

NAME: STAN JENSEN
AGE: 50
RESIDENCE: MOSS BEACH, CALIFORNIA
YEARS RUNNING: 13
YEARS RUNNING ULTRAS: 9

Photo courtesy Leadville Picture Co.

I ran cross-country in high school, and then continued to run occasionally for fun and exercise, including a 10K once or twice a year. In 1989 I helped a friend train for her first marathon, and I ended up running it with her. A friend of mine, Bob O'Conner, introduced me to trail running and trail marathons, and before long I was running trail marathons every month and really enjoying it. Bob later talked me into running my first ultra: the 1993 American River 50.

In 1994 I paced Tom O'Connell in the Western States 100-miler. He was attempting to run something called the Grand Slam. I'd never heard of this, but it sounded intriguing. What is the Grand Slam? In 1986 Fred Pilon wrote an article in *UltraRunning Magazine* that coined the term for finishing all of the 100-mile races at that time: Old Dominion, Western States, Leadville, and Wasatch. In 1986 several runners tried to finish all four races, but only Tom Green succeeded. Since 1988, runners have had the choice of finishing either Old Dominion or Vermont, but they still need to finish the three others (for a total of 4). And for those who want to take it even farther, there is the Last Great Race, which was conceived by Angeles Crest 100 race director Ken Hamada, and first run in 1989. The Last Great Race consists of six 100-milers: Old Dominion, Western States, Vermont, Leadville, Wasatch Front, and Angeles Crest.

What does it take to finish a series like the Grand Slam or the Last Great Race? I don't really think that a person needs to be exceptional in any way to complete these series, but it doesn't hurt. You need to be prepared, of course, and motivation and some luck are essential too. There is no specific formula, but here are some of the basics:

Experience—Finishing four or six of the harder 100-milers in about 16 weeks (May through late September) is not something that you should try if do not have the experience to back it up. It's not for someone who has only been running ultras for a year or has never finished a 100-miler.

Conditioning—Physically, the challenge is to recover from the last race and recharge for the next one. You'll need to be able to spend most of the time between the races recovering and not much time training, since some of the races may be as little as two weeks apart.

Time—No matter how you look at it, you must commit to a long period of time during which you'll travel to and run four or six races, each of which takes about five days of your time (you arrive on Thursday and leave on Monday). Not to mention the planning time that is involved before and during the series. There is the task of catching up on work, mail, bills, and so on that piled up while you were gone. And don't forget the preparations that must be made for the next multiday trip. These things get especially tough between Wasatch and Angeles Crest, which are just two weeks apart.

Money—With entry fees, travel, lodging, and any expenses for crew and pacers, you should plan on anywhere from $3,000 to $5,000 for the Grand Slam, and even more for the Last Great Race.

Motivation—When you're halfway through Wasatch, feeling exhausted from finishing Leadville three weeks ago, and you discover that your drop bag doesn't have the socks you were counting on, or you twist your ankle, you'll need to have some strong reasons for not dropping out. (Hint: see "Money" above.)

Luck—Yes, you will need this for the races, but you'll also need it in order to get into Western States, since it is a required event and there's no automatic entry for those attempting the Grand Slam. You'll also need to send in your Leadville application within the first two weeks of January to get in.

Planning—You'll need a good travel agent to make the hotel, plane and rental car arrangements, but you'll also need to make sure you take care of the race paperwork (entries and volunteer work forms). You also want to make sure you bring the right equipment to each race and plan your drop bags, flashlights, and so on. Nobody wants to DNF because they forgot a simple item.

When I was laid off work in October 1997, it seemed like 1998 might be a good time to try the Grand Slam, so I signed up. In August 1998, I injured myself during Leadville and had to drop out of the Slam after finishing the first three races. My sister told me that she'd come back one more time to help crew me, so I signed up for the Slam again in 1999 and decided to go for the LGR as well, since 21 people had Slammed in 1998, but only two had done the LGR. As of 2002, 123 runners (104 males, 19 females) have completed the Grand Slam, ranging from a 23-year-old man to a 66-year-old woman. One person has even completed the Grand Slam six times. In 1999, 25 people signed up for the challenge, and I was one of them. I felt my training was there, and I had planned and prepared for the series as much as I could. I was ready to go.

Old Dominion: Woodstock, VA, June 5-6, 1999

I flew into Baltimore (to save money) on Wednesday and drove for three hours to Woodstock, arriving around 9:00 P.M. and soon going to bed. The next morning, I slept in, bought a map from the forest service and drove the runners' route. I wanted to remind myself of the terrain, footing, and turns before the race, as well as note some landmarks that would tell me when I was getting close to the aid stations. I figured that I drove about 70 miles of the course in a little over five hours and ended up feeling much better about what I'd be facing.

Friday morning was a late start and I joined Rob Grant and his wife Linda, for breakfast. After that it was a quick trip to the store for some bagels and Gatorade for Saturday and then back to the room for a final check of the drop bag contents. Registration and a simple weigh-in started around 1:00. After I got my bib number, I went back to the hotel to label my drop bags and bring them back to the fairgrounds. After that, I hung around to talk to friends and meet as many of the Grand Slam entrants as possible. (Of the 25 this year, 13 were running Old Dominion.) The briefing started around 5:00 P.M. and was over in a few minutes, so we went back to the Ramada for a pasta banquet. After setting three alarms, I turned in early.

The alarms went off after a very short night and I got up and started getting ready. I got dressed, grabbed a bagel and a cup of coffee, and with one last, longing look at that warm bed I headed out the door. It was only a quarter mile to the start, but I wanted to be able to drive back when the race was over, so I drove to the start. I checked in with the starter, visited the restrooms, and then milled about aimlessly, waiting for the race to begin.

The starter pistol went off at 4:00 A.M., and we circled the racetrack in the dark. I found myself running with last year's second place woman, Rebekah

Trittipoe, and the original Grand Slammer, Tom Green, so I backed off and let them go ahead. My game plan was to run alone, run easy, and meet my goals: 1—finish, 2—beat last year's time (27:14), and 3—break 24 hours for the first time. We ran through downtown, crossing the main street under the supervision of a sheriff and reaching the first aid station (mile 3.0), where I stopped to refill my hand bottle. I was carrying a 20-ounce hand bottle for Power Ade and I had a 20-ounce fanny pack bottle that I kept filled with plain water. As we ran along the road in the dark, I could see fireflies off to the side and smell honeysuckle. Approaching the Burnside Bridge, I could see the flashing lights of the sheriff's car as he led the pack up the hill. The leaders were going out quickly, perhaps hoping to make time while it was still cool.

The first crew access was at the 770/758 aid station (mile 19.6) and I arrived about 15 minutes later than the previous year, but I was not worried. I got fresh supplies from my drop bag, said hi to a few people, and headed out. I carried a PBJ until the next uphill, and then I ate as much as I could and tossed the crust. I amused myself by looking at names on the mailboxes and noticing the neighborhood cemeteries that seem to be placed every few miles. As I turned a corner I found myself at St. David's Church (mile 25.4), where they refilled my bottle with Power Ade.

It was only about 8:30 A.M. and 25 miles into the race, but already runners were feeling the effects of the heat. I encountered a runner who had cramps, and I gave him a packet of rock salt and a basic electrolyte lecture and left him to recover (he did go on to finish). Before I knew it I was at the Four Points aid station (mile 32.6). There were lots of crews there, and I missed having one. I got supplies from my drop bag and ice for my hat. I headed up the pavement and was surprised to catch up with Rebekah again. Her ankle was causing her pain, so we talked for a while as we turned onto the trail again. She told me to go by, and I wished her good luck as I passed. Within a short distance I caught up with another runner and was shocked to find that it was Tom Green again! He always beats me in 100s. By hours! I must be going too fast. I calmed down and ran through "the systems" checklist again: legs, energy, hydration, peeing, and so on. Everything seemed to be okay, and I was only 35 minutes faster than last year, so maybe I didn't need to worry. Tom and I ran together for a while until we encountered Dennis Herr lying in a small stream. He got up and ran with us a while, then I left the two of them behind. I arrived at Peach Orchard (mile

38.7) and was overjoyed to find that they had Mountain Dew, the ultrarunner's nectar. Two cups of that and I was off and running again.

I caught up with another runner in the next section who informed me that I was on a 20-hour pace. Yikes! I really shouldn't be running that fast. I crossed Passage Creek and reached Crisman Hollow (mile 43.1) for the first weight check. I was down four pounds, but that did not worry me. I headed down the road, which seemed to go on forever, but was mostly runnable and shaded on one side. I just focused on trying to drain both bottles, take in some electrolytes, and eat.

As I crossed the line marking the 50-mile point, I was surprised (and worried) to see that it took me only 9:20. My trail PR is 9:11, so I must be running too fast! *Calm down, Stan, this is more of a road course than a trail course. Oh, okay.* The road at this point was open to the sun and it was 3:00 P.M., so I was moving kind of slow from the heat. However, I knew it was runnable, so I took off.

As I came into Edinburg Gap (mile 56.6), I made my only mistake of the race. I saw a familiar face and was racking my brain to remember who it was. I remembered to refill my bottles and grab a PBJ, but I forgot to get a supply of electrolyte capsules from my drop bag. The sheriff helped me cross the road and I was climbing up the hill when I realized my mistake. Okay, I can get by on the extra rock salt I still have in my fanny pack. *Mike Morton! That was Mike Morton, the WS record holder. Sheesh!* That internal monologue went on as I climbed the rutted and rocky ATV trail to the ridge. I didn't remember it being so tough or long from the previous year. At last I crossed the ridge and was able to make a semblance of running. Peter's Mill Pond (mile 59.6) had fresh fruit, and the volunteer told me I was in 17th place. No! That was still too fast! About a mile farther on I saw another runner, walking downhill. As I approached, I heard the unmistakable sound of a runner whose stomach wasn't happy. I asked him if he needed salt or water, and he passed on all but a peppermint candy. I told him to hang in there and off I went again.

When I arrived at Little Fort (mile 64.3), I ran into a small logistical problem. I had planned my drop bags for a slower pace and had a flashlight in this drop bag that I would not need for another three hours. I solved the problem by taking the flashlight belt (with spare batteries) and leaving the flashlight with the volunteers in case anyone else needed it (and sure enough, someone did). I headed out slowly from the aid station and up the hill, running whenever I could. Arriving at Mudhole Gap (mile 69.5), I took a cup of chicken noodle soup, crossed the creek, and headed down the trail. It was dark under the trees, even though it was still about 5:30 P.M. After the last creek crossing and the sharp left turn, I was on the jeep trail and one of the volunteers came running by to set up glow sticks on that section. I spotted the left turn onto the trail and started to finish off my electrolytes (yes, I'd remembered to get them at the last aid station). One more junction (where I hear some people got lost), then across the road and into Elizabeth Furnace (mile 75.0) by 6:45 P.M. I passed the last weight check within a pound or so.

Sunset wasn't for another two hours and it was still warm, but my next drop bag would be too late, so I switched to a long-sleeved Capilene top and put a flashlight in my holder. It was cooler by the creek, but I was warm, even with the sleeves rolled up. I could hear a couple of runners ahead as the trail went in and out of canyons, slowly climbing toward the ridge. I caught up with them as we slowly climbed the last steep section to Sherman's Gap. It's a tough climb, but you're at the top within 90 minutes of leaving the aid station. Going down the other side was steep and slippery, since fallen leaves covered the rocks. I hung back, and the two of them slowly pulled ahead.

It was about 8:45 P.M. and getting very dark. I didn't need my flashlight for the road, but turned it on whenever a vehicle drove by. I arrived at the Veach East aid station (mile 82.8), had some soup, and gave Bill Ramsey a big surprise when he saw me: "What are you doing here *now*?" he asked. I can't say as I blame him for being surprised, because he's a much better runner than I am, especially in 100s. He and his brother headed up the hill, and I soon followed. I discovered that I could still run pretty well downhill. My flashlight was working, my legs felt good, a dose of No-Doz was keeping me alert, and my Montrail Vitesse trail shoes kept me from worrying about the rocks. I think I covered that 4-mile stretch (2 up, 2 down) in just over an hour.

Veach West (mile 86.6) had a cozy fire going, but I was on my way home: no more trail sections, no major hills, and "only" 13 miles. I grabbed some supplies, including a fresh flashlight and another PBJ, and took off. As I climbed to the road crossing, I found that running the uphills was easier at night than during the day, because I couldn't see how steep or long the hill was and I'd just run until I felt the effort. Before long I saw the light of the

770/758 aid station (mile 91.0).

Refilled, refueled, and restocked from my last drop bag, I headed out of the aid station and up the hill. I had seen no other runners for some time now. In a few minutes I arrived at Mount Top (mile 93.2), where Race Director Pat Botts was working. She said I was too clean, so I offered to drop on the ground and roll around, but she said it wasn't necessary. Since I'd planned that to be my last stop, I refilled both bottles. Crossing the summit, I could see the lights of Woodstock in the distance. The road isn't too steep, but the switchbacks seemed to go on forever. I ran as long and fast as I could, taking a short walking break every 20 minutes or so, even on the downhill. Before long I was on pavement again, crossing the bridge and seeing the fireflies in the fields. Two more hills and then I was heading down to the Water Street aid station (mile 97.4), where I thanked the volunteer as I ran past. At last, the fairgrounds! I ran through the gate, around the bleachers and track, and across the orange line in the dirt. When I was told my time, I couldn't believe it! I finished in 21:23:59, in 13th place. Everything just seemed to work right.

That Old Dominion was perhaps one of my best races ever, and I hoped, with five races to go, it was a sign of good things to come. Now I had four weeks to prepare for the next challenge. What follows are some of the high (and low) moments from the other events, as I ran my way through the summer.

Western States 100: Squaw Valley, CA, June 26-27, 1999

Western States was the second race in both series, but it was my third time there and I felt very confident, especially since I'd made it through the snow in 1998. I knew the course, I'd trained on it, I was in generally good shape, and I was still on cloud nine after my run at OD four weeks earlier. I just had to be careful not to get cocky and make a simple mistake. I did have problems when I arrived at Foresthill (mile 62), but a friend diagnosed that I'd been taking too many electrolytes and switched me to plain water. By the time I reached the river (mile 78), I was feeling fine and even passed 14 runners in the next 7 miles. When I reached the last aid station, Robie Point (mile 99), I decided to run nonstop to the finish and managed to break 27 hours by 45 seconds! I was very happy with that finish. Next stop, Vermont.

Vermont Trail 100: South Woodstock, VT, July 17-18, 1999

I ran Vermont without a crew, just as I had at Old Dominion. I don't think it mattered, since a crew isn't really needed at VT and I'd run it the year before, so I knew it pretty well. One mistake I made was to tell my hosts at the B&B that they could meet me at the Lincoln Covered Bridge (mile 36) at 11:00 A.M., since that was my time from the previous year. This caused me to run the first few miles faster than I wanted in the heat and humidity in order to meet them (which I did). One thing I did do well was to notice how hot and humid it was (I heard 95 degrees with 95 percent humidity!) and concentrate on staying hydrated and cool, which kept me going. I hooked up with Allan Kaplan near mile 60. We worked as a team to both break 24 hours. Three down, three to go. I had a little over a month to get ready for Leadville, which is where my Grand Slam attempt fell apart the previous year.

Leadville Trail 100: Leadville, CO, August 21-22, 1999

Leadville was the biggest production of all the races, partly because I'd DNF'd the year before and partly due to the altitude and acclimation required. I arrived the Sunday before, my crew arrived on Wednesday, and my pacer came in on Friday (translation: expenses). It rained the night before the race, which sent me to bed worrying about race conditions. The race itself went pretty well until my legs turned to rubber by mile 40, probably due to lactic acid buildup caused by running too hard in the thin air. I picked up my pacer at Twin Lakes (mile 60), which was fortunate since my flashlights both died and we ended up sharing one of hers. On the way back from the turnaround, it started to rain and I was cold and miserable, but thankful to have a pacer with course experience. We reached the Fish Hatchery (mile 76) ahead of the crew and I really had to fight the desire to quit there. I focused on putting on warm clothes and getting food. It took almost four hours to climb over Sugarloaf and get to the next aid station, May Queen (mile 86). After that, it was just a matter of maintaining forward motion, as fast as possible, even on the last muddy road. It wasn't until I saw my second sunrise of the race that I realized I was going to finish. I was *so* happy to crest the last hill and see the red carpet at the finish line! I find it amusing to note that I ended up as the 105th of 210 finishers: right smack in the middle of the pack at 28:17:03. Whew! The Grand Slam was all but complete, and just two more races to go in the Last Great Race series. Now I had to focus on recovery with Wasatch Front just three weeks away.

Wasatch Front 100: Kaysville, UT, September 11-12, 1999

Wasatch is the final race in the Grand Slam, but most people know that if you finish Leadville, you've got it made. I had the experience of pacing at Wasatch in 1996 and finishing in 1997, so I felt prepared and ready to run. A little too ready, perhaps. Things went well for most of the race and I found myself leaving my crew at Upper Big Water (mile 60) on a 30-hour pace. By the time I reached Scott's Peak (mile 69), I was dizzy and had tunnel vision due to some electrolyte imbalance problems. I staggered down the road to Brighton (mile 74), and my sister got a medical volunteer to check me out. They convinced me to lie down in a sleeping bag in the back room. My sister checked on me every 15 minutes, and when I showed signs of malingering, she dragged me back into the main area and got me to eat and drink again. I spent 130 minutes at that aid station, but managed to recover and finish the race, and the Grand Slam. One series down, one to go.

Angeles Crest 100: Wrightwood, CA, September 25-26, 1999

In some ways, the Angeles Crest 100 was anticlimactic. Less than two weeks before, 10 of my new best friends and I had finished the Grand Slam and four of them were now back home, recovering and relaxing. On the other hand, seven of us were gathered in Wrightwood in preparation for our sixth 100-miler of the summer. I can't recall ever feeling as relaxed as I did the day before the start as we sat around after the weigh-in and watched other runners mill about nervously. Some of them were probably getting ready to attempt their first 100-miler. I tried to keep that in mind as I took off Saturday morning and used it whenever I had a mental or physical low point. One low point happened when I was coming into the Vincent Gap aid station (mile 14) and a friend called to me to look up for a picture. When I looked up and smiled, I stepped down on a loose rock and rolled my ankle. For a brief moment I thought I'd blown it again, just like at Leadville in 1998. I stopped running and limped down the trail a while and then gradually put some weight on it and tried running again. I was enormously relieved to find that it wasn't badly turned. From then on I took things more seriously and tried to make sure that I wouldn't make any other simple, avoidable mistakes. I didn't really think about the end of the Last Great Race until I left the last aid station and was 99 percent sure that nothing would stop me from finishing. My long summer was almost over. When I crossed the finish line, there was nothing to indicate that it was anything other than the finish line of AC, and it wasn't until the award ceremony that it really sunk in. There were seven LGR finishers in 1999, more than in any other year. I still don't have an explanation for that. Out of the 25 people who signed up in 1999, I was one of 11 who completed the Grand Slam. Ten finished the Grand Slam in 2000, nine in 2001 and 2002. Four people finished the Last Great Race in 2000 and only two in 2001. The Last Great Race was not officially held in 2002 due to the fact that the Old Dominion 100 and Angeles Crest 100 were canceled.

Why don't more do these series? Perhaps some are intimidated by the challenge or don't have the time and/or money. Some people aren't interested in running one 100-miler, let alone four or six of them in one summer. Some people like 100-milers, but prefer smaller events and shun the larger ones like Western States and Leadville. Then again, some people want to do the series, but don't get accepted into Western States. Of those who attempt the series but don't finish, I think some forget that each 100-miler is part of a 4- or 6-part series and they go out too fast or forget to take care of themselves and end up as a DNF, which ends the series for them. Most 100-milers have a 65 to 75 percent finish rate, so the odds of finishing four or six in a row are pretty low.

The Barkley Marathons
60 hours to run 100 miles
36 minutes a mile
I don't care how tough the course
I don't care how steep the hills
I can run 36 minutes a mile
All it takes to finish
I must only not quit
Over 300 runners have thought this
Only one has backed it up
The others have heard a voice
A pitiful, plaintive voice in the wilderness crying
"Mommy, I can't take it anymore."
"Mommy, I want to go home."
And the voice was their own
Humility Awaits
at the Barkley

(from the Barkley Marathons homepage)

Going Nowhere Fast on Fatal Terrain at the 2000 Barkley Marathons

NAME: BLAKE WOOD
AGE: 41
RESIDENCE: LOS ALAMOS, NEW MEXICO
YEARS RUNNING: 27
YEARS RUNNING ULTRAS: 8

In 1977, James Earl Ray, murderer of Martin Luther King Jr., escaped from Brushy Mountain State Penitentiary into the surrounding hills. He was captured 54 hours later, only a few miles from the prison. A local ultrarunner, Gary Cantrell, thought to himself, *In 54 hours, I could have been 100 miles away!* He later decided to hike through the area, and was told by the ranger, "Just check back in with us when you give up." It was worse than Gary had imagined, so naturally he began planning a race on those trails, and "the Barkley Marathons" were born.

The Barkley consists of a 20-mile loop around Frozen Head State Natural Area, near Oak Ridge, Tennessee. Although it is advertised as a 100-mile run (5 loops) with a "60-mile fun run" (3 loops), it really is just a matter of seeing how many loops you can do. This was the 15th year this event had been held. Five loops had been finished exactly once, in 1995, whereupon Gary made the course even harder by decreeing that the third and fourth loops be run in the more difficult "backward" direction.

The run is limited to 30 or 35 starters. Typically there no are more than half a dozen "fun run" finishers. A time limit of 12 hours is imposed for each loop, although you can take up to 40 hours for the "fun run." You're probably thinking, *Why in the world would it take someone as long as 12 hours to run each 20-mile loop?* There are three reasons: (1) The course has been designed to climb every mountain available, and boasts 20,000 feet of climb and descent per loop. (2) Most of the trails haven't been maintained for years, and are covered with downed timber and brush. Much of the "run" consists of cross-country scrambles straight up and down insanely steep hillsides. "Little Hell," "Big Hell," "Leonard's Butt Slide," "Zipline," and "Ratjaw" are all aptly named 1,000- to 1,500-foot vertical climbs of this variety. These routes are often through thickets of sawbriers—vines with rosebushlike thorns. Finally, (3) the course isn't marked at all—you have to follow the route off a topo map and written description.

To verify that you actually made it around the course, nine paperback books are placed along the route. You rip a page from each and present them to Gary at the end of each loop. If you lose one, tough luck—runners have been disqualified for coming up one short, even though there was no question that they actually made it to all the books. The book titles are chosen appropriately. This year they included the following titles: *All Fall Down, So Little to Die For, Sin and Its Consequences, Fatal Terrain, Going Nowhere Fast, Curl Up and Die, Next Week Will Be Better, Top of the Mountain,* and *Journey into Darkness.*

Although Gary sincerely wishes participants the best, that doesn't stop him from good-naturedly taunting everyone who decides they've had enough before finishing five loops. A bugler stands by to play a mournful

"Taps" each time a runner gives up.

The entry fee is $1.55, a license plate from your home state, and an essay "Why I Should Be Allowed to Run the Barkley." Gary makes the choice of who gets in, based on his own whims. He always admits a couple of "sacrificial virgins." This year, for instance, there was a good runner who told everyone how disappointed he would be if he couldn't complete five loops in under 50 hours. He ended up dropping out midway through the second loop.

One year, two runners made a navigational error and ended up outside the fence of the Brushy Mountain Penitentiary. They were held at gunpoint by the guards until it could be determined that no prisoners were missing, and that their crazy story about a 100-mile race in the hills above the prison was true. Even then, the guards refused to give them a ride back to the campground where the race starts. They made them climb back up the mountain the way they'd come. Barkley is the only race in which participants have been forced to continue at gunpoint. You never know what might happen.

The night before the run Gary puts on his "raw chicken feast," where he barbecues a large amount of chicken over an open fire for the runners and their crew. The feast got its name one year when Gary got frozen chicken instead of fresh, and it ended up charred on the outside without being fully cooked inside. One runner later quipped: "What's the difference between the Barkley chicken and the Barkley runner?—The Barkley chicken is burnt on the outside and raw on the inside, and the Barkley runner is burnt on the inside and raw on the outside." Barkley, by the way, is the name of the guy who supplies the chicken.

Barkley, in all its eccentricity, attracts some of the best ultrarunners in the country. They come to Barkley because there is something irresistible about a run that no one finishes, year after year.

I've been running competitively since age 15, but only started ultrarunning in 1992, when I began my career as a physicist at Los Alamos National Laboratory in the mountains of northern New Mexico. Now, at age 41, I'd managed to finish most of the hardest 100-milers in the country, and had won Colorado's Hardrock Hundred the previous summer in record time. I'd finished the Barkley "fun run" in '97, '98, and '99. In 1999, I became only the third person ever to even attempt a fourth loop (David Horton had also done this in '98). However, I didn't make it far before losing the trail in the dark, while experiencing vivid, sleep-deprivation-induced hallucinations of animals and runners who turned back into logs and rocks when I tried to talk to them. It was *very* weird.

This was going to be the year I finally finished the whole thing. In fact, in the weeks before the run, I found myself thinking not *Can I do five loops?* but rather *Can I beat all the other excellent runners at five loops?* Privately, I set a goal of 56 hours. I felt like the only obstacles that might get in my way would be injury or weather. But every year is different, and you take the Barkley as it comes, weather and all.

At 9:00 A.M. on April Fool's Day, Gary lit the traditional cigarette signaling the start of the Barkley Marathons. Most of the field stuck together for the initial hour it took to reach book 1, but the speedsters all took off up Jury Ridge while I stopped to take pictures, record the time, get something to eat, and fill my water bottles. I had decided to bide my time and avoid the fatal mistake of going too fast on the first loop. Working my way slowly up through the field, I arrived back in the campground, as planned, in eight and a half hours. Turning my pages in to Gary, I endured the nerve-racking process watching him slowly count out all 10.

On the second loop, it got dark enough to use my flashlight shortly after book 1. I always enjoy seeing flashlights in the dark ahead or behind me. It creates a strange sensation of remote camaraderie—whoever they are, they're in it with me, but there's the delicious mystery of trying to guess who. I was surprised when two lights appeared on the trail immediately above me. "Who goes there?" I called out. "I'm embarrassed to tell you, because we're dropping out!" It was David Horton and another runner. David had been throwing up, and the other runner was dropping because (as he put it) "I had to watch David throw up." Their fast pace on the first loop had done them in. I was glad I made the decision to start slowly.

Little Hell is easy to negotiate in the dark in the forward direction— you just keep going uphill and you can't miss. I could see three lights ahead of me, but I couldn't guess who they were. By the time I had climbed Ratjaw and reached the water drop at the top of Frozen Head, they had already left. It was about 1:00 A.M., and a heavy fog had settled on the ridge. I began to feel occasional raindrops.

I was puzzled to see only one light ahead of me while running toward book 8. When I reached Indian Knob, I found another runner with his shoes off, tending blisters. He told me the other two runners had given up and returned to the campground by a shortcut. I debated whether to wait for him before descending Zipline, but decided against it. He was still working on his feet, I was in a hurry, and I didn't want to be held up if he was slower than me. I took an approximate bearing off my map and started down. After an incredibly steep 1,250-vertical-foot descent, I perfectly nailed the start of the trail that would take me to book 9 at the base of Big Hell. By then it was raining hard and I was soaked to the skin. I became chilled despite the hard climb up Big Hell. I made it back to the campground at a few minutes after 4:00 A.M.—only 10:15 for the nighttime loop! All right!

I took a hot shower to warm up before getting into my dry clothes, while my wife, Rebecca, stood in the rain to scramble some eggs for me. At one point one of my daughters came to tell me that four runners had just come in, and that one of them was already heading back out again. She was mistaken on this latter point, but it really focused my attention on getting back out on the trail!

I started loop 3—a backward-direction loop—with a small pocket flashlight to provide just enough light to see me through the last 45 minutes of darkness. It had stopped raining, but there was fog and a vicious wind when I met two runners near the end of their second loop below Chimney Top. They confirmed that I was the first third loop runner. I expected my fellow New Mexican Randy Isler would be chasing me up here, thinking he was one of the four who came into camp while I was there, so I was very surprised when I ran into him at book 10. He was really bummed, having missed a turn during the night and ending up miles off course, and beyond the cutoff. As he put it, "To have worked so hard, and have it end like this!" I felt really sorry for him.

It had started raining again, making the descent down Ratjaw difficult. The dirt was rapidly turning to slippery mud. By the time I reached the bottom, it was pouring, the mine road was flooded, and the beautiful patches of violets that normally adorn the road were now underwater.

The slippery mud on the north boundary trail made this a slower leg than I had hoped—it took me five hours to get back to the campground from book 2 at the Garden Spot, an hour more than I had planned. The rain finally let up an hour before I finished my third loop in 10:45, for a fun-run time of 31 hours flat—comfortably under my 32-hour plan. I was

dismayed that my quads were starting to get sore, and the constant wet-
ness was taking a toll on my feet, which were badly blistered.

After changing into dry clothes and going through my checklist while
sharing my daughters' dinner, I headed out for the fourth loop just after
4:30 P.M. This was the loop I had been dreading—the backward nighttime
loop. I had fallen apart on this loop last year before reaching Chimney
Top. However, this year I had a big advantage—I had enough time to get
down Big Hell in the daylight.

I had planned to nap at the base of Big Hell, but decided to push on
since I didn't feel sleepy. Darkness fell as I headed up the trail toward
where the Zipline ascent began. It seemed to be taking a very long time—
had I gone past it? The trail didn't look at all familiar. My sense of time
was messed up, so I couldn't trust the internal clock that was telling me I
should be there by now. I decided to trust my intellectual knowledge of
where I was rather than my feelings. I pushed on, and soon reached the
base of Zipline. Halfway up the climb I found myself in a thick fog. My
flashlight beam disappeared into white fuzz within about 15 feet, so I
could see nothing except the immediate area around me. Not being able
to pick my route ahead, I got tangled up in patches of sawbriers. After
what seemed like a *very* long time, I began to sense large rocks around
me—I must be near the caprock, but couldn't see enough in the fog to be
sure. Nothing looked familiar. Should I go left or right? Forcing down
feelings of despair, I decided to follow a trail I'd passed a short distance
below. According to the map, it should lead me on a very roundabout
route to the book, but that seemed to be the only way I'd find it. I followed
the trail and suddenly realized I was standing right beside book 8—the
trail was not the one I thought it was, but was a different one that leads
directly to the book from the ridgeline. Sometimes it's better to be lucky
than good!

I reached Frozen Head at about 9:00 P.M. The fog was so thick that I
couldn't see the power line that ran down Ratjaw, even when I was standing directly under it. As I filled my bottles at the water drop, it started to
rain very hard. My first thought was to try to descend Ratjaw before it
became too much of a quagmire, so I headed down. It already *was* a quagmire, and I spent a lot of time slipping and falling in the mud. I had just
started down when suddenly lightning lit the world up around me like I
was inside a flashbulb! Then came the thunder. It continued like this all

the way down, in a drenching rain on an extremely steep, thornbush-covered slope that was slippery as ice. Probably the worst time I've ever spent outdoors. About halfway down, it occurred to me that in a lightning storm, it was probably a bad idea to be hanging on to the old downed power line that I'd been using to sort of rappel on the steepest sections. I finally made it to the bottom of Ratjaw in one piece, thankfully out of the fog so I could identify the correct cross-cutting road to pick up my page at book 7. I splashed along the violet-covered road, now under ankle-deep water.

The road steepened on the climb toward the top of Little Hell, and I was forced to walk. Rivers of water ran down the road. The lack of mind-stimulating running or route finding was putting me to sleep, but I was too wet and cold to take a nap. I'd doze off on my feet, and wake up to find myself just standing there. At one point, I opened my eyes, and found myself standing right by the top of Little Hell. Lucky I opened my eyes there or I might have walked right past it!

Now that I had the difficult descent to negotiate, I woke up. This was the crux of the whole race—David Horton's 1998 fourth-loop attempt had ended when he got lost descending Little Hell, and I had gotten lost here myself in broad daylight in previous years. The heavy rain had erased the scuffmarks made on earlier loops, and the thick fog made it impossible to see any landmarks whatsoever. There was only one chance—take and follow a bearing and hope I could figure out where I was at the bottom. This I did, pulling my compass out of my shirt every 10 yards or so to check my direction. After a long descent that was off the usual ridgeline route, I reached a trail, which I assumed must be the one passing by book 5.

Was I above or below the book? I decided to go upstream, because eventually I'd find the New River crossing, and I knew that from there I could run back down the trail to the book. I found the river crossing and started back down the trail. I ran for a long way. "Must have gone too far—better go back." Back to the crossing, watching carefully for the broken wall containing the book. Nothing. I remembered that I had earlier timed the book to be a 3-minute run below the crossing. I checked my watch and started running. After a long time I checked my watch again. Only one minute had passed. So much for my sense of time! I continued, and found the book. My blind 1,200-foot vertical descent of Little Hell in the darkness, rain and fog had brought me out within 100 feet of my target. Surely one of my greatest orienteering feats!

The New River was swollen with runoff, and the rocks we usually hopped across were underwater. I waded the widest spot in muddy, knee-deep water and found book 4 at the base of Leonard's Butt Slide only after a long search. The mine road beyond the top of the Butt Slide was completely underwater, but as I was already soaked to the skin it didn't matter. It continued to pour. I soon found myself in the meadow where the road ended. Or was I? Something didn't look right . . . I knew that the road split a few hundred yards before this meadow, and that the correct route was the lesser-traveled one on the right. Could I have missed it? I decided I'd better go back to check, and sure enough, I had missed the turn. Now that I was in the correct meadow, Coffin Springs was at the saddle just upcanyon from me, only a few hundred yards through the trees. Nothing looked familiar. Before, there had been a single stream in the canyon bottom. Now there were rushing streams in every gully. I climbed for a long time, seemingly in the right direction, but began to fear that I'd lost my way. I decided to backtrack. Wait! Here was a spot I recognized—another runner had fallen facedown in the mud on an earlier loop. Now I knew where I was, took a bearing and soon reached Coffin Springs. I *had* been going in the right direction before, just not far enough.

From here on in, the fourth loop was straightforward, though not easy. In fact, it was a real S.O.B. The North Boundary Trail was slippery, difficult to find in the darkness, rain, and fog, and very slow to negotiate. I couldn't see well enough to be sure that each step wouldn't send me head over heels on a muddy patch, so I was forced to do a careful shuffle rather than run. I had figured it would take me four hours to return to the campground from book 2, but this stretched to five hours, and finally six hours. It stopped raining at first light, as I crested Bird Mountain for the final downhill stretch to the campground. It had been a *very* long night. My feet were blistered and sore. The fourth loop had taken me 15 hours. Still, this fourth loop was something to be proud of. Although I took wrong turns at many spots along the route, through a combination of luck, orienteering skill, and knowing when to push on and when to backtrack, I had made it. This in horrible conditions that chased the remaining runners away and left everyone in the campground wondering how I was surviving out there. Completing this fourth loop was perhaps my greatest ultrarunning performance.

Back in the campground, I decided that I would get as much sleep as possible before heading out on the fifth loop. I didn't have as much time as I had hoped—only 80 minutes before the 48-hour cutoff for beginning the final loop. After I changed into dry clothes, Rebecca threw a sleeping bag across me in the back of our car, and I was instantly asleep.

The alarm woke me up, and I felt surprisingly refreshed and alert from my 45-minute nap. I retaped my feet, but they had swollen during my nap, and hurt like crazy when I forced them back into my remaining pair of dry shoes. I was surprised that people kept asking me if I was planning to go out for a fifth loop. Of course I was! It started to rain again while I sat in the car talking to friends. With five minutes to spare, I walked up the dirt road out of camp in the pouring rain. My feet were extremely painful, and a pull in the back of my right knee was aching and tight from the 75 minutes of inactivity. This fifth loop was going to be grim business.

I was scrambling up the hillside below book 2 when I heard voices. This was not unusual—I'd been hearing imaginary voices in the rain and wind for most of the past two days. Suddenly, a huge white animal bounded past me out of nowhere, heading up the hillside. I recognized it as Randy Isler's dog, and could now make out the voice calling "Argus! Argus!" Randy was waiting for me at the road just below the Garden Spot, soaked and bedraggled in the pouring rain. He had hiked all the way out here in the storm to give me moral support. What a guy!

I was soaked to the skin and starting to get cold as I plunged down Leonard's Butt Slide. The Barley Mouth Branch boomed and roared off to my right. I'd certainly make it to the New River crossing by six hours elapsed, and knew that this point had always been exactly halfway through the loop timewise. The second half should not slow as much in the rain as what I'd already covered, so I felt comfortable that I'd make it with at least 30 minutes to spare. Was I actually going to finish the Barkley?

I reached book 4 and got my first glimpse of the New River. I knew right then and there my answer. My run was over. What was usually a small, clear, cascading stream was a muddy, foaming, raging torrent! I got my page and decided I might as well continue to the crossing, hoping to find some weakness in the barrier before me. But there was none.

I stood at the crossing for about 20 minutes, marveling at the sight and sorely wishing I had a camera. Half a dozen or more huge booming waterfalls launched into space where rain-fed streams hit the line of cliffs above the crossing. The crossing itself was at least 30 feet wide, a rolling, boiling flood with large pieces of trees carried along, disappearing beneath the current and reappearing farther down the rapids. Before my eyes, the mountains were coming apart. It was an amazing and beautiful thing to see. I *really* wanted five loops, but wasn't even tempted to try to cross, and didn't think twice about my decision to turn back. Attempting to cross would be suicide. I was disappointed, but relieved at the same time. The race was over; I knew I could have done it, but was stopped by the raw, naked forces of nature. I hadn't given up, and didn't feel like the course had beaten me.

However, this was no ordinary 100, where after dropping out one can climb into a car and be whisked away to a hot shower and a warm bed. This was Barkley, and I still had a miserable 3-hour run to get back to the campground.

Leonard's Butt Slide was a grim climb. It killed me to lift my knee to hip level, and the climb required this maneuver with every step. Now that I was heading back to camp, every ache and pain that I'd suppressed before started to hurt. It was still windy and pouring rain, and was now late afternoon. I wrapped myself in the space blanket that I was still carrying from the previous night, but was getting very chilled—walking just didn't generate enough heat. I realized that at this rate, I'd never make it back before dark, when it would get colder still. With that incentive, I started running as best as I could manage, regardless of how my knee felt. It loosened up as I ran, however, and gradually began feeling better.

The road back from Coffin Springs seemed to take forever. It clung near the ridgetop for several miles, and thus was exposed to the full force of the storm. It was windy and very cold. Every few dozen yards a huge stream roared down the hillside, flooding the road. It was amazing to see this much water, and incredible to imagine that it was all coming from the rain on the few hundred feet of slope between me and the ridge.

Finally I made it back to the campground, and told Gary what had happened. It appeared to be with genuine reluctance that he blew "Taps" for me. Nearly everyone had left. My family had set up our folding chairs, cooler, and stove in the rest room—the only dry place left in the campground. After a shower, it felt really good to be warm and dry again.

Several people have asked me if I'll go back to try it again. In previous years, I'd always felt that I could have done more, if only I'd been stronger, so the answer was always, "Of course!" I didn't feel that way this time. I sincerely gave it my best, although the fact remains that I *didn't* finish five loops, so I guess I'll have to try again. Every year at Barkley is unique and exciting, so although 2001 is sure to be different from 2000, it is equally certain that it will be interesting in its own way, and that's the real reason to keep going back to try again.

Blake did go back again, and he and David Horton teamed up against the Barkley. David Horton (next) tells their story.

Running Book to Book at Barkley

NAME: DAVID HORTON
AGE: 53
RESIDENCE: LYNCHBURG, VIRGINIA
YEARS RUNNING: 26
YEARS RUNNING ULTRAS: 24

Photo by World of Color

No American had ever finished the 100-mile Barkley Marathon, and in 2001, Blake Wood and I decided to work together to try to be the first. I had been there eight times, and I wanted it bad. It was Blake's fifth year in a row there, and he wanted it just as bad. We knew it would be easier if we ran together. We could help each other find the books, and we could talk to each other to keep from getting lonely.

My wife can understand why I would run a 50- or 100-miler, or why I would want to run across America or the 2,100-mile Appalachian Trail. But she doesn't understand this Barkley thing. You get nothing out of it. There's no T-shirt, no award. She cannot understand why I go down to Tennessee time after time after time, only to come back broken and defeated. But there's an unbelievable pull there. People often ask ultrarunners what their ultimate goal is. For some it is to do Western States or to finish Hardrock. Some want to finish Leadville or run across America. But many dream of Barkley. It is the ultimate in the ultrarunning world right now, and it is a race that no American had ever completed. I've always felt I could finish it someday. And I hoped that 2001 would be the year.

I started running consistently in March 1977 to get fit and lose a little weight. It was like a drug, and like an addict, I started running a little more and a little more. I ran a few marathons, then I heard about the JFK 50-Mile Run, which I ran in 1979. I finished 24th out of 400, and I thought to myself, *Hey, I've found something I can do!* After a few more 50-milers, I discovered the Old Dominion 100, and ran it in 1980, followed by several other 100-milers. It was around that time that I came across the book *Flanagan's*

Run by Tom McNab. It is about a 1929 race across America, and reading that book motivated me to run really long distances. In 1991, I ran the full 2,160 miles of the Appalachian Trail, and then in 1995 I ran across America. Like an addict, I needed just a little more. I was always on the lookout for tough, long, and hard races.

Any 100-miler is tough. But Barkley is not your average 100-miler. In the Barkley Marathon, there is no marked course, and for about half of each 20-mile loop there's not even any trail. You just run through the woods. The trail, where it does exist, is tough. There's one section, 6 miles in length, which is hard to complete in less than four hours. It is a boundary trail that goes straight up and straight down, and it has never been cleaned up or cleared, so there are hundreds and hundreds of dead trees. You climb up and over them, under them, and around them. Then there are a couple of places with a lot of briers. You get ripped to pieces. A choice you have to make is to wear pants and burn up if it's hot, or wear shorts and get ripped up. Fortunately it was cool enough in 2001 to wear thin nylon pants. There are also some hills that are so steep, with real loose soil and leaves, that for every step you take you slide half a step back. Then there are a couple of places where you have to take compass bearings and go straight through the woods through some of the thickest forest you've seen in your life. It is an unbelievably tough course.

There are roughly 50,000 feet of gain and 50,000 of loss over 100 miles. That's an average of 500 feet of gain and loss per mile. You try to put that in a mile and that's a hard thing to do, especially with no aid stations and no defined course. There are nine books along the way, and you have to navigate to each one of these books and tear out a page. Then at the end of each lap you turn all nine pages back in to prove that you have been where you were supposed to be. And if you lose one page, you are DQ'd. The race director, Gary Cantrell, tells everyone roughly where the books can be found. So you know where the books are. It's not trouble locating the books that makes the race impossible. At the end of each loop you end up back at the campground, where there is aid, shelter, people, and your vehicle. Starting another lap is unbelievably difficult because you have to choose to go out again. People DNF because they complete a lap and they just don't want to go out again. But you have to focus. You have to eat, drink, and gather your supplies for the next loop. You have to think, "What am I going to need for the next 8 to 12 hours?" Then you have to leave this safe, comfortable place and head out into the wild again. It is really tough because after the first lap, you know what lies ahead. And it is not something you ever want to face again.

Having not finished Barkley so many times before was weighing heavily on my mind. Before I left Lynchburg, I went to Wal-Mart and bought $150 worth of food, drinks, and other supplies. There I was buying all this stuff, and the farthest I'd ever been was four laps two years prior. And here I am, two years older, and the only thing I can think as I'm buying all these groceries is how stupid this was. Here I was, 51 years old, buying all these groceries that I would probably not even need. I'd never even made it to the fifth lap. And the previous year I'd dropped during the second lap! But I had to be stupid and spend the money; otherwise, without the food, I would have no chance of completing the race.

The night before I didn't even want to talk about the run. People would ask if I was planning to finish the 100-miler. It is hard when you've tried as many times as Blake and I have, and people keep asking you, "Are you going to do it?" You don't want to be too cocky or too confident. You just tell people, "Yeah, that's what I'm trying to do."

Race Director Gary Cantrell doesn't tell you when the start is until race morning. He blows his bugle and an hour later the race starts. In 2001, we heard the bugle at 8:00 A.M., signaling a 9:00 start. I'd prefer a 7:00 or 7:30 A.M. start. All I could do was just sit there and wait. And that wasn't a fun thing to do.

Blake and I started out pretty conservatively, and the first three loops went by uneventfully. Well, as uneventful as 60 miles at the Barkley Marathons can go. We were feeling good, and thought we just might have a chance of finishing. Then on Sunday night, during the fourth loop, we got lost and had some trouble finding the books. As we were finishing the fourth lap early Monday morning, we had been talking a lot about the kinds of books we like to read. I told Blake that one book I had really enjoyed reading was *Endurance*, Alfred Lansing's classic book of Ernest Shackleton's survival in the South Pole and Antarctic region. We talked about how much we liked the book, and about how tough Shackleton was and what he had gone through. It helped take our minds off our own discomfort.

As we finished the fourth lap, Blake was really hurting and I didn't think he wanted to go on. He was struggling, and we'd run out of food the last three or four hours. We were in bad shape. I told Blake that we had to get in and out of the aid station really quick because we had to run the last lap quicker then the fourth lap in order to beat the 60-hour time limit. I really didn't want to go on, and I didn't think he wanted to continue either. I had pretty much resigned myself to going home with another DNF. I sat there, drinking and eating, thinking that the race was over. After all, if Blake didn't go on then I wouldn't have to go on either. And I really didn't want to go on. There was nothing wrong with me physically; I just really lacked the motivation to go on after already spending 48 hours and 80 miles in those woods. I reluctantly said, "Blake, are you ready?" And to my disappointment, he answered, "I'm ready."

Here we go again.

We walked out as the crowd gathered there cheered us onward. Other than Blake the previous year, we were the first Americans to ever start the fifth lap of this race. It was really an emotional time, but in my mind, it was over. I thought we would just go to the first book and come back. Or maybe the second book, or *maybe* we'd even go to the third book where there was a shortcut we could take back to the campground, and everyone would be amazed that we'd gone that far. I felt horrible. The thought of another lap was horrendous. I said "Blake, I *really* don't want to go on. I *really* don't feel like doing this.

"I *really, really* want to stop."

Blake was just quiet for a little while, then he said to me: "What do you think Ernest Shackleton would have done?"

That was like taking a knife and sticking it in my heart. I was crushed. I knew what Shackleton would have done. He knew what Shackleton would have done. Shackleton would have gone on! Shackleton didn't have a choice. When you are there in a situation like that, you go on. Kind of like Shackleton, we were in a special situation. We had the opportunity to make history: to be the first Americans to ever finish the hardest 100-miler in the world. We stood quiet for a few moments, then, just like Shackleton, we went on.

Blake pulled away from me and stayed a little distance in front of me, and we didn't talk for a long time. After a while, my food and drink began to digest and I started feeling better. I never considered quitting again. A little while later at the end of the last lap Blake was struggling and I was able to return the favor and help him. We went on and finished the race together. So many times you want to give up, but you cannot. That's what ultra-running is all about. That's what life is all about.

The last mile was one of those special feelings knowing that you've done something special and you've done something special together. Seeing the people cheering and clapping. They were looking at us, amazed. They couldn't believe that we were coming out of the woods. They couldn't believe that we were finishing in under the 60-hour cutoff. You could see the excitement in their eyes. One person later told me that seeing us finish was one of the most special things he had ever seen in his life. It was great to have them all there and see the expressions of joy on their faces. They were witnessing something special that had never happened before and may not ever happen again. They sensed a feeling of accomplishment just being there. It was just really, really special. I laughed and I cried. There were a lot of people there, including a lot of my good friends. I called my wife at the finish line but she was not home. I was so disappointed. I wanted to tell her, *Honey, I finally finished.*

I finally finished.

It felt surreal. I'd been beat to death and I'd gone through what may be the hardest thing I could ever go through. I was still alive, but I was really on the edge—just broken down physically and mentally. There was an unbelievable feeling of accomplishment, but there was also an unbelievably raw feeling. I felt like I was worn down to the core—down to my inner self. There were no layers left. Everything was one big nerve. I was totally spent, both mentally and physically.

Blake and I were the first two Americans to finish the Barkley Marathon. Our time was 58 hours, 21 minutes—just shy of the 60-hour cutoff. There was no time during the entire event that we could allow ourselves to relax or sit down to rest. I didn't know I could do that. I'd stayed up one night many times in other 100-mile races, but never had I stayed up for two nights in a row. We started at 9:00 Saturday morning and finished about 7:30 Monday night. That just blows my mind.

Ultrarunning is a part of my life. I am an ultrarunner, and I love to race. I want to continue racing for a long time. Running races like that is a stress-ful thing, and often the rewards are few to none. Finishing at Barkley was so much greater to me than finishing in Central Park after running from LA to New York; more special to me than going from Georgia to Maine on the AT. Finishing at Barkley was 10 times greater than anything else I have ever finished. There have been 80 to 100 people who have run across America, and about 6,000 people have through-hiked the AT. But no American, other than Blake and myself, has completed the Barkley Marathon. It is that difficult. Someone once said, "Man cannot enjoy that which he acquires without hard work and toil." And what do we enjoy the most? The things we work the hardest for. That's why I enjoy Barkley. It is the hardest thing I have ever had to achieve.

UltraRunning Magazine *chose Blake's and David's performance at Barkley as one of the most notable finishes of 2001.*

Magical Moments in New England's White Mountains

NAME: STEVE PERO
AGE: 51
RESIDENCE: DUBLIN, NEW HAMPSHIRE
YEARS RUNNING: 27
YEARS RUNNING ULTRAS: 9

I started running in 1976, when I was 25 years old. I had been lifting weights at a local health club when a trainer told me that I should begin to work the inside of my body now that I had gotten the outside of my body into good physi-cal shape. He said that I should begin by running. So I began to jog, painfully, to and from the gym. Before long, I realized that I liked running and began to concentrate on that, never returning to the health club. It was not long after that I was introduced to road races. I entered a small 5-mile road race and had so much fun, I knew it was something that I could do and enjoy for a long time. I soon discovered that I wanted to run longer and longer and started thinking about running a marathon. A couple of friends and I entered the 1978 NYC marathon. I finished in 3:46. One year later I ran it again in 2:59. Five weeks later I ran another marathon in 2:48:06, my PR to this day. I was now qualified to run the Boston Marathon. I ran that and 13 more Bostons, along with two more NYC marathons and many more—about 26 marathons total.

I ran my first ultra in 1995. I had been running shorter trail runs in New England and found that I preferred the softer surface of trails to roads. My friend Howie Brienan convinced me to run his inaugural 50K trail run just south of Boston called the Trail Animal Don't Run Boston 50K. I won that race in a time of 6:35. Needless to say, I was hooked!

It was also in 1995 that my sister Elaine was diagnosed with cervical can-cer. I drove her to the hospital for radiation treatment every day, which meant giving up my regular lunchtime runs. I did not run a step for seven months, which taught me that running wasn't everything. After a while I no longer missed running as I cared for Elaine. It was during these times we spent together that the seeds of change were beginning to take root in my life. Focusing on my sister not only put me back in the real world as far as running goes, but it also was the beginning of the end of my marriage. My former wife not only disliked my running, she also thought that I was overly concerned with Elaine.

As time went on, Elaine's condition worsened. I was voted by my brothers and sisters (I'm the oldest of 6) to be Elaine's health-care provider while she was being cared for by hospice. This involved stopping on the way to work and on the way home to help clean her up, empty her bladder bag, and change her IV solution. The hours we spent together gave us lots of time to talk. Elaine had many things to say to me, but one thing she really tried to get across was that I needed to live life to the fullest. She knew of my desire to complete a 100-mile trail run. She also knew of my failing relationship with my wife. Elaine told me that I should do two things: find a woman who would love me, and run that 100-mile race. As she put it, life is way too short. And as a 38-year-old mother of three young daughters with maybe three months left to live, she knew what she was talking about.

Elaine hung in to have one last Christmas with her daughters, then lapsed into a coma on the day after Christmas. She passed away a week later, on January 3, 1996. It was that very day that I began my quest to run my first 100, and as Elaine put it, to begin living my life. After two years of training, I ran the 1998 Vermont 100-mile trail run. I spent many hours during that run thinking about Elaine, replaying over and over what she said to me during the last days of her conscious life. I finished my first 100-miler in 19:45, and one year later my wife and I separated.

This was also that year that I met Deb at an ultra in Rhode Island. I do not remember much about our first encounter, but our paths crossed again at an organized training run. I'll never forget her smile: a very warm smile that would draw me to her in the coming months. Over the next seven months, Deb and I grew close to one another. A serious relationship was forming.

We were training together for the 2000 Bear 100-miler in Idaho when we decided it was time for a long hard training run. We wanted to do the Presidential Traverse and get shuttled back to our car, but we couldn't get the logistics worked out. I suggested that we do an out-and-back to the halfway point. Deb, being Deb, answered "Why not do the whole thing?" This "Double Prezi" she was suggesting had not been done by too many people due to the unpredictable and rapidly changing weather in the White Mountains, combined with the time it would take to run the complete trail out-and-back. I thought she was crazy, but being an ultrarunner, I was intrigued and willing to give it a go.

The White Mountains are in northern New Hampshire. They are not very high compared to the western ranges, but can see some of the most severe weather in the world. Mount Washington, the highest at 6,288 feet, occasionally records winds in excess of 200 miles per hour. This is because the range sits at the confluence of two jet streams. In addition, the fact that the range rises 3,000 to 4,000 feet above the surrounding terrain has resulted in the same alpine conditions and barren rocky landscape typical of mountains 10,000 feet higher. The tree line is at about 4,000 feet. The section of the White Mountains where Mount Washington is located is called the Presidential Range. There are nine peaks above 4,000 feet that create the Presidential Traverse, or the Prezi as we like to call it around here. The Presidential Range extends about 22 miles, and the official Presidential Traverse follows the Appalachian Trail from one end to the other, adding the summit loops to each peak for a total of closer to 24 or 25 miles and a lot of elevation gain. The trail above the tree line is lined with large boulders of every shape and size, with seldom a flat place to plant your foot. Cairns mark the trail, as well as well the familiar white blazes of the AT. It can be an extremely inhospitable place in bad weather, and bad weather can happen on any day of the year. Hikers have died of hypothermia up there even in August.

Weather forecasts on the day of our run called for a chance of rain. At least we would have a full moon, clouds willing. We loaded up with food, water, money for the hut meals and the restaurant on top of Mount Washington, and just about every bit of running clothing we had. The weather started out cool and breezy, typical for September in the White Mountains of New Hampshire. But as we got farther into our run, the sun came out and it became unseasonably warm, leaving us with all of those unneeded clothes to carry.

The trails to the summits of the Presidentials are very rocky, but those who hike them are rewarded with great views from the peaks. I don't remember being tired at all during the out part of our Prezi out-and-back. It was just a time spent on the trail with the new woman in my life. Deb and I were still getting to know one another, and what a way to do it!

We reached the crowded summit of Mount Washington at just about noontime. I really hated it after being alone on the trail with Deb for the past two hours. It felt like rush hour in Boston. We went inside to get something hot to eat and got back on the quiet trail as quickly as possible. Our next stop would be the Lake of the Clouds Hut, one of my favorites. We stopped there to get water and use the rest room before hitting the trail again. From this point on it was pretty quiet—just Deb and I—not only because we were getting farther from Mount Washington, but also because it was getting later in the day.

The next memorable part of our run was descending Crawford Path, the trail that leads to the end of the first half of our run. It seemed to go on forever, but we soon arrived at the Crawford Hostel and went inside to fuel up, rest, and prepare for our nighttime journey back through the Whites. We started out about 6:00 P.M., back up the Crawford Path, and reached the top just as the sun was setting. We hugged and kissed as the sun went down behind the horizon. We decided that on our return trip we would forgo the summit trails, sticking instead to the main trail. We did this because the white blazes on the AT would be easy to see in the dark, minimizing our chances of getting lost.

The mica embedded in the rocks up there fascinated us, and caused the rocks to glow in the beams of our lights. We called them our trail stars. We reached the Lake of the Clouds Hut at about 10:00 P.M. The crew was sitting around, having a few beers and playing cards. When we told them what we were doing, they stopped their card game and made us some delicious soup. We donated a little money to their beer fund on the way out as we thanked them.

Next up was Mount Washington for the second time in one day. We reached the summit at midnight under a full moon, clear skies, and a very slight breeze. This was a rare weather combination that we'd most likely never see again in our lifetime. This truly was a magical moment: a moment given to us to share together. It really meant something to me to be here with Deb, at the highest point in New England under these conditions. There was not another person I'd want to share this with more.

The rest of the run was uneventful. We were tired, mostly walking by now, and the skies were becoming more and more threatening. We'd occasionally stop to rest and refuel, huddling together behind rocks to escape from the wind. The rocky trail was beginning to wear on our already sore and tired bodies. We finally reached the Valley Way Trail, and the long downhill to the car. The rocks were very wet and slippery, and there were spiderwebs all across the trail that broke across our faces. We were tired and getting aggravated with the spiderwebs and rocks. Soon we saw the trail register that marked the end of our journey. We signed out at 6:00 A.M., 20 hours after we started. Just as we crawled into the warm car, it began to rain.

Those 20 hours that I spent with Deb marked a turnaround point in my life. It was 20 hours spent on some of the most rugged terrain in the northeast United States. It was also 20 hours spent with the woman I was most likely going to be with the rest of my life. We shared stories and many laughs along the trail and Deb gave me a kiss on every peak. The Double Prezi only strengthened our bond, which was already growing stronger every day.

Love and Marriage at Hardrock

NAME: DEB PERO
AGE: 48
RESIDENCE: DUBLIN,
   NEW HAMPSHIRE
YEARS RUNNING: 7
YEARS RUNNING ULTRAS: 5

I was standing on the narrow ledge at the top of Grant Swamp Pass when I saw the person in front of me dodge around a rock outcropping, and then suddenly disappear. I walked around the rock, and there he was, already 150 feet below on what looked like an impossibly steep slope of loose rocks.

"We have to go down *that?*" I asked fearfully.

I didn't start running until 1996. I was nearly 42, and had volunteered at the start of the Boston Marathon. The spectacle of thousands of runners was awe-inspiring. Something about it called to me, and I vowed to myself to begin running. I ran 9 miles total that next week and entered a local 5K race the next weekend to seal the deal. I joined a running club and ran a few more local road races. I was really enjoying it. Before long, however, the familiar soreness and stiffness gave way to stress fractures, knee surgery, and eventually a physician's stern warning to stop running. But by this time, running was something I really liked doing. I had made some new friends, and I wasn't half bad. Determined to find a way to do it, I began running some trails near the house, thinking that a "softer" surface might be easier on my body. I asked my doctor about this. His recommendation: If I wouldn't quit entirely, then I should run no more than 15 miles a week. (I eventually learned not to wear last week's race T-shirt to my doctor's appointments!) I soon entered my first trail race, which was so much fun I never looked back.

Along the way I met and began running with Steve. He helped me get into ultrarunning, but he also helped me get through a couple of the hard-

est years of my life. He was encouraging and offered a lot of helpful infor-
mation. He became my very best friend. Fast-forward four years. I'm with
Steve, on the verge of running one of ultrarunning's toughest races, the
Hardrock 100. And I'm scared to death.

We arrived in Silverton, Colorado, two weeks before the 2001 Hardrock.
Just the drive over the mountains from the airport scared me (Coloradoans
evidently do not believe in guardrails). We assisted with the course marking
as a way to see the course and get used to the altitude. Every night we would
go over the course booklet to see what the next day's hike would be.
Warnings such as A FALL HERE COULD BE FATAL! did little to calm my fears.

As it turned out, however, the daily hikes gave me great confidence, as
each day I found that I could do what the night before I feared impossible.
Climbing up a very steep snowfield several hundred feet high to Virginius
Pass (13,100 feet), kicking steps in the snow, and knowing that a slip could
send me sliding down hundreds of feet into rocks below, for some insane
reason did not seem so awfully bad. But there was one section of trail that
kept giving me night sweats. Pure panic. The Bear Creek Trail out of Ouray
is a classic cliff trail, cut into the edge of canyon walls that tower 300 to 400
feet above a raging torrent. Sometimes the trail is only two feet wide, and at
several points recent rock falls require scrambling over boulders. I do not
like ledges. No, that's an understatement. I am *petrified* of ledges. I did not
think I could do this trail. To make matters worse, we knew we would hit
this section at night during the race. A friend of ours had almost backed out
of the race when he saw this trail for the first time. He was ready to pack it
up and go home before the race even started. And he was a seasoned ultrarunner. How could I do this? I was having nightmares and losing sleep over
this section of trail. I even refused to participate in the course marking on
that section.

Toward the end of the first week in Silverton, I developed a hacking
cough that seemed to get worse as race day approached. Now instead of
feeling stronger during our daily excursions, I was having more and more
trouble. We drove to Durango and spent a day at lower altitude, but it did
not help. I visited the local doctor, whose theory was that the chemical used
to keep the dust down on the dirt roads had irritated my lungs and triggered
some asthma. I have always had mild asthma, which typically does not
require much treatment. But she didn't think I should use an inhaler
because of the altitude, where I'd already have elevated heart rate. Bottom

line, she didn't give me any medication at all. So the last few days I rested, worrying about how I'd feel come race day.

By the time race morning came, I was exhausted from night after night of coughing, nightmares, and little sleep. The alarm went off about the time I finally closed my eyes. We drove the half-mile to the gym, thinking we'd really be glad not to have to walk the distance back to the hotel after the race. We parked, then walked to one of the local diners that opened early for the runners. It was already full. The runners were nervously picking at pancakes, gray faces pinched in anticipation of what lay ahead. My own breakfast of eggs and toast sat like a rock in my stomach. I didn't feel well at all. *Must be nerves,* I thought to myself, trying to think positive. In spite of the anxiety I felt concerning the race, I was also immensely happy to be here, and most especially to be sharing it with Steve. These past two weeks had been the happiest I'd experienced in a long time—a very romantic get-away in the most beautiful scenery imaginable. The people, the scenery, the quest of Hardrock itself were like a dream come true. I was really here! Hardrock! The toughest 100-miler on the planet! Best of all, we were going to do this together.

After breakfast, we walked back over to the gym. A clock at the start/finish line was counting down with about 40 minutes to go till the start. Hundreds of runners and crews were milling around in the gym. Some sat silent on the bleachers in somber anticipation of what the next two days would bring. Film crews from *National Geographic* and *Sports Illustrated* were interviewing the speedier runners, lending an odd Hollywood glitz to this otherwise unpretentious mining town. We ventured outside just before the start. It was barely light, and the cool, damp air settled around us. We were shivering, but I think it was due more to pre-race jitters than the cool temperature.

We all counted down the seconds to zero, and then we were off. The race starts in town, runs down a short side street, and then heads up, out of town. The first of many river crossings soon followed. Cameras were everywhere as families and filming crews watched as we plunged into the ice-cold rushing water, grabbing onto the rope that had been stretched across to make the crossing less hazardous. Crossing Mineral Creek is the baptism of initiation. This was the real "beginning" of the race. And it would be hours before we'd see the first aid station, and probably close to two days before we'd have dry feet again!

Right away, I knew something was wrong. Shortly after we crossed the river I began having "blind spots" in my vision. I've since learned that this was due to lack of oxygen reaching the blood vessels in my eyes as a result of the asthma. Even at this relatively low altitude (9,500 feet) I had to keep stopping to rest. Steve and I dropped back farther and farther in the field, until we were very near dead last. We had planned to run this together, and he was sticking with me. I was struggling, even at this snail's pace. We had originally thought we would be able to finish around 40 hours, but now, only several miles into the race, we were forced to rethink everything. It was going to be a long couple of days. It was tough physically because the altitude combined with the asthma was really beating me up. I couldn't breathe well at all. It was tough mentally because I kept feeling we should be much farther along than we were, and I was feeling bad that I was holding Steve back. It was an emotional seesaw. I so much wanted this to go well, and was angry and disappointed that I was having this problem. On the other hand, Steve and I were together, and it was the closest I'd ever felt to him, struggling together, leaning on each other, sharing the incredible vistas and beauty of the San Juans.

Late in the day, we began the climb up Mendota Saddle, which leads up to Virginius Pass. We hoped to reach Virginius midafternoon, but were several hours behind that goal. Virginius is about 33 miles in, and we had been going for close to 12 hours now. Mendota Saddle is a long, slow trudge. As we walked, we talked about many things. We talked about the future, about us. As we approached Virginius, I told Steve how much I really loved him. He responded likewise. I'm not sure how it all happened, but we decided then and there that we wanted to get married as soon as possible. We were nearly at the pass, and were both bursting with happiness at what we knew was the right decision. "We have to tell somebody!" I said. And just then, we were at the aid station, and Steve said to the crew there, "We have an announcement to make!" I think they all knew what he was going to say before he said it, because Steve and I were grinning like schoolkids.

This little aid station, which has to be the coolest and most unique of any in ultrarunning, is located at 13,100 feet, in a tiny, 10-foot-square notch between boulders with extremely steep slopes in either direction. In fact, a fixed rope is provided to go down the other side. That's how steep it is. Every year, this crew climbs up that slope, hauling water, a tent, a stove, and aid. This includes a few beverages not usually included in traditional aid station fare. They are a fun bunch. They are climbers rather than runners, and think nothing of setting up and hanging out for 12 hours in any kind of weather on this precipitous ledge.

"We just got engaged!"

They all cheered, and offered us congratulations and a drink of something worthy of the occasion. Looking at the fixed rope I was about to have to descend, I thought better of that, so we settled for some hot chicken broth, served in Styrofoam cups. It tasted better than the finest champagne! I believe I could have simply floated down that mountain. One other runner, Bob Ross, was present when we arrived. He joined in congratulating us and headed down the mountain while we still celebrated. As we would soon find out, he alerted the folks ahead as he passed through. We were congratulated at every stop. It was lots of fun.

Darkness fell as we made our way down, down, down into Ouray, the lowest point on the course. The Ouray aid station is a big one. Runners check in, find their drop bags, refuel, rest (many take naps here), change clothes and shoes, and prepare for the long cold night ahead. I was actually feeling better at this point, but it was also lower altitude. I was still flying high from the engagement. So high, in fact, that I was not even thinking about what lay ahead: the Bear Creek Trail. The point that I was sure would be my undoing. Steve and I were talking about the future, making plans, and I barely noticed that we were now on the feared switchbacks in the canyon. We could hear the river below, flowing fast and furious. Shining our light over the edge, we saw *nothing*. Blackness, total and complete, met our flashlight beams in an eerie emptiness. For some reason, though, I was not frightened here. Go figure! We actually passed several other runners on this narrow trail, which required sliding by them near the ledge. Yet after all the time and energy I had spent dreading this section, this was the best I had felt the entire race. Maybe things were going to be okay after all.

Leaving the canyon and finally back on "solid ground," we headed up toward Engineer Pass. This is a long, slow climb in the "witching hours"— the hours between 1:00 and 4:00 A.M., which I always find the hardest. We reached a tiny aid station, somewhere in the woods along a jeep road. It was not much more than a tent and a campfire. Two gentlemen were manning the station and a couple of other runners were sitting by the fire. We were feeling pretty good at this point, considering we'd been on our feet for nearly 20 hours. We were getting ready to sit down by the fire and warm up and rest a bit when one of the volunteers said something that shocked us. "You'd better get going soon. You're only 15 minutes ahead of the cutoff time."

What?

We couldn't believe we were that far behind pace. This was a real blow to our confidence. Rather than taking the time we should have to rest and eat, we panicked and just refilled our bottles and headed out. As it turns out, this was a miscommunication. The aid station volunteer was giving us the cutoff for a predicted 48-hour pace, *not* the cutoff for that aid station. We thought he meant we were in danger of being pulled because we were near the absolute cutoff. This little misunderstanding did as much as anything to end my race, and severely demoralized us both as we trudged up the pass. We just couldn't believe we were that far behind. It would prove to be a costly misunderstanding.

The trail to Engineer Pass was littered with bodies. There were probably at least a dozen runners and their pacers, sitting and lying along the trail, moaning. If we all weren't so pathetic, it might have been humorous. We found one friend curled in the fetal position right on the trail, asleep with her headlight still burning. It was very cold, so we physically picked her up and helped her up to the top. From there the course takes a jeep road down to the Grouse Gulch aid station. She said she could make it from there. The Grouse Gulch aid station is known for its wonderful food and hospitality, a warm tent, and a place to lie down. It is strategically placed before the biggest climb of the race, Handies, at over 14,000 feet. So we were really looking forward to Grouse. When we got there, however, it looked like a MASH unit. The tent was packed with sick and exhausted runners. There was barely room to sit, and getting help from the overworked volunteers was out of the question. They were too busy tending to the wounded. Grouse is the largest dropout point because of its easy access back to the start, and many folks here were waiting to make that trip. So again, we passed through without getting the aid we needed. I was feeling bad by this point—the combined effort of trying to overcome the asthma and the altitude, plus not eating at the last aid station had finally taken its toll. I was wasted and nauseated. And then there was "the cutoff." We feared that if we rested too much, we would miss it.

Steve thought that if he could just get me over Handies, maybe I'd make it. He literally pulled me up that climb. I was throwing up, and had to sit down every few minutes. At one point I just collapsed on a rock and cried.

Runners passed us, giving a questioning look at Steve, who just answered, "She's having a bad moment." We finally reached the top of Handies, but I don't know how I made it. I literally crawled up the last steep pitch on all fours. I was so wasted that I couldn't manage more than a slow walk on the relatively easy descent.

As we reached the road that leads to the Sherman aid station, I was convinced that I just couldn't go on. I was still nauseated, and more tired than I've ever been in my entire life. We were 70 miles and about 30 hours into the race. I so much wanted to cross that finish line with Steve, but we were still under the mistaken impression that we were racing against cutoff times. Mentally, that derailed me. I may not have been thinking totally clearly (who is after 30 hours of this kind of physical exhaustion?) but I knew I couldn't make the cutoffs, because I couldn't possibly go any faster. It didn't make sense for us both to fail, so I needed to drop out. It was that simple. If I dropped out, then at least Steve would have a chance to finish. He was unwilling to go on without me. I was unwilling to let him stay. He insisted that we were in this thing together, but I told him that his finish would be my finish too. I told him he had to go on without me. He was still feeling good and moving strongly. I was only holding him back. He very reluctantly agreed to go on. He really did *not* want to leave me. His dream, and then *our* dream, had been to run Hardrock, and finish it together. It was gut wrenching to watch that dream slip away, then to finally give it up for good. I think, though, that he realized my condition: pale, depleted, lungs gurgling from mild pulmonary edema. He knew I could not continue. We stood a moment in the road, silently embracing. I tried hard not to cry, but the tears came anyway. He kissed me gently and turned to go. As hard as it was to realize I was not going to finish, it was even harder to watch Steve walk away, broken-hearted, with tears in his own eyes. I felt so guilty, like I had utterly failed and disappointed him. This was so damned unfair.

I was done. I lay down on a cot in the tent at the Sherman aid station, trying to hide my tears as he left. This wasn't the way it was supposed to be. It was as low a moment as I can remember when they cut my wristband off, signaling I was officially out of the race. I eventually caught a ride back to town. It was a lonely trip back. I showered and changed clothes, and tried to lie down, but I couldn't stay there. I drove back to the finish to cheer the runners coming in, and of course, to be there when Steve crossed the line. I kept trying to get word of where he was on the course, but it was difficult.

He was going into the second night on the course. There was some severe weather shortly after he left Sherman and I was concerned. Many runners got caught up high with lightning cracking all around. Finally someone came back into town and reported that Steve was looking very strong and was just leaving the last aid station. At that point I knew he would make it. I watched and waited in anticipation. What a thrill it was to see his familiar loping stride appear in the darkness, rounding the corner in town, heading toward the finish. He crossed the finish line, kissed the Hardrock (a tradition), and then kissed me (not a tradition, yet).

We were married in October 2001, and it was our intention to enter Hardrock in 2002 and run together as a married couple. Unfortunately, the race was canceled due to wildfires in the area. Hopefully, we'll get to someday stand on Virginius Pass on the anniversary of our engagement. And maybe we'll accept that drink this time around.

Finding Self-Confidence at the Arkansas Traveller 100

NAME: FRANCESCA CONTE
AGE: 30
RESIDENCE: CHARLOTTESVILLE, VIRGINIA
YEARS RUNNING: 9
YEARS RUNNING ULTRAS: 2

Photo by Butch Adams

The days prior to the Arkansas Traveller 100 were tough. By Thursday I was ready to start, and Friday was just a waiting game. That night I could barely sleep, and the more I fretted about it, the worse it got. I watched television to keep my mind off the race. I could not concentrate enough to read. When I was left alone with my thoughts I rehearsed the race over and over again, trying to plan for the unexpected, thinking about how good it would feel to cross the finish line. Despite the fact that I got just a couple of hours of sleep, I was ready to run when the alarm clock went off.

I ate a Powerbar, drank some sports drink and took a salt tablet, just like I do before every race. The weather was perfect for a late-summer race in Arkansas: Rain from the night before had subsided, leaving the air crisp, almost cold. We hopped into the car and turned on the heater full blast. I always enjoy driving to the starting line, using the time to collect my thoughts and try to relax. I was in charge of the music, and nothing could have been more appropriate than "Sweet Home Alabama" by Lynyrd Skynyrd. Good music just before a race is crucial. If you are going to have a song in your head for over 20 hours, it must be a good one.

Starting a race late is one of my worst nightmares. We got there with just moments to spare, and I really had to go to the bathroom. I bolted toward the Porta-Potti as everybody else moved toward the starting line. My heart was racing. The feeling was purely irrational, since starting a minute late in what was to be a 20-hour run does not really matter. I was freaking out just the same. I made it to the finish line just in time, kissed Russ, my boyfriend, and we were off. As soon as the gun went off, a very strange thing happened: All the pre-race anxiety, doubt, and stiffness disappeared. I immediately felt I was alone and that I could run forever. It was a wonderful calm feeling, and it made all the stress and preparation well worth it.

I first started running when I was a teenager. I was pretty sedentary at the time, and my dad, concerned about my lack of exercise, convinced me to give running a try. Since then I have always enjoyed the freedom that running provides. I love that Forrest Gump feeling that I could just keep running and running and running. Even then I did not realize how much I loved it until I discovered trail running. Running in the woods is about the most beautiful thing I have ever done. I went to college in San Diego, a city not very conducive to trail running. Every day it was the beach, the road, or the desert. Once I moved to Virginia, though, I found myself in a running paradise. There were more trails and trees, and running in the woods became a real passion. I saw an advertisement for the Mountain Masochist 50-Miler, and, even though I had never even run a marathon, I decided to do it just for the pleasure of running that long on trails. I finished the event, but I can still remember the pain.

Through ultrarunning I met, fell in love with, and started training with Russ. He was my true mentor and, very simply, taught me everything I know about ultrarunning. Russ brought me back to square one. He taught me how to drink, eat, train, and mentally tackle races.

Leading up to the Arkansas 100 I was running 80 to 100 miles per week for about six weeks. This varied at times because I just needed to physically and psychologically back off. Training with Russ made everything easier. We tried to incorporate one long run during the week. We usually got up early and headed out to the Appalachian Trail to run between 12 and 18 miles. We always jumped into the nearest and coldest swimming hole when we were done. That was my favorite part of the run. We did one weekly speed session, usually consisting of fartleks or mile repeats on a measured course. We also did longer tempo runs and hill repeats, alternating all of these on different weeks to keep training interesting and fun.

The weeks and days before the race, I slept as much as my body allowed. Sleeping is very important and very often overlooked; even the slightest sleep deprivation can greatly impair performance. Good nutrition is just as important. Training hard puts an incredible amount of pressure on the immune system, as well as joints and muscles. I tried to get enough vitamins and proteins by eating plenty of fruits, vegetables, red and white meat, and fish. Women have special nutritional requirements such as iron and calcium, so some red meat and milk were always in my high-protein Mediterranean diet. I also snacked anytime I found myself a little hungry.

The race started in the dark on a paved downhill road. What a great way to warm up! I forced myself to slow down and relax. No matter how many 100-mile races I run, I always have to remind myself they are very long races and must be run smart. What seems like an easy pace early in the race will become labored soon enough. A group of lead runners took off, and I could not tell if there were any women among them. Reminding myself that the first few miles are not the time to worry, I just relaxed and tried to control my pace. During the week prior to the race my legs seemed tired and stiff, but as soon as the race began, all the pains and worries were gone. I think it was simply an effect of the adrenaline, but it sure helped with the confidence. Minutes felt like seconds, and before I knew it the sun was rising and we were at the first aid station. I can still recall the reddish tint of the sun coming through the trees. It was beautiful.

Aid stations are one of the biggest highlights of this race. Many have a theme, and the volunteers put a lot of effort into having a great time. There is the Chili Pepper aid station, managed by employees of a local restaurant. They had Mexican food, which turned my stomach to even look at, and there was one very loud, very big, and slightly drunk guy who kept trying to have a conversation with me. *Sorry buddy, I have a race to run.* The Flamingo aid station was also very inventive. There was a large cutout of a basketball player dressed up in a Hawaiian hula-style outfit, and as the runners entered the station, they were given flowers and their picture was taken. I hardly spent any time at the aid stations—just long enough to refill my water bottles. One of the things I regret about competitive racing is that I can't socialize and meet people at the aid stations.

After a few miles of gravel roads, the course turns onto the Ouachita Trail. At that moment my life seemed perfect. Single-track trail is my favorite surface, especially when it is relatively smooth and rolling, with just a few obstacles to keep it interesting. Time stops and, if my legs are rested, running becomes effortless. All my concentration is on my feet, trying to find the best footing among the rocks and roots. Some trails are as fun as roller coasters, and the Ouachita Trail is no exception. Although we would run this portion of the course only once, I wished it would go on forever.

This sounds odd, but the hardest part of the Arkansas 100 course was the unexpected amount of running. I have an almost religious appreciation for walking breaks, and because the hills at Arkansas were not too steep, I found myself running more than I was used to. I ran for a while with a new-found friend, Ray, who had won this race several times in the past. The joy of this encounter was unexpected, since I had run alone every other race, and I have never had the energy to share small talk with other runners. With Ray it was different, and the conversation became very pleasant. We had covered about 30 miles by this point, and I was getting very tired. Ray and I learned a lot about each other. I was very happy to be running with somebody and surprised that a friendship could develop so quickly in such strange conditions and circumstances. Once, when I stopped to use the bathroom, Ray passed by to give me some privacy and, as he did, ruffled up my hair. It was one of those small gestures from a person I barely knew that truly meant a lot. I have not talked to Ray since that day, but I am sure that when we meet again he will seem like an old friend.

Alone again with my thoughts, I began to focus on the competition. I was in the lead, but in a 100-mile event, the real race does not start until mile 70, so my lead meant nothing. Michelle Burr, my nearest competitor, passed me around the 50-mile mark, and we exchanged a few words. I let her set the pace and tried not to let her build too much lead between us. When we arrived at the next aid station she stopped to fix one of her shoes. I left the aid station feeling energized, again in first place. I tried to maintain a faster, yet comfortable pace to distance her. I caught up with Ray again, and he cautioned me to pick up the pace as much as I could to get over Smith Mountain and its tricky footing before nightfall. Picking up the pace after about 70 miles of running is no small feat, but I knew it was good advice, and my goal was now to run wisely and preserve my lead.

As I climbed over Smith Mountain, I remembered the Pay Day candy bar I had put in one of my drop bags. My mouth watered just thinking about it. The plan was just to eat a bite, and carry the rest with me. However, once I got to my drop bag, I ate the whole thing. One of the things that really helped me at Arkansas is that I tried to eat as much as I could. Energy gels were my staple, and I ate anything that looked good at the aid stations. I had moments of extreme fatigue, but I never bonked. Toward the end of the day I tried to get some protein by eating a turkey-and-cheese sandwich. By then I could have eaten a live cow. I felt very tired, but never too tired to run. I kept my fluid level up, even at night, drinking almost two bottles between every aid station. I have had lower points in other 100-milers, so I never really considered quitting, especially because I was in the lead. I was so excited by the prospect of winning that I would have quit only if a car had run me over. By mile 90, though, I must admit that was not such a bad prospect at all.

As darkness fell I was surprised at how good I was feeling. I was quite tired and fatigued, but my legs were not hurting as they had in other races, and this allowed me to simply fly on the downhills. I was alone in the night with my flashlight, with city lights in the distance, and the only sounds were my footsteps, night owls, and my breathing. The last few miles were on a very rocky dirt road, but they were mostly downhill. I tried not to think about Michelle behind me, tried not to think about the distance, tried not to think about finishing. I just relaxed as much as I could and focused on increasing my pace. I was tired, maybe as tired as I have ever been, but I was not in unbearable pain, a nice change for once. I turned left onto a gravel road and I knew the finish line was approaching: I kept looking behind me for Michelle's flashlight, but saw none.

I was ready to be done. My time did not matter, but my position did, so seeing nobody behind me was a relief. Then I saw a flashlight coming toward me and I heard my name. I almost cried when I realized it was Russ. "I am so tired!" I complained. Russ was encouraging, and he told me that I was on the edge of breaking 19 hours. He pushed me to run the last mile as fast as I could. Although I did not care about breaking 19 hours, I gave it my best simply because I figured it would get me to the finish line sooner. I was so exhausted that, even in that last mile, I could not bring myself to run a very small hill. Then I saw the first cars and I knew the finish line was there. I gave it everything I had. Like a miracle, my legs started moving fast. The cheering, the lights, the end of a very long day: I ran as fast as I could and crossing the finish line was pure ecstasy. As I took the last step, I thought I had never been so happy. I was happy the running was over for a while, I was happy I had won, and I was happy I would soon take a shower. Thanks to Russ, I crossed the finish line breaking 19 hours with a whole minute to spare.

Russ hugged me and took me inside. Somebody shook my hand; I think it was the race director. Somebody else offered congratulations. Russ left me sitting by the roaring fireplace and went to get my bag. I found myself sitting down with a stupid smile on my face. This was my fastest time ever. In just under 19 hours, I had come in first woman, fifth overall. An indescribable feeling of satisfaction simply overwhelmed me.

We went back to the hotel and I took one of those glorious showers that seem to have the power to wash away not only the dirt, but also the fatigue and hard work. As I lay in bed my muscles were getting more and more sore, rendering sleep impossible. We drove all through the next day until 1:00 A.M. on Monday, when I finally collapsed in a hotel room. I slept an unconscious sleep, closer to passing out than I have ever been. I do not remember falling asleep, and I do not remember anything about that night. But Arkansas did leave me with many great memories. It also left me with the worst case of poison ivy I have ever had. It lasted for weeks, and left scars that are still clearly visible. But scars fade over time. Arkansas left me with something that will not. Throughout my whole life I have rarely had confidence in myself. After Arkansas, however, I felt confident, thinking that maybe my other wins were not all about luck. I have gained so much faith in myself that I've begun to believe I am worth something. As a woman, it has also given me a sense of strength, which at times makes me forget about the risks. I fear less simply because I can run 100 miles.

In races like the Arkansas 100, the real competition is between me and my own body and mind, not with other runners. Fast times come from within me. It does not matter who is around. All that matters is how much I am willing to endure. My first goal is to always enjoy it. I like the competition and I like the challenge, but what I like the most is the freedom of putting my shoes on and covering so much ground in so little time. I hope to never get caught up in racing so much that I forget what it is all about. I always want to allow myself to cut a run short, or to take the trail with the better view, even if it does not fit into my weekly mileage. I always want to smell the pine trees. I always want, in every race, to take the time to look up at the sky at night, because remembering how lucky I am matters more than winning.

From Head Injuries to Hardrock

NAME: MARC WITKES
AGE: 36
RESIDENCE: DURANGO, COLORADO
YEARS RUNNING: 19
YEARS RUNNING ULTRAS: 12

I was only 21 when the car I was traveling in slid out of control during a snowstorm and collided head-on with a truck in the oncoming lane. I was with some college friends, returning from a cross-country skiing weekend. Rescue crews were quickly on the scene, and the driver and two passengers walked away from the accident with barely a scratch. But the Jaws of Life were needed to extract me from where I was trapped in the front passenger seat. I was still in the seat belt, which saved me from going through the windshield, but I suffered a serious brain contusion when my head hit the glass.

An ambulance ride through the night sped me to the nearest hospital. Still unconscious and paralyzed on the right side of my body, I struggled to stay alive while my friends gathered and comforted each other in disbelief. A resuscitator was quickly inserted into my throat to help me breathe.

Soon after, the local police knocked on my parents' door to tell them some of the worst news ever. My parents dressed quickly and drove 300 miles to be with me as I lay in a coma in an upstate New York hospital. Days went by, and the situation changed little. Finally, on the tenth day, I awoke to a new world of which I knew little. The impact to the brain erased my short-term memory, and my long-term memories were terribly shuffled as well.

While I was transferred to a rehabilitation hospital, my mother sat with me in the back of the ambulance and comforted me as best she could. I could speak only in whispers, my vocal cords damaged from violently ripping the resuscitator from my throat.

My condition steadily improved while in the rehabilitation unit. I started in a wheelchair, and physical therapy eventually enabled me to move around with the use of only a cane. Occupational and speech therapy helped me regain lost memories. I remembered that I had once been an ath-lete who enjoyed running and bicycling.

I first started running with a friend to get in shape. I ran 2 to 4 miles two or three days a week, and steadily improved. Shortly after high school grad-uation, in the spring of 1984, my friend and I made a bet to see if we could run a local 10-mile race. We ran it, and I got hooked. I continued running during my stay at Ithaca College. I ran my first marathon during freshman year. I was miserably underprepared and was the last finisher in just over five hours. By my sophomore year, I had improved considerably and was running 7-minute miles for the shorter races. I usually finished in the top three for my age group, mostly because there were so few competitors in my bracket. I also took up cycling while at Ithaca. I started racing, doing a few time trials and many long solo tours. Before the accident, I was running four to five days a week and cycling another two to three days.

The doctors insisted that only my excellent physical condition had enabled me to survive the automobile crash and return to normal function.

My recovery progressed and I began to get stronger, due in part to doing push-ups and countless "wheelchair" laps around the hospital corridors to build strength. I pleaded and begged my therapists to help me get back on my bicycle. Tethered to two therapists, who walked beside me, I returned to my beloved bicycle and was thrilled to briefly ride through the parking lot without falling over. My balance and coordination were still very much lim-ited. Physical recovery progressed quickly, and I was eventually allowed to go for a run on the hospital's front lawn.

That first run after the accident was maybe a quarter of a mile, but it was miraculous! I nearly cried. When I first arrived at the hoipital, the doctors thought that I might be able to walk, or even run again, but no one could say for sure. Now here I was. Just a quarter of a mile, and it was very slow, but I was running. I was just thrilled to be able pick up my feet and do more than a walk. It felt brand new and wonderful. But man, did it hurt! I was very stiff and the whole right side of my body was miserably atrophied. It would take another six months before I would gain back the muscle tone that I had prior to the accident.

Finally released from the hospital, I began a 2-year stint in outpatient therapy. Once an A student, I returned to college twice in desperate attempts to finish my education, but withdrew both times. Intellectual recovery was going to take some time. Hallucinations, personality changes and compulsive behavior were obvious direct results of the extensive brain damage I suffered. I got into trouble with my parents and the law, and it was a very confusing and difficult time in my life, to say the least.

Eventually I relocated to Durango to once again try to finish school. This time I was able to graduate. I also continued to ride and run more than ever. In fact, this is where I was introduced to ultradistance triathlons and running.

When I arrived in Durango in 1991, I met Earnst Baer at a local run. We started doing long runs together on the weekends, and everything just evolved from that. From 1991 to 2000, I ran in a handful of ultras, including a Leadville 100-mile attempt where I dropped at mile 76, and a Hardrock attempt where I dropped at mile 30. One of the differences I quickly learned between ultrarunning and shorter distance running was that ultras were not just longer, but more challenging and much more fun. Of course they require greater training and commitment. But long distance running is not impossible for anyone who is willing to overcome the obstacles, and I'd had some experience in that area.

Many ultrarunners are drawn to 100-mile events because they provide an excellent opportunity to test personal limits. They are also a great source of camaraderie. I wanted to run a 100-miler for many of the same reasons. I chose Hardrock because it is practically in my backyard, and the scenery and race organization are unparalleled among 100-milers. Living and running in Durango, Hardrock is all we talk about all year long. We train on the course every chance we get. Now it was time for me to give it a second shot.

I left for the race Thursday morning after getting off work at 7:00 A.M. I rode up with another local Hardrock participant. We got there in time to enjoy the scenery, socialize, eat, and attend the pre-race meeting and weigh-in. I slept in the local hostel that night, and other than being a little restless, I actually got a good night's sleep. It didn't hurt that I had been awake the whole previous night at my job as a hotel night auditor. I wore my race clothes to bed to save time in the morning.

In the early-morning hours before the race start, I felt nervous and excited. I was really worried about my feet, which were giving me problems. I had been given a cortisone shot one week before to help relieve the pain associated with Morton's neuroma in both feet. I tried to put my worries aside and focus on the positive. The weather was perfect and there was much energy in the air that morning. It was very exciting. We were all about to undertake an incredible journey, and we were all in it together. I said a small prayer at the race start and reminded myself of my goal: finish within the 48-hour time limit and have an enjoyable experience.

Having made the costly mistake of going out too fast at too many previous races, I started the 2001 Hardrock very slowly and conservatively. I made sure that I walked anything that was remotely steep. I felt good during most of the event except for a touch of altitude sickness and dehydration around the Telluride aid station. I felt like quitting for the first time at the Telluride, but my friend, Brad Hatten, came along and told me to eat, drink, take some aspirin, and start moving again. Which I did.

Not by coincidence, the highest points mentally for me were also some of the highest points. Perched high on top of the magnificent passes with extraordinary views below, I felt high as a kite. I was high on life and living, and lingered there for a while, just taking in the beauty and wonder of it all. But low points usually follow high points, and Hardrock was no exception.

I tripped over a rock in the 95th mile, and suffered a bad hamstring pull. I was in so much pain; I seriously wanted to quit. The area is heavily forested and I knew the only way out was to walk. Again, I just kept moving forward, trying to stay focused on the goal at hand—just 5 painful miles away. I was in horrible pain. It took me probably three hours to cover the last 4 miles. I was moving incredibly slow due to the intense pain, but I was moving. At one point I came to a big tree across the trail and it took me about 20 minutes to duck underneath. I wasn't sure that I would make it until I was within a half-mile of the finish; I literally had to drag my hurt leg around with every step.

The finish finally arrived, and I was completely exhausted, and completely elated. Running and finishing Hardrock is such an incredible experience. I have to say it is one of the best experiences of my life. What a great triumph! If there's just one lesson that the 2001 Hardrock taught, it's to never give up. I can do anything that I set my mind to, both on and off the trail.

I don't think much about my accident anymore, only how lucky I am to be alive and still running. I'm very thankful for that. It's been an incredible adventure and it's not over yet! Every day is a new challenge for me as a runner, a writer, a member of the community, a son, a brother, a boyfriend, and an employee. Sometimes I forget about the events of my past and I let small things bother me when they really should have little bearing.

Still, I know that I am one of the luckiest people around, and I will continue to run, read, learn and work hard every day to improve my physical and mental functions. Life is never going to be the same for me after the brain injury that I suffered 15 years ago. But, I'll still try to live one day at a time, one run at a time, to the best of my abilities.

Portions of this essay are adapted from an article Marc wrote in February 2002 for the Durango Herald.

Mother's Day at Massanutten

NAME: HARRY BRUELL
AGE: 34
RESIDENCE: BOLIVAR, WEST VIRGINIA
YEARS RUNNING: 13
YEARS RUNNING ULTRAS: 6

Virginia Happy Trails Running Club

I was a competitive cyclist in college, racing intercollegiately and in local and regional USCF races. After leaving college I began running for fitness as an alternative to cycling. I lost my fiancé to cancer in 1993 and began running longer and longer distances, as it helped me find peace and deal with my grief. My first ultra was the JFK 50-miler in 1996. My longest previous run was 19 miles, and my only previous race was a 5K. I finished that first JFK in about 9:22. Over the next four years I went on to run JFK four more times, buckle at Old Dominion, and complete a number of 50Ks.

At the end of 2000, my running started to drastically improve. I ran a 50K and would have been fourth in a competitive time if I hadn't gotten lost. I then came in second in the Laurel Highlands 70-miler. I was more than two hours behind the winner, but nearly an hour in front of third place and very happy with my time of 13:27. I was third in my next race—a local Fat Ass 50K—losing by only 8 minutes. I gained time on the trail sections and lost time badly on the road sections. I seem to do better the harder and rougher the trail. My next race, Catoctin 50K, seemed right up my alley—a hard trail race with lots of hills in the heat of summer. I led the first half, got caught at the turnaround, and then pulled away on the second half to win by 15 minutes, only 11 minutes off of the course record.

I was looking forward to more high-quality running the rest of the year, but got injured in early November. About this time I also began to endure some major stress at work. Early November began an 8-month ordeal involving executive turnover, a huge work increase for me, and a massive restructuring. My injuries, including tendonitis of the right lower shin, left hip, and left foot, as well as other injuries, seemed to follow one after another. My training was cut short and included a 6-week section during December 2001 and January 2002 of no running whatsoever. The Massanutten Mountain Trail 100 over Mother's Day weekend of 2002 was to be my return to racing after the series of injuries and the first since my win at Catoctin. I was looking forward to a fast race, and with my family there to support and encourage me, as they had done in all of my races, I thought I had a great chance to do well.

My wife (Jenny) and kids (Leo, age three; and Taya, age one and a half) drove with me to the race on Friday. It is only about an hour from our home, so we took the easy drive down on Friday afternoon in time for the pre-race dinner. We had a long-standing dinner obligation that night back in Bolivar, so Jenny and the kids drove back home, leaving me to spend the night alone at the race site. This was the first time I'd been away from them before an event, and I missed them. I slept pretty well, though I had lots more time to think about (and get nervous about) the race than if my family had been there.

The morning of the race got off to a great start. It was cool, but I was well rested and felt good and ready to run. I had given Jenny a schedule of projected times and she, the kids, and her mother were going to meet me later in the day. Driving from aid station to aid station on rough mountain roads with two small children is often harder than running the race, so we didn't plan to meet until the afternoon. That allowed them to spend the day relaxing. And I would need them more at night anyway.

I started out at a pretty regular 5 miles per hour pace, hoping I could maintain that pace as I had at Laurel Highlands 11 months earlier. Unfortunately, I had given Jenny a conservative schedule based on my going 4 miles per hour. It was going to be interesting to see how she would find me since she was working off the slower schedule. I ran the flats and downhills and walked the steep uphills. I think I was in seventh or eighth place at the first aid station (8.7 miles) and then slowly moved up from there. When Jenny arrived to meet me at one of the early-afternoon stations, I had already gone through two or three hours earlier. That's how far ahead of schedule I was. Surprised and anxious to catch up with me, Jenny left the kids with Grandma at the Jawbone Gap station and set out to find me. The kids had been cooped up in the car long enough, so they were perfectly happy playing with Grandma at Jawbone Gap, nibbling on aid station food, and cheering for runners. Jenny missed me at a few other stations, finally catching me at the Route 211 aid station at 57 miles. She was happy to see me finally and wanted to do more for me at the station. I didn't need any special food, drink, or flashlights; I just needed to see her. It was overwhelming to me that I had the unconditional love and support of my family. After my tragedy in 1993 I never thought that I would marry or have a family. I am thankful every day for Jenny, Leo, and Taya and sometimes—especially after running for 10-plus hours—it all starts to feel overwhelming to remember the extreme grief and now the extreme happiness. I had also been through a tough period of work stress and injuries that had taken another emotional toll over the past eight months, and it was slowly starting to come undone for me emotionally. I was so happy to see her that I started crying as I left the station. But I had to keep going and continued across 211 and back into the woods. I was in second place.

I had a hard time in the next 8-mile section leading up to the Jawbone Gap aid station where I saw the kids for the first time. My legs were starting to hurt from running the downhills. I was also wearing some very heavy orthotics designed for mild walking, not mountain running, and the bottoms of my feet were suffering. My physical condition was declining and I was beginning to have less fun. My mind-set had been to come out and run fast and do well. The MMT 100 is known for its difficult course, but it really is my kind of course. Plus, I had finished in the top three in my last three races. There were no top national runners at MMT and I thought I had a chance to win or place very well. I was not surprised to be in second, but frustrated that I couldn't catch the guy in first. You need to have a sense of inner peace and calm to do well at an ultra. I certainly was not in that place. I didn't really have a goal of finishing MMT. My goal was to run fast as long as I could. When I started not being able to run fast, I stopped having fun. That mind-set was quite a contrast to the attitude I had in my last 100 (and only 100 finish at that time). At the 2000 Old Dominion I started very, very slowly and was in last place after 20 miles. I walked the hills and ran very conservatively on the rest. I kept this pace up the entire race until the last 3 miles, which I covered at a 6-minute pace. I finished in 24th at around 23:11. Miles 97 to 100 were almost a 5K PR for me, and I felt great at the finish with lots of energy to spare. I didn't want to finish the MMT with fuel in the tank. I wanted to push as hard as I could and run the fastest race possible. I had done this at Laurel the year before and it worked, though I realized that this could backfire at MMT and result in a DNF. I needed to try, but it was taking a toll both mentally and physically.

I had a feeling that I was going to drop when I left my family at Jawbone Gap. There were only 2.8 miles between Jawbone and the next station, and I had to walk the whole thing. I came out of the woods and the trail went about 50 yards on the road up to the next aid station. Leo, who had been waiting patiently for me, had been distracted and missed seeing me come out of the woods. When I got to the aid station he ran up crying because he'd wanted to see me come out of the woods. He was clearly near the end of his rope and quite tired after a long day in the car. So I ran back along the road, back into the woods, and back out again so that he could see me come out. He was so excited, and just wanted me to hold him. Taya was teething and running a fever. Grandma was excited for me to go on, and Jenny was willing to do whatever I wanted. I usually go through aid stations with very little or no stop time. I have only sat down twice in my life at aid stations, and that was to change shoes. I realized, though, that it just didn't make any sense to go on. I was not going to be able to run fast—or run much at all—because my quads were shot. I probably could have recovered a little, but would most likely have to walk a good portion of the next 33 miles. I had 22 hours left before the cut off, so I had more than enough time to finish. If I could have gone just 3 miles per hour I could have finished in the top 5. However, my goal had been to run fast and I hadn't planned on slogging to the finish. And, most importantly, it would have been a huge sacrifice for my family, already tired from a full day of crewing. I stretched out on a blanket, and Leo climbed on top of me. I was just so happy to see them all, and they were happy to see me. I know that they would sacrifice everything to support me to the finish and make me happy. And I'm sure there will be times that I will need that sacrifice from them, but this was not one of those times. It was more important to me to stop. We had all been through enough for one day.

My kids were overjoyed that I stopped. They were ready to go. Grandma, however, was not so happy. She had gone to Old Dominion in 2000, but had missed all of my good finishes in 2001. One of her other daughters had helped us at Laurel Highlands and told her how much fun it had been to be part of my crew. Grandma Helen is a huge sports fan, was enjoying the experience, and just wanted to keep going. Jenny understood completely what happened. She was disappointed for me and absolutely would have kept going, but she was also probably happy to relax and have some family time. Which we did. We drove off the mountain, got some pizza, and headed home to rest. We went out for Mother's Day brunch the next morning and had a really nice day, though I was quite sore.

I had my only other DNF in Vermont in 1998 when I twisted an ankle and could barely walk after 50 miles. That DNF was a huge disappointment and I had a hard time bouncing back. Unlike Vermont, the MMT did not discourage me. I got new orthotics and within two months was back in race shape and ready to go. I went back up to Vermont to erase the old DNF. I had a good run, not pushing too fast but still taking over two hours off my previous 100-mile finish—and enjoying the experience. I then went back to Catoctin just three weeks later and finished in second place.

I learned several very important lessons from my experience at MMT. First, I have to be mentally prepared for a 100-miler, and be at peace internally. If my mind is on other things, like work problems, I will have a difficult time. Second, I need to remember that each race is a "race of one" and that all ultras are races of attrition. I got too caught up at MMT worrying about racing the guy in front of me rather than just running. My best races have been those when I just run for fun and don't worry about whether I'm first or last.

Give Me a Mountain Race Any Day!

NAME: GREG LOOMIS
AGE: 29
RESIDENCE: SAN ANTONIO, TEXAS
YEARS RUNNING: 18
YEARS RUNNING ULTRAS: 4

Photo by Phil Mislinski

I was introduced to running at an early age as I watched my father get into the sport. As Dad got more and more into running and began racing marathons and 10Ks all over the East Coast, the family went to watch. Some of his big races included the Cherry Blossom in Washington, DC, the New York City Marathon, and of course Boston, where I watched Bill Rodgers win in 1980, and Salazar and Beardsley duel in 1982. I also watched Dad PR with a 2:34 in the cold rain of 1983. I remember asking my mom if he was going to die after watching him shake uncontrollably with an IV in his arm, wrapped in blankets in the medical tent after that one. Maybe it was these impressions, or perhaps the 1- or 2-mile runs he would let me run with him from time to time, that gave me my love for running. Or it may have been the many track meets I watched my older brothers compete in. They broke and rebroke all of our school records from the 400m to the 2-mile. I idolized them so much that I begged to be allowed to take the maturity and strength test as a seventh grader so that I could run with my brother Jeff for our school's varsity cross-country team during his senior year.

My biology teacher was the coach then, and daily practices provided not only physical training for my 93-pound body, but an opportunity to train my mind as well. I learned about lichens, fungi, symbiotic relationships, and tree identification, and through those practices I fell in love with the natural world around me. Without really knowing it, I became a trail runner.

The next summer I began running longer and longer distances, making loops out of my favorite trails and desolate dirt roads. I even managed to do a 12-mile run before the start of the cross-country season. I wrote my own training schedules as running books and magazines replaced the Hardy Boys as my reading material of choice. I'd also sneak peaks into my dad's training log, in awe of the 100-plus-mile weeks and ultralong runs he had put in before marathons. I was very impressed.

I spent a week at cross-country camp each year before school practices officially began. Those weeks were some of the best times of my life. Our routine included two runs each day on the most beautiful trails and dirt roads of rural Alfred, New York. During my senior year, I accomplished one of my running goals: running 100 miles in one week. Then came my freshman year of college, when my running took me to places like Notre Dame and Kansas State, and my longest run grew to 19 miles. That summer I watched Ann Trason battle for the overall lead in the Leadville 100-mile race through the mountains of Colorado and knew that was something I wanted to someday do.

When I graduated from Ithaca College in 1997 I decided the next step for me was to move up to marathon and even ultramarathon distances. So I entered the Finger Lakes Fifties 50K that summer. I found that ultrarunning was very different from shorter-distance racing. Sure, an ultra is a race. But you can talk to the other competitors, stop to walk whenever you want, and even eat during the run. It was quite a change from cross-country racing, and it was more fun too. The next step came the following year when, with a few successful road marathons and experimentation with the outer edges of my limits, I managed a 38-mile Boston "Marathon" by running from my apartment to the Boston Marathon start line, then running the race.

Finally, in 1999, the finishing touches were added and I became what I am today: a trail ultrarunner. After running two 30-mile training runs and marathons on back-to-back weekends, I figured I was ready for a 50-miler. So I entered the Finger Lakes Fifties 50 in July. I began the race with two conservative hours of easy running that included walking breaks every 15 minutes. Then I began to press a little harder and moved up through the field. With a long break to change shoes and socks, eat, and take in some caffeine at 30 miles, I was on my way into the unknown. Despite temperatures in the 80s and a few long struggles with uphills, it wasn't too bad. Not only had I finished my first 50-miler, I won the race!

After that grand debut and another win at the Mount Hood PCT 50-miler, I was completely hooked. Finding success in ultrarunning helped me shed the sheepish and shy personality I had as a youth and become a self-confident, take-charge individual. Because of this attitude shift, I was able to attract the eye of a beautiful gal who will someday be my wife. But success can also have its downside. In my case, I let it go straight to my head. My first attempt at running 100 miles at the Superior Trail 100 ended with me a broken and beaten man at mile 65.5 after 13 hours on the trail. Humbled and much smarter, I entered and finished the Massanutten Mountain 100 the next spring. It did not end there, as I ran two more 100-milers that year, four the next, and seven this year. Like I said, I was completely hooked. I was an ultra racer.

Ultra races are not like shorter-distance races. They are not me against the competition. Ultras are more of a competition between me, myself, the course, and the distance. Ultrarunning pits my mind against my body. It is about being outdoors where few dare venture, either with friends or alone with just my God. Ultras are a test of what the magnificent human body can do and what the mind will allow. I can think of no other way to truly feel alive. Running is not just what I do: It is who I am. For me, sleep-eat-work-TV-then-repeat is not enough. I need to see things. I need to see a squirrel scramble in the snow, then jump up onto a branch and run full tilt with no fear of falling. I need to hear a deer snort out a warning that I am perhaps not where he thinks I should be. I need to feel the wind, the breath of Mother Earth herself, tickle my ears and cause the trees to sway and dance around me. I run to be fit and healthy, to be fast and strong, and to accomplish feats that seem unobtainable to many. I enjoy the discovery of that which I am actually capable: of how far I can push myself. It is why I live.

In 2001, I trained to win the Arkansas Traveller 100. My training that year brought back memories from my cross-country days five years prior during my senior season at Ithaca. I was training hard for one particular race just as I did back then. Back then, it was the regional championships, and the dream of making a trip to the national meet. This time it was for the dream of winning a 100-mile race. Back then, I sacrificed schoolwork and a social life to ensure that every day I slept enough, ate well, and continued to methodically prepare for the big day. I rose at 6:15 every morning during that fall semester to put in an easy run. Then later in the afternoon we would bang out the miles and speedy repeats with one goal in mind: to qualify for nationals. Much had changed since those days, but the parallels were still there as once again, I was making sacrifices toward a running goal.

On the big day of the AT 100, I went out too strong and things started falling apart early. It turned out that I had sacrificed too many long runs and hill workouts in favor of speedwork, and now I was paying the price. I knew as I came into the aid station at 64 miles that it was not going to be my day. Sure, I could have finished. I could have walked the last 33 miles and still come in under the cutoffs. I'd done it before on the last 35 miles of the 2000 Massanutten Mountain 100. But was it worth risking real injury and not being able to run for weeks? I didn't think so as I limped into the aid station at 67.7 miles and announced that I was dropping.

After that failure, I felt the need to run a flat and fast 100 again, and to prove that I still had it, I wanted to run a 15-hour race. I chose the Rocky Racoon 100 because of its reputation as a fast course. Even with a fast, relatively easy course, I had my work cut out for me. Mountain races and rough terrain I am good at, but the flat steady running of the Rocky Racoon would present a whole new challenge.

I woke early on the Friday before the race, and drove three hours to Baltimore to catch a flight to Huntsville, Texas. Upon learning my flight out was going to be an hour late, I switched to an earlier flight in hopes of making my connector in Detroit that would eventually get me to Houston. I made the connector, but my luggage didn't! So I arrived in Houston with only my carry-on bag. Luckily it contained most of what I needed to race. The shoes on my feet were not my favorite, but they would have to do. I did not have my homemade supersugared drink that had become a staple for me, and I had to go to Wal-Mart and buy some Slimfast and a flashlight. My camping gear was also not there, so I got a motel in town. After eating some pizza at 10:00 P.M., I finally got into bed at 11:00. The alarm was set for 4:00 A.M. I awoke feeling surprisingly refreshed and ready to run, but discovered in the 30-degree morning air that I had no hat. It too was in my lost bag!

The race began in the dark and I started out at a comfortable clip, trying to be conservative. I ended up running the first 20-mile loop (of 5) with Kevin Bligan and Blake Wood. The course seemed confusing on the first go around with three out-and-back sections and a few tricky turns. But it was very well marked with ribbon and yellow pie plates, and I never felt lost. The trails were pretty smooth; a mix of sandy pine-needle-covered paths with some rooty sections. It was almost completely flat with a few rolling gentle grades. I ran the entire loop without taking a walk break—which was unheard of in the mountain ultras I was accustomed to. Kevin, Blake, and

I finished the first loop in 2:46. This is about where I hoped to be. It wasn't 8-minute miles, but it was quicker than the 9-minute pace I hoped to hold for a 15-hour finish. But would that really be possible?

I drank a Slimfast, grabbed a piece of banana, stripped off my Patagonia vest, and started off on loop 2 feeling pretty good. By now Scott Eppleman had pulled ahead, and Blake and I moved off in pursuit. I took the Gatorade at each of the four aid stations, but knew that at only 50 calories per cup, it would not be enough to sustain my run. I had been nibbling on pretzels, M&Ms, and crackers, but none of this was enough either, and around 30 miles into the race I was starving and starting to bonk. Although I was in second place, only four minutes behind the leader, I had no choice but to back off the pace.

For the next 10 miles I questioned the reason for trying to race my guts out and wondered what happened to the me that used to run these races just to see if I could finish. When did I stop racing against me, and start racing for the win? I decided to jog and enjoy myself, and ended up coming through loop 2 in just over three hours. I had dropped several places in the standings, and my 15-hour goal was now out of the question.

I was pleasantly surprised to see that my lost bag had arrived at the start/finish area! When I reported it lost at the airport, the baggage claim guy asked for a delivery address and I told him Huntsville State Park. He said they would try to drive it out to me, but I really didn't expect it to show up here, 65 miles away from the airport. I immediately switched into more comfortable shoes, then I drank a Slimfast, got some of my homemade drink mix, and headed out for the third loop. Feeling good but still behind energywise, I started walking all the tiny hills and tried to eat more at the aid stations. I was beginning to enjoy the design of the course as I got to see many of the other runners on the out-and-back sections. Everyone was shouting words of encouragement, and I felt part of a special crowd. Many of my friends were there, running well.

I was amazed at what was going on up front as Scott and Blake continued to hammer at a sub-15-hour pace. I was also shocked to see Ann Heaslet up there with them. She is a very fine runner, but I was surprised to see her running that pace. Just behind me were three women, including my hero Sue Johnston, and my friend Michele Burr. They kept nipping at my heels, and it made me wonder how they were all running with ease while I was struggling. I began to feel the onset of the stomach problems that have plagued me before in these long events. I was a bit nauseous too, so I tried to hold off on the food for a while and just drank instead. (Note: I thought at the time that it was my running that caused the stomach problems. Later research showed that it was probably the highly sugared drink that I was consuming.)

Morning turned into midday, and now it was time to start thinking about nightfall. I finished the third loop now a little over nine hours into the race, and stopped to get another shirt and find a flashlight. It would be dark and cold by the time I finished loop 4. My legs were tired but my feet felt good and nothing was structurally wrong. I drank another Slimfast, ate some baked potato, and headed out with 60 miles under my belt. Three laps down, two to go.

During a 100-miler, miles 60 to 80 are always the strangest for me. I go through huge swings from feelings of invincibility to utter despair. My legs were starting to get stiff, and I found myself longing more and more for big hills and mountains. The endless miles of flat running were beginning to take their toll on my hamstrings. I love to climb. It always offers a different muscle recruitment pattern (walk breaks!), not to mention the mental lift of ascending a mountain to beautiful vistas and the resulting downhill. Rocky Raccoon offers miles of runnable trail with views of a lake and that is about it.

I had moved up in the field again as I passed Mark Henderson, who after 70 strong miles had suffered corneal edema and was stumbling along with blurred vision. His pacer was there to help him find the way. I ran into the 80-mile mark with Chris Clark of Colorado and finished the fourth loop at the 12:14 mark. After putting on my vest, gloves, eating a cup of chicken noodle soup, drinking a Slimfast, grabbing a bottle of my staple drink and my flashlight, I was ready to rock. However, the seven minutes I spent in the aid station left me unbelievably stiff; even the walk out was torture. As I began to loosen up and run, I tried to figure the math for a sub-17-hour finish. It would be possible, but I was hurting. I hoped the three Advils I took at the aid station would kick in soon.

After running another 5 miles with Chris, chatting about various subjects such as Hardrock and traveling, I was feeling better and decided it was time to push harder. This is why I do these races: the challenge of pressing on, even when I feel so sore, so tired, and have legs that barely function. I looked at my watch and saw I was at 14:31 at the tip of the turnaround.

Hmmm, I thought. *If I run the last 10 miles in 2:08 I can break 16:40!* The magical 10-minute pace was there for the taking. But I would have to push hard. With my bottle in my left hand and flashlight in my right, I tried to "float" the downhills as my quads could no longer provide any braking. I just flew down the hill, trying not to fall. I walked the uphills as strong as I could manage, and I ran the flats as long as I could bear before taking a walk break. At the aid station I had a cup of broth, filled my bottle with Coke, and moved on. I knew I had to get out of there quick. I had to press on. I climbed up a tiny hill and could see the warm glow of the finish line lights across the lake.

Soon all of this will be over. I have got to run. I have less than one hour to break 16:30. Go, go, go!

The glow sticks lit the way and I called out to each as I ran by. At this point I had not seen another runner for an hour, which was strange for this course. I longed for company.

Where is the last aid station . . . where is it? I know I'll have three miles to go from there . . . thirty minutes! I can do it.

Finally I was there. The last aid station. I drank a cup of Coke, and didn't even bother to fill my bottle before I ran out. My watch said 15:58. I could still do it. With a huge effort to run strong, I managed to get within earshot of the finish and then, as if to taunt me, my quads cramped up.

"Oh God, please let me finish this thing before I fall apart!" I prayed out loud.

My watch said 16:21, and there it was. The finish line was just down the road. I turned and ran for it, crossing in 16:28. *Yes!* I was fourth in a stellar field. Sure, I was more than a minute-per-mile behind Scott and Blake and my original goal. But the strong last loop and the finish under 16:30 really made my race. I had lost the overall race, but in the race between me, myself, the course, and the distance, I *won!*

As with any ultramarathon, the Rocky Racoon taught me a few things. The main thing was that in spite of being so stiff and sore that it seemed impossible to run, I could indeed still run. I proved to myself yet again that, when it comes right down to it, I can put myself through a lot of suffering. It also reminded me that it's a lot more fun to race against me, and not for the win. Last, but not least, I learned that *running* 100 miles is tough. Give me a mountain race any day . . . at least there I can walk!

Iron Will at the Laurel Highlands Ultra 70-Mile Trail Race

NAME: RUSSELL GILL
AGE: 39
RESIDENCE: CHARLOTTESVILLE, VIRGINIA
YEARS RUNNING: 16
YEARS RUNNING ULTRAS: 5

I remember once watching the Hawaii Ironman Triathlon on television. Ironman champion and veteran Paula Newby-Frasier was literally crawling toward the finish line. She looked as if she was dying right there on the course. Her mind and body had been pushed to their limits and she was suffering the consequences. I recall thinking to myself, how would I respond if I were in her place, if I was pushed to my limits? Would I quit, or would I press on like a true Ironman? Little did I know that I would soon come close to finding out.

I was always an athlete. I played a lot of sports in high school, mainly baseball and basketball, and was fortunate enough to get a scholarship to play basketball for Hendrix College in Conway, Arkansas. I enjoyed running, so after my junior season of basketball I thought about joining the cross-country team. However, the college would not let me run cross-country because I was a scholarship athlete. Finally my senior year, our season was over and I was no longer under scholarship, so I joined the team. After college, I went on to graduate school and ran cross-country again. I was running a lot of road races, and eventually started running marathons. After one particular marathon I went for a pretty hard run and ended up pulling the IT band in both legs. It took about six months to recover. I had never really been injured before—even playing basketball—so that was new to me. During my recovery I saw an article on trail running, about how off-road running was easier on the body than its paved-road counterpart. That sounded good to me. I realized that if I wanted to extend my running career then I needed to get off the pavement and onto a softer surface. So trail running, and subsequently ultrarunning, came from a desire to protect my body for the long term. It is funny that you would consider running 100 miles a form of protecting your body. But trail and ultrarunning really are different, in more ways than one.

When I was doing a lot of road racing, I never really connected with people. That is totally different in ultra distance running. I think there is a correlation between the friendliness of ultras and the fact that many ultras are run in the woods. The kinds of individuals who love to be in the mountains or the forest are the same kind of people who love life and love meeting new people. It is all one big experience. You get that personality type in conjunction with an ultradistance athletic event, and it has a profound effect on the kind of individual you meet. Anytime you meet people who are unique and different, whether you agree on things or not, it has an impact, and you take some of that person back with you. From my perspective, that's totally different from road racing. From a more physical, or athletic perspective, ultrarunning has made me a healthier individual. I think that my long-term prognosis for being a healthy adult is better because I do run ultralong distances. I live a healthy life so I can perform well in these events. But all of that was about to be put to an Ironman-caliber test.

It all happened at the 2000 Laurel Highlands 70-Mile Ultra. The Laurel Highlands Trail runs from Ohiopyle to Seward in southern Pennsylvania. The trail makes for a difficult course: very technical with a lot of climbing. On top of that, it is run in the middle of the summer. The event is also known for its limited number of aid stations. I knew it was going to be hot and tried to train for it. I grew up in Arkansas, so I'm used to heat and humidity. But in training for Laurel Highlands I made myself run in the afternoon at least three days per week. I made sure I had plenty of water, and I was taking electrolyte tablets as well. Heat training is like speed work. If you do not do speed work, you do not get any faster. And if you do not train in the heat, you can not acclimate. So for three days a week I trained specifically for the heat. Then the weekend long run always started in the morning, but would extend into the heat of the day, so I'd get some more heat training there. I did that for about six weeks to prepare for Laurel Highlands. I thought it would be enough.

On Friday I drove up to Somerset with five of my friends who would also be running. That night there was a pre-race dinner with pizza and pasta. Tim Hewitt, the race director, warned all of the participants during the pre-race briefing that the weather would remain extremely warm and humid. He told us to be sure to drink as much as possible during the race and carry as much fluid with us as we could. The heat, humidity, and lack of available water during the race with only five aid stations for the 70-mile distance would prove to be a tremendous challenge for everyone.

The race started at 5:30 A.M. in an attempt to get a head start on the heat. It was a typical summer morning, and even at that early hour it was over 80 degrees and the humidity was already stifling. You could tell from the very beginning that it was going to be a scorcher. As runners stood around waiting for the race to begin, many shared their concerns regarding the weather. Everyone seemed more concerned about the weather conditions than the distance. Tim warned us again that there were very few aid stations and we would need to carry enough liquid to get from one to the next. Then, at his command, we were off and running.

I started out at what I felt was a fairly conservative pace. The course is point-to-point with little mileage markers along the way, so whether I wanted to or not, I could tell my pace by looking at my watch each mile. I went out at around a 7- to 8-minute-per-mile pace, then as it got hotter and hotter, that slipped to a 9- and 10-minute-pace. Then we started climbing and my pace slowed even more to 12 minutes per mile. My body was starting to break down.

The Laurel Highlands Trail winds beautifully through the southern Pennsylvania mountains. It is rocky, with some very technical sections. The trail is named after the laurel flower, and the purple blooms are everywhere. There are also lots of ferns, so I felt at times as if I was running through a prehistoric forest. It was really pretty that year, even with the oppressive heat. There is probably 13,000 feet of gain over the 70 rocky and rooty miles. The trail crosses several creeks along the way, and at each crossing there would be runners, literally lying down in the water trying to get cooled off.

I was running ahead of my five friends when the strangest thing started happening. I came into one of the aid stations and one of my friends was there, cleaned up with changed clothes and everything. He had dropped out and hitched a ride to the aid station. This continued for a while, and by about 50 miles, four of my friends had dropped out and were there. It was really a challenge for me to keep going, suffering, knowing that my friends were done for the day. And then to make matters worse, on more than one occasion I entered an aid station with a couple of runners, and they would drop out and I would be the only one leaving. This should have told me something. Eventually I was running the race all by myself. I don't think I saw any runners the last 20 miles. That was really tough.

I considered quitting 100 times. I was at the last aid station at around 57 miles, contemplating quitting, when I suddenly remembered seeing Ironwoman Paula Newby-Frasier on television. I recalled her posture and the look on her face as she gave every last ounce of energy she had to get to that finish line. I told myself, *This is what I wanted. I wanted to see how I would react. I wanted to see what I would do.*

I felt like quitting, but if I didn't go on then I had the answer to my question, and it was not the answer I wanted. If I kept going, then my answer, be it good or bad, would come later. So I kept going. The challenge motivated me. By this point in the race I knew that I was suffering from severe dehydration, my muscles were cramping, and I was having a difficult time keeping food down. I had been taking an electrolytee capsule (E-Caps) every hour during the day and felt this was probably the only thing keeping my muscles from locking up. Electrolytes help the body absorb fluids, and are depleted through sweat. Realizing it was time for another E-Cap, I reached into my pocket to find that I was all out! Because I had planned on being finished by this point I hadn't brought enough capsules with me. Now I knew this was really going to get interesting. Luckily, one of my friends who had dropped earlier in the day met me at a road crossing with about 10 miles remaining and had a couple to spare.

It was really dark for the last four hours of the race. My original goal was to finish in 14 or 15 hours, so I had not planned on needing a flashlight. But I did have a light at the very last aid station just in case something like this happened. Thanks goodness for planning ahead!

With just 5 miles to go in the race, I was really suffering, not just physically but mentally as well. I was so close, but just not close enough. When you start running a ultra race, 5 miles seems like nothing. But at the end of a long race, with 5 miles to go, it seems like you have Mount Everest yet to climb, especially when things are going badly. And things were definitely going badly. But quitting with just 5 miles to go was out of the question. I finally broke through that mental barrier in the final few miles and realized that I was close to finishing. There was a certain amount of euphoria, and a certain sense of accomplishment that I had really overcome some major obstacles. I was about to pass the test, and it felt really good.

I could see the lights of the finish from about a half-mile away, and although just 2 miles back I could barely run at all, now all of sudden I felt I could give Carl Lewis a run for his money as I sprinted toward the finish line, toward the answer to my Ironman question. I had faced the limits of human strength and endurance, and I had succeeded.

Out of approximately 150 starters, only about 26 finished. I finished in eighth place. The course, heat, and humidity really took a toll on everyone that day. Although I had run longer races in much faster times, this one took more from me mentally and physically than anything I've ever done. It hurt so much, yet it had a profound effect on me. It taught me that I could feel that low and hurt that bad and want to quit that much, and still make it to the finish. Laurel Highlands put me as close to the edge of my physical and mental limits as I've ever been. My friends took a picture of me after the race and when I saw it, it scared me. I didn't recognize myself. I started the race weighing 164 pounds and after my weight had dropped to 151! In 100-milers I would have been pulled from the race due to the weight loss. I had no idea I had lost that much. My whole face was covered in white salt from dried perspiration. I probably should have stopped, but it is one of those things that either out of ignorance or perseverance, I kept going. The great thing about that race is that I have been in other tough situations since then, and I can always remind myself that no matter how tough it seems, I've seen tougher. Sometimes there will be races where it is just smarter to stop. But it is great to have an event like the 2000 Laurel Highlands to be able to draw back on and say "I did it!"

The next year, runners enjoyed low humidity with the high temperatures in the low 60s. Go figure!

Running with Mom at the Wasatch Front 100

NAME: CATRA CORBETT-McNEELY
AGE: 38
RESIDENCE: FREMONT, CALIFORNIA
YEARS RUNNING: 7
YEARS RUNNING ULTRAS: 4

Photo by Ammon McNeely

My mom has always been my number one fan. She watched me train for and run my first marathon. Then, even though she thought I was nuts, she watched me take the next step as I ventured into ultrarunning. She has always been there waiting for me to come home from a race to share all the stories and pictures of where I ran, what I did, and so on. She so much loved hearing about my races. She is, by far, my biggest supporter. My number one fan.

At 8:10 A.M. on March 31, 2002, I found my mom dead of an apparent heart attack. I was devastated. My father died when I was 17, but this was different. This time I was all alone. Prior to that fateful morning, my thoughts were focused on running the American River 50-mile run the following weekend. But my mom's sudden death left me confused, unsure what to do. Could I run the AR 50? Could I even continue running at all? I honestly wasn't sure how I could go on. I turned to my friends and family in the ultrarunning community for advice, hoping they could help me decide what to do. I was greeted with open arms and more love and compassion than I ever thought possible. I was swamped with e-mails, cards, prayers, and poems. It was so uplifting. Thank you, ultrarunners.

My mom has earned her wings and is now an angel in heaven. She will be with me in every race from here to eternity. Yes, I would keep running. And I would start that very weekend with the AR 50. I would run it in memory of Delores Corbett. In celebration of my mom's life. I had no choice but to keep running and enjoying life. That's what Mom would want me to do.

I woke up the morning of the AR 50 feeling sad because I knew that I would return to an empty house after the race. There would be no mom to lovingly listen to my stories. Even that morning, I wanted to quit. I wanted to tell the officials that I was not going to run. But somehow I managed to get ready and put on a happy face, even though the pain was overwhelming. I knew Mom would want me to go ahead and run it. I decided to start the race, and see how I felt from there. Everyone there who knew about my mom's death gave me hugs and told me how sorry they were. It strengthened me to know how much everyone cared. That strength allowed me to take off fast from the very beginning. I felt surprisingly fine. I was lost in my thoughts of how lucky I was to have had such wonderful parents. I felt my mom all around me through the whole race, giving me strength and guidance. This was my fourth year at the AR 50, and for some reason it felt so easy this year.

There were beautiful butterflies everywhere, fluttering all around me. I felt like they were running with me, somehow leading me toward the finish line. I was running fast, way ahead of my 9-hour goal. The race seemed like it went by so quickly, and I finished in 8:44. My mom would have been so very proud of me. I knew then that she was smiling down on me and would continue to give me the strength to finish all my races. That is a gift from her. On Mother's Day, I was able to give her a gift in return.

It was at the 2002 Massanutten Mountain Trail 100 run. I was so very focused. I was running strong. I passed many runners during the night. I proved to myself out on that course that I can do better then I ever thought I could. Late in the race I looked at my watch and realized I could finish in under 29 hours. My goal had been to finish in less than 30, and here I was over an hour ahead of schedule. This would be my special gift for my mom. It was Mother's Day, after all. It had been only six weeks since her death. I realized on that tough race course that she is the one who made me so strong and focused. She was with me, guiding me through those mountains and leading me to a strong finish. Thanks, Mom. Happy Mother's Day.

My mother has inspired me to run thirteen 100-mile races in 2002. That might seem extreme, but it has not been at all. I feel like my mom has been there with me the whole way. Even when things are going really bad, and I feel very alone and scared, something happens to remind me that she is there with me. That is exactly what happened at the 2002 Wasatch Front 100-miler.

First let me go back to last year's Wasatch Front 100, my second year pacing my friend Linda. She had major problems and dropped at the Brighton aid station (mile 75.43). I tried everything to get her going, but nothing worked. I asked the officials at Brighton if I could continue on my own. They said yes, so off I went. I arrived at the last aid station and saw a man there whom I had seen out on the course earlier. He was really struggling. I looked at my watch and realized he would not make it under the 36-hour cutoff unless someone helped him. So I asked him if he wanted to finish in under 36 hours. Dejected, he said he couldn't. I told him he could, and he would, if he would let me pace him. He agreed. His name was Robert Tuller. He worked so hard to get to the finish. I made him run and shouted encouraging words to him along the way. I never gave up on him, and as a result he never gave up on himself. I knew he could finish under the cutoff, and eventually he did with nine minutes to spare. It was such a great feeling to be able to help him achieve his goal. All he needed was a little help and encouragement to get him going.

Now fast-forward to race day, 2002. I felt great at the start of the race, and great on the early climbs. Then all of a sudden the weather changed, and I started getting cold. The rain and wind started, and I found myself alone on the trail being blown sideways by the storm. I was cold, wet, and becoming delirious. I just wanted to get to the Big Mountain Pass aid station (mile 39.24). I'd underestimated the weather, and placed all my warm clothes and rain gear in drop bags that were waiting for me at the Lambs Canyon aid station (mile 52.97). I knew I could not make it to Lambs Canyon the way I was feeling. I broke down and started crying. I talked to my mother, asking her for the strength to keep going. I just wanted my mom to tell me I could do it, but it seemed that she wasn't there. There was no one who could help me. I have never felt so hopeless and alone in a race. I felt like a little girl all alone in the big scary woods. There was nothing I could do. I just had to accept the fact that I made such a dumb mistake. I had come to terms with the fact that I could no longer go on. I planned my drop bags poorly and there was nothing left to do but to give up and quit. I arrived at Big Mountain Pass over an hour slower than I had planned and I despondently told the aid station people I was going to drop. All of a sudden I heard a voice say *"You* are *not* going to drop!"

It was Robert Tuller. I could not believe he was there! He said that he had come to the race, ready to run, but when he woke up, he just didn't feel up to running the race. I was shocked. Robert quickly recognized my predicament and took total control. He asked me what I needed, and I told him that I had no warm clothes. That they were in drop bags at Lambs Canyon. He instantly had a plan. He put me in a warm car with a nice family who didn't even seem to mind that a strange, wet, dirty runner was invading their space. I warmed up and ate while Robert drove to Lambs to retrieve my drop bag. When he got back, he helped me get into warm, dry clothes. All the while he kept telling me that I would finish the race. I began to feel more positive about the situation, and soon believed what he was saying. Yes, I would finish. I told him that it was strange, almost like he was supposed to be here, helping me. Everything happens for a reason. This person whom I was fortunate enough to be able to help last year was now here, unselfishly returning the favor. If Robert had not been there, I would have dropped. Period. But he was there, and he knew just what to do. He made me believe in myself enough to get me out of that aid station and moving toward the finish line.

I left that aid station a new person, feeling so much better than I had when I stumbled in earlier. I felt like myself again. I made it to Lambs Canyon, and Robert was there again. He helped me with my clothes, and again, I left the station with lifted spirits. I never saw him again after that. My friend Jenn came out to crew me through the night. I had some tough times alone out there, often struggling to stay awake. I just kept moving forward. I just wanted to get to the Brighton aid station to see my friends, Jenn, Butch, and Tommy. Tommy would pace me to the finish. As I climbed from Desolation Lake toward Scotts Peak aid station (mile 70.61), I became very delirious and sleepy. On several occasions, I heard a runner catching up with me on the trail. Each time, I would stop and move off the trail to allow her to pass. But there was no one there. This went on for 30 minutes. I turned around at one point and clearly saw that there was a person with a light not far behind. A few moments later I stopped to get something out of my pack, fully expecting to see the light behind me, but again, the runner was gone. I finally realized it was my mom. She was following me just to make sure I was okay all alone in the middle of the night. I began to talk to her, and I know she was listening, because she got me to Brighton. At that point I knew she would also get me to the finish. I feel my mom with me at times when I need her. I tell my friends that when they are struggling in a race, they can ask Mom for help. Some have told me that they have.

I met Tommy at Brighton, and never thought again about dropping. All of that was erased, thanks to Robert and my mom. My original plan was to be out of Brighton by 7:00 A.M. Tommy and I left at 7:01. I was back on schedule, and feeling much better. Our adventure along the last 25 miles was epic. We got stuck in a lightning storm, and waited it out for 15 long minutes. I fought hard to climb those muddy trails. Boy was it tough! I was so happy to finish this one. I earned that beautiful plaque and belt buckle. I really gave it all I had, and more. My original goal was to finish in under 35 hours. I crossed the finish line in 34:52. Talk about a race full of stories.

I couldn't go home after Wasatch to share my incredible stories with my mom. But then again, I didn't have to. She was there with me to see it first-hand. Thanks, Mom. I love you.

Satisfied with Second Place, For Now

NAME: CLARK T. W. ZEALAND
AGE: 30
RESIDENCE: LYNCHBURG, VIRGINIA
YEARS RUNNING: 20
YEARS RUNNING ULTRAS: 4

I attended a small Christian grade school where finances were sometimes scarce. This made athletics low on the list of important activities and made a sport like football or basketball inconceivable. However, cross-country running required almost no financial investment for the school or athlete. All you needed was a pair of shoes. I ran in a pair of basketball shoes, not aware that real running shoes even existed. They were all I had.

Gary Schubert, my fifth- and sixth-grade teacher, made running enjoyable for the kids by creating a recess running club. He tracked how many playground laps each person ran on a big bar graph that was prominently displayed for all to see. This resulted in a major competition among the students. We ran practically nonstop, morning, lunchtime, and afternoon, just to see who could top Mr. Schubert's chart. The competition drove me to run a lot, and when another teacher made a statement one day that "I looked like I had a good stride and could be good at running," I signed up for my first cross country race. My father was a gifted and natural athlete, which further prompted my interest in running. My father ran some 10K road races with me and constantly encouraged me to develop my running talent. Bill Dunford, my high school coach, was also a strong, positive influence as he emphasized the importance of running for enjoyment while not compromising competitiveness. My high school years helped me develop as a runner and become a real student of the sport. I was willing to do almost anything that would make me better. This included going an entire year with no junk food—as a teenager!

When I was offered a track scholarship to Liberty University in

Lynchburg, Virginia, I jumped at the chance. There were no athletic scholarships in my native Canada, and an offer to pay my education costs was too attractive to refuse. In addition, I liked what Liberty had to offer in educating the whole person, mentally, physically, and spiritually. Running at an NCAA Division I institution was an experience I will never forget. My running matured, and I quickly discovered that my speed was not great compared to some of my competitors—nor was it my strongest factor. During my years at Liberty, I met David Horton, a professor at the university. He talked me into going for a "easy 20-mile run in the mountains" as he had done with numerous other college track runners. I had no idea what I was in for when I agreed to go with him for a "little jog in the mountains." The run was 26 miles—half on fire roads, and the other half on the Appalachian Trail. I was not ready for the over 6,000 feet of elevation change we would encounter on that run, and it rocked my world, to say the least. However, I was determined not to let this old "legend" leave me on the trail! I suffered a lot toward the end of that run but kept working hard, and he never ran away from me. I was sore for days, but I knew deep down that when my college track running days were over, I'd be coming back for more of the ultrarunning scene.

My brother Mike and I decided to run our first ultra in the spring of 1999. When we realized that the GNC 50K was also going to be the 50K national championships, we thought, "Why not start with the best?" and so we jumped in with both feet. We were not prepared for such an endeavor and yet I found myself cruising fairly easily at 6-minute pace for most of the race. However, I underestimated the need for caloric intake and started bonking at 25 miles. I split 2:43 for the marathon but by then I was really hurting, and was soon passed by five of my competitors as I struggled for a ninth-place finish in 3:22. I learned so much that day about the deep-down strength I needed to develop in order to compete in this sport. I knew it would take a couple of years of training and racing to really gain the necessary experience, so I left there encouraged about the future.

I didn't run another race until November when I decided to attempt the JFK 50-miler, the largest and oldest 50-miler in the nation. This was also when I first raced against Courtney Campbell, one of the best trail runners in the nation, who also lived in Virginia. Courtney was a veteran of the sport along with most other competitors in the field. As the race developed, I found myself passing a suffering Courtney, as I moved into second place. Someone told me that the runner in first place was bonking and was actually walking! I had about 8 miles to go and thought, "Wow, I might actually win this thing!" Little did I know, Courtney was beginning to feel better and was gaining ground on me. He passed me back with 4 miles to go. I finished that day in second place. Even though I ran 6:06, good enough for an all-time top 10 performance and the Canadian record, I was beginning to realize that this was the start of a great rivalry between friends.

I met Courtney next at the Holiday Lake 50K++, David Horton's first race in the annual Lynchburg Ultra Series. We dueled all day, and with 3 miles to go, we were once again running neck and neck. However, this time it was early in the year and neither one of us felt like racing to the line. So we agreed to run in together and enjoyed our last 3 miles talking. We crossed the line together, but since my last name starts with Z, David Horton listed me second in classic Horton style! We had fun that day, but Courtney and I both knew we wouldn't have this kind of luxury at our next meeting: the upcoming Bull Run Run 50-miler.

I was unable to train very hard for Bull Run because I was very busy coaching track at Liberty University. Traveling to track meets every weekend didn't give me much of a chance to get in those 20-plus-mile training runs. I had, however, done more road training than usual, including some speed workouts consisting of a 10-mile tempo run at a sub-6-minute pace. I felt adequately prepared for the race and expected to have a decent run. Most of all, I wanted to have fun.

My best crew person, Josh Oppenheimer, got a great deal on a hotel room for us. The only problem was that the hotel was in downtown DC, about 40 miles from the race start. We had trouble finding the hotel, and ended up driving in circles around DC late Friday night. We finally found the hotel and got in a total of four hours of sleep before the alarm went off the morning of the race. We left early for the start, unsure of where we were going. We ended up getting there twenty minutes before the start. Plenty of time.

The pre-race temperature was approximately 45 degrees with a fine mist. Despite the dreary weather, the pre-race atmosphere was relaxed, with runners milling about, talking about various things. I was in good spirits, ready to get started. At 6:15 A.M. sharp we were off and running. More than 275 runners bolted down a short stretch of asphalt before taking a sharp right onto a narrow trail. I knew that I needed to get in the front prior to this bottleneck to avoid being caught on the narrow trail behind a slower runner. Courtney Campbell took the lead as we made our way down to the riverside trail. The first couple of miles were extremely rocky requiring some fancy footwork, but soon the trail flattened out and followed the river. Courtney and I ran together like this for the first 18 miles; then we came to a hilly section and he slowed a bit. He followed me for another mile and then fell off pace, maybe for a quick bathroom break.

Except for some high humidity, the weather was perfect all day. It remained overcast and never got above 60 degrees. The aid stations, placed every 5 miles, were very good and staffed with friendly people. Most aid stations were "full service," offering an electrolyte drink, cola and Mountain Dew, water, and a wide variety of foods to choose from. I continued on and was feeling great. I knew I was running well and went through the halfway point in 3:07. This was good, considering the fact that before the race started I had set a goal. I wanted to break the course record.

Goals are very important to set, in every area of life. I have a lot of specific short-term and long-term goals. My most important long-term goal is to be healthy enough to run ultras for a long time and to have some kind of significant impact on the sport of ultrarunning. Short-term goals include being competitive in every race I run. Everyone, regardless of experience or talent, should set goals. The course record was 6:30:50, and based on previous race times and my recent speed work, I was confident I could break that. At 34 miles I was 22 minutes ahead of Courtney with no one else contending for the top spot. I was feeling really strong and started thanking the Lord for such awesome strength, because it certainly wasn't coming from me alone.

At 40 miles I went through an aid station and took one cup of Gatorade and one cup of Mountain Dew. I had combined these before with no trouble, but for some reason, it gave me problems this time. Soon after leaving the aid station, I threw up, draining myself of all the calories I had in my stomach. And the next aid station wasn't for another 4.5 miles. After approximately 2 miles on an empty stomach I began to feel light-headed and I knew I was in trouble. I needed to get to the aid station to refuel, so I just kept pushing myself. I thought that if I could get there and get some calories and then carry a water bottle with Mountain Dew in it, I'd be okay for the last 5 miles.

I finally arrived at the 45-mile aid station and began to drink like I had never drank before. Josh told me that Courtney was only eight minutes behind so I took off with a full bottle of Mountain Dew in hand. Just 5 miles ago I could taste victory. Now, with just 5 miles to go, I was running scared. I thought that if I could get up the last hill (49.5 miles) without Courtney catching me, I'd be home free. Knowing that my blood sugar was really low, I just kept sipping from my bottle. Let me tell you, nothing tastes better in the last miles of an ultra than Mountain Dew. I would sip a little and begin to feel better as the sugar high took hold. Then after a few moments I'd begin feeling dizzy and nauseous again, so I'd take another sip. I was bonking. I'd hit the wall, and was in such bad shape that everything looked and sounded as if I was in a tunnel. Running in a straight line was impossible. By the 48-mile point I had drained my bottle, but I knew that all I had left to do was go through a tricky, rocky section, then up the last hill into the finish. I also knew Courtney was closing in on me, and I was fading fast.

That last rocky section was interesting, to say the least. I don't remember running through it at all, and I have no idea how I got through it without tripping and breaking an ankle or bashing my head. But somehow I made it through and came to the last hill. With both hands on my knees I began to climb. That was one tough hill. I finally got to the top and had only half a mile to go when I heard a voice closing in behind me. It was Courtney. My heart sank and I began to run as hard as I could, which was neither fast nor in a straight line. Like the predator feeding on his prey, Courtney took note of how bad I looked and charged past me. I tried to respond, but it was hopeless.

Feeling absolutely awful, I staggered across the finish line in 6:29:00, a new course record! Unfortunately, Courtney finished a little over a minute ahead of me, so I guess the course record is his. It is easy to think that if I had not thrown up, or if my blood sugar had not dropped so low, or if I'd been able to train more . . . things might have been different. But Courtney ran a great race, and I am satisfied with second place knowing I gave it all I had that day.

One important lesson ultrarunning has taught me is to have a good attitude, no matter what happens in a race. After all, it is the hard times and challenges in life that truly test your character. To be an ultrarunner means week after week, I push myself to the utmost limits of what I can do. With each test, I learn how to push those limits farther. Then, the next time I'll be able to push even harder.

My hat is off to Courtney. It was a good race. But there will be a next time.

Miles of Mentoring at Massanutten

NAME: BETHANY HUNTER
AGE: 24
RESIDENCE: LYNCHBURG, VIRGINIA
YEARS RUNNING: 6
YEARS RUNNING ULTRAS: 4

It all began when I signed up for Dr. David Horton's running class at Liberty University. I hoped it would rekindle my interest in running. Little did I know that it would be the beginning of my ultrarunning career and a wonderful friendship.

I played volleyball and basketball in high school, but did not have the talent necessary to play at the collegiate level. Shortly after graduation, I took up jogging just to stay in shape. I did not really even enjoy running at first. I remember when I could only run one mile without walking. I eventually got to the point where I was consistently jogging about 3 to 5 miles, five days a week, a routine that I would continue for the next two years. After a while, I began to get burned out with running, so I decided to take Dr. Horton's running class, hoping that at the very least it would keep me running for a few more months. I knew some of what Dr. Horton had accomplished in the world of long-distance running, and I was intimidated. After all, this was the guy who had run across America! He was also the head of my department at the university so I felt compelled to do well in his class. One of the requirements for the class was that we run in a race of any distance. Thinking I would take the easy way out, I set my sights on a local 5K. That all changed when one day after class Dr. Horton asked me to consider entering one of his events, the Holiday Lake 50K++. I just looked at him like he was crazy. After all, I had never run a single race before in my life! But he sparked something in me that I could not ignore. After he suggested it to me a few more times, it occurred to me that maybe he saw something in me that I had not even seen in myself at that point. After all, he knew better than anyone what it took to run an ultra. I decided to do it, but I put off sending in my entry form until the last minute just in case I lost my nerve and chickened out.

In preparation for the event, Dr. Horton gave me some training advice, and told me to shoot for a long run of three hours. I think up to that point my longest run had been about an hour and a half. If I could run for three hours, he said, then I would be able to finish his race. I put that long run off week after week, because I was afraid I would not be able to do it. That long run was almost as daunting as the race itself to me. Not knowing about the concept of tapering, I waited until the weekend before the race to go for the long run. I just knew, for my own self-confidence, that I had to make those three hours. It was a cold, snowy February day, but I ended up running for four hours in spite of the weather. It was extremely hard, compounded by the fact that I did not take water or food with me. I had never run long enough to really need either. But I survived, so the following Monday I turned in my race application and hoped for the best. Dr. Horton gave me some last-week pointers about getting enough sleep, cutting back on my mileage, eating right, and so on. It was now or never. Even though I was scared out of my mind, I was determined to finish, even if I had to crawl across the line.

All week, the more I thought about the race, the more nervous I became. One minute I was sure that I could do it and the next minute I was wondering what possessed me to try something like this in the first place. The night before the race felt like the longest night of my life. I just wanted the morning to come and the race to start. The anticipation was wreaking havoc on my nerves. The race was held at a park about 45 minutes from my home. Cabins were available for the runners to stay overnight, but I thought I would sleep better in my own bed. Boy was I wrong! I think I woke up about once every hour because I was afraid of missing my alarm. I had my bag packed with my whole outfit laid out and ready to put on. I was living in a dorm room at the time, and while everyone else was going out on Friday night I was getting ready for bed. It was a lonely feeling, because none of my friends really understood what I was about to do or what I was feeling that night. They just thought I was crazy! I think I got three or four hours of restless sleep that night.

I rode up to the race with two other Liberty students. Both had run ultras before and chatted comfortably the entire 45-minute car ride as I sat in the

backseat in a nervous daze. They joked about all the problems they might
have during the race while I kept going over a mental checklist of all the
things I might need for the race, trying to see if I had forgotten anything. I
was so nervous I barely spoke two words the whole time in the car. I had
eaten a banana and an energy bar for breakfast, and they felt like rocks in
my stomach. The weather was rainy and cold, which made me even more
nervous. The thought of running in muddy, wet weather only compounded my fears.

Dr. Horton gathered the runners at the starting line about 5 minutes
before the official starting time. I do not really remember what he said
because I was so nervous about the race. I glanced around at the other people who looked like "real runners" and I felt way out of my league. All I
could think was, *How did I let him talk me into doing something like this?* I
started out very conservatively because I was so afraid of going too fast and
not being able to finish. He had told me several times that the first part of
the race did not matter. What mattered was if I was able to run the second
half or not. He also warned me not to get sucked into running someone
else's pace. If someone was running harder or faster than I was, then I
should let them go. I repeated his advice over and over in my head, just hoping I would have something left at the end.

The Holiday Lake 50K++ is an out-and-back "loop" course around a
lake. It is a great course for someone to do his or her first ultra. The first loop
is run counterclockwise, the second loop clockwise. The plus signs in
"50K++" are for the notoriously long "Horton miles" that are the cause of
much debate and controversy at his races. I have yet to discover how far the
course actually is! The first few miles are run on a single-track trail around
the perimeter of the lake. From there the course becomes a combination of
gravel roads, pavement, and dirt trails. It is a relatively flat, fast course with
no huge climbs. The uphill sections are gradual, and are not too long
(although that perspective can change after running 20 miles). I was actually enjoying myself on the first loop when Dr. Horton rode by in a truck.
He stopped a few hundred yards up the road, and jumped out of the truck
to shout words of encouragement and take pictures as I ran by. He told me
that I looked too happy to be running a 50K. I could tell he meant every
word and truly wanted me to do well. His excitement was contagious and
gave me hope that maybe I *could* actually do this. He told me to take my
time and make sure I stayed hydrated. How quickly things can change! I

went from feeling wonderful one minute to feeling like my legs were attached to lead weights the next. The turnaround point halfway through the race was an especially low point for me. I had just run for three hours, and now I had to turn around and do it again! Dr. Horton was there again, and he assured me that I was running well, and reminded me to keep running a nice, even pace. I told several runners that we all must be crazy to be doing what we were doing. The hardest section for me was near the end of the race when the course went up a steep gravel road to an aid station. My legs felt like Jell-O at that point and the road just seemed to stretch on forever. In reality the road section is probably less than half a mile. By that time though, any slight uphill was a huge effort for me. Once I made it to the aid station at the top of the hill, there were about 6 miles to go to the finish. Those 6 miles, which had seemed so effortless and enjoyable a few hours earlier, now seemed to take forever. Finally the trail came out on a road with about a quarter mile to go to the finish. I was extremely happy at this point because I knew I had done it. I could see the light at the end of the tunnel. I could hear voices cheering the runners across the line. Luckily the last section was all downhill so I was able to coast to the finish line. I crossed the finish line to the sound of Dr. Horton announcing my name to the crowd. It was the most incredible feeling to know that I had made it. I had completed my first ultra—my longest run ever. I had done what most people would never even consider doing, and it was an amazing feeling. The sense of accomplishment was unlike anything I had ever experienced before.

I love to watch people finish their first ultramarathon, because there is no other feeling in the world like it. An ultramarathon is something that no one else can do for you. It all comes down to you at the moment when you face your own limits and you push on. Dr. Horton came over to me at the end of the race and gave me a congratulatory hug with a huge grin on his face. I was happy, but too tired to show much enthusiasm at the moment. My legs ached more than they ever had before in my entire life. I was too sore to even sit down. And besides, it would have required too much effort to stand up again! I instead just kept walking/hobbling around trying to keep my muscles from cramping up. A friend and fellow student came over to me and asked if I would do the race again next year. I told him absolutely not, and that I thought people who ran ultras were completely nuts! He laughed, and said he would ask me again once the soreness had passed. I saw him at school a few weeks later and he repeated his question with a knowing smile. I sheepishly answered that I would definitely be running again next year because, naturally, I had to beat my time from this year!

I think ultrarunners must have a very poor memory or no one would ever do another race. You tend to forget the pain and misery and only remember the thrill of accomplishment. Sometimes you even welcome the pain because it causes you to overcome your own weaknesses and become a little stronger each time. With a 50K under my belt, I soon began thinking of doing a 50-miler. Another of Dr. Horton's races, the Mountain Masochist suddenly became very enticing to me when only a few months before I had used terms such as *crazy* and *insane* to describe people who did 50-mile races. All of a sudden I was one of those crazy runners wanting to run 50 miles and willing to pay money to do it! I completed the Masochist in October of the following year and I was hooked on ultras from that point on. I have run about 15 ultras since Holiday Lake four years ago. At first I had no expectations beyond doing one race, but I quickly found that I was addicted to the sport. I approach every race with the mindset of doing my best, no matter the outcome. That is why I love the sport of ultrarunning. The challenge is not so much against other people, but against yourself and your own mind. You leave past races behind when you step up to the starting line. During every race you are faced with a moment of truth, a point in the race when you either quit or persevere to the end. Every person that finishes an ultramarathon has accomplished a great feat, simply because they finished.

After doing several races over the last few years, I needed a new challenge to keep from getting burned out. For me that challenge was doing a 100-mile race. Running a 100-miler had been a vague dream of mine for the last two years, but I had not given it serious consideration in the past. The distance was too daunting to me before this year. However the timing seemed right this year and I did not know if I would ever have the chance again. Once I started thinking about doing a 100-miler, I asked several runners what race they thought would be good for my first 100-mile race. I love to run on trails and I especially love running on technical, rocky courses. I am not an extremely fast runner, but my strength seems to be that I can run fairly consistently for long periods of time. Because of all these things, everyone agreed that I would like Massanutten. Dr. Horton had asked me last year what I thought about doing a 100, but dropped it when I did not appear to be overly enthusiastic. He brought it up again this year, and really got me thinking about it. After a while I thought about it all the time. He always told me he would never talk anyone into doing a 100. It is on a different level than a 50K or 50-miler. People have to want it for themselves or they have no business being out there. You cannot finish a race of that distance on someone else's enthusiasm or desire. The fact that he even brought it up gave me confidence that I could do it. Every single person I talked to about Massanutten, including several people who had completed the race themselves, told me without hesitation that I could do it. I think all the positive feedback, along with my own desire, convinced me that it was time.

I mailed my entry form for the 2002 Massanutten Mountain Trail 100 in March, which gave me about two months to train. At Dr. Horton's suggestion, I increased my weekly mileage from about 50 to 60 miles to 70 or 80 miles per week. I ran everywhere from treadmills to roads to trails. Saturday mornings were the best part of my training when a whole group of people would go for a long run in the mountains, including the ever-present Dr. Horton. Looking back, I can see where my training could have been more consistent. Not enough training on technical trails along with two missed weekend training runs are probably what hurt me the most at Massanutten. My last "training run" was the Promised Land 50K held two weeks before Massanutten. I was not terribly pleased with my performance there, but I had my sights already set on MMT. I had a brief period of panic thinking that my rough time at Promised Land was a precursor of things to come at MMT. Dr. Horton helped me put it in perspective by saying that the Promised Land was only one race. He reminded me to look at my training and realize that I had done everything I could do to prepare for the MMT. And no matter the outcome, the MMT 100 would only be one or two days in my life. His advice helped me forget about my doubts and focus on the task at hand.

My first 100-miler was going amazingly well up until about mile 70. Then my left knee started hurting to the point that I had to stop running completely. I began to walk and would continue to walk a lot over the next 25 miles. After several hours of continuous walking, however, I began to get mentally discouraged. I started to cry, simply because I felt sorry for myself and it felt good to cry. Dr. Horton was pacing me then and told me it was okay to cry, as long as I kept moving forward. He told me story after story of times in his ultrarunning career when he had similar experiences, times when he felt "raw," as he called it. The hours and miles crawled by slowly, probably more so for Dr. Horton because he had to put up with my whining and tears! After a while, he tried to get me out of my mental funk by suggesting that I try running small sections that were fairly flat. He knew that my pain was more mental than physical at that point and wanted to get me back in the race. My lowest point of the whole race was at the second-to-last aid station. We had 12 miles left, but it felt more like 1,200 miles to my tired body. I was tired of walking, tired of crying, even tired of eating. All I wanted to do was sit down for a long break and rest my legs. I think we stayed at that aid station for a grand total of five minutes, our longest stop of the whole race! We both knew that staying longer would only make it harder for me to go on. I felt so depressed and weak leaving that aid station that I began to cry again at the thought of several more hours on the trail. I could barely make myself run another 12 steps, let alone 12 miles. But I knew that in spite of everything, I had to finish. Too much work and sacrifice had gone into this race for me to quit. Too many people were pulling for me, including Dr. Horton, and my mother who had come all the way from Texas to crew for me. As we were walking to the last aid station at 95 miles, Dr. Horton promised that we could sit down and rest once we made it to the aid station. The prospect of resting gave me enough hope to push on. However, he tricked me! Just as the aid station came into view, he said that we should only stop long enough to eat and fill our water bottles. I knew he was right, but all I wanted to do was sit down, even if just for a few minutes. Then an amazing thing happened: I realized that, compared to the last 25 miles, I actually felt pretty good. The hours of slow walking had helped the pain in my knee subside. Perhaps I would get through this thing after all.

Dr. Horton knows me well enough to know what motivates me. He told me that we had an hour and a half left to finish under 31 hours. My response was that I didn't care, even as I began to walk faster. He added fuel to the fire by telling me that another woman had come into the aid station just as we were leaving. My answer to him was that she could beat me for all I care, but then I unconsciously began to go even faster! Once we reached the top of the last climb with less than three miles left to go I could finally see the light at the end of the tunnel. We ran down the mountain to a gravel road leading to the finish. Well, he ran and I sort of hobbled along. The last mile seemed to go on forever. But then we were there. The finish line was in a grassy field decorated with fake, pink flamingos. I have no idea why the flamingos were there other than to be a strange sight to tired eyes. I crossed the finish line, surprisingly unemotional, too exhausted to smile or even cry. I kissed the ground and gave my mother a hug. I sat down in the grass and I remember thinking how long ago the start seemed to me. I could not comprehend that I had just run 100 miles in the mountains. But I had. I finished in 30:56, and was the fifth-place woman.

Perhaps the biggest thing I learned that day is that I can accomplish anything if I want it badly enough. As Dr. Horton has told me so many times, the decision to quit is a mental decision, not a physical one. In retrospect maybe I could have finished without Dr. Horton, but it would have been a lot harder and a lot slower. He helped me in so many ways, but it was mostly his belief in my ability to finish the race that brought me through to the end. His support and faith in me carried me through those long painful miles. But it's more than just the last few miles, or even the last race. Dr. Horton has been there, showing complete confidence in me through the years. He pushes me when I need it most and encourages me when I am down. I would not be the runner I am today if it were not for his influence in my life. A person like that can make all the difference between success and failure—both on and off the race course.

Growing Up at Western States

NAME: ANN TRASON
AGE: 42
RESIDENCE: KENSINGTON, CALIFORNIA
YEARS RUNNING: 20
YEARS RUNNING ULTRAS: 19

Photo by Keith Facchino

I was first exposed to ultrarunning in high school when I was selected to attend an Olympic training camp. Part of our workout was to run the first 4.5 miles of the Western States 100-miler course. I about died, but I remember thinking that it was the most awesome thing I'd ever done. It was such a beautiful and magnificent run, and to think that it was just the first 4.5 miles of a 100-mile race! I was definitely impressed and intimidated.

I got back into running around 1985 after laying off it for a few years. I experimented a little with other endurance sports like the triathlon, but I found that I really liked running the best. I also enjoyed backpacking, so when I saw an ad for the American River 50-Mile trail run, I thought it would be the perfect combination of the two. From the outside looking in, it did not even seem like a race. It seemed more like an adventure, a quest to see if I could run 50 miles through the woods. I thought, *Wow, this looks kind of interesting!* And I signed up.

Let's just say it didn't go quite as expected.

To look at the results, you might say I did really well. I won, and I set a course record. But I absolutely hated it. I just mentally cracked. Back then, there was very little information available about proper training, nutrition, and so on. I had no idea how to run 50 miles. I didn't even carry a water bottle, and it was the hottest year we ever had! I mean, I really hated it. When I finished, people started telling me that I should pursue ultrarunning, and that I should run the Western States 100. And I was like "You guys should be committed!" It was really, really hard. I had never run on such rocky trails before. I thought trail running meant running on fire roads and well-groomed trails. It was a real eye-opening experience, to say the least. As far as I was concerned, my ultrarunning days were over.

I met Aaron Warnam at the American River 50, and I guess he thought I had some potential because he was not ready to see me quit. He invited me to come up and run the first 30 miles of the Western States course before I abandoned ultrarunning forever. So we went up during the summer of 1986 and ran the first 30 miles. And I loved it. I mean, it was everything I'd ever dreamed trail running could be. It was gorgeous. We were running through the wilderness, surrounded by mountains. It even smelled beautiful. As we ran, Aaron explained the historic significance of the area. He told me stories of gold miners, the Donner party, and so on. I realized that for once I felt really comfortable on the trail. I felt right at home. Those 30 miles with Aaron changed my view of ultrarunning forever, and I signed up for Western States that year.

I've been running ultras now for over 19 years. Ultrarunning has changed my life in many ways. I've had experiences I never would have had without ultrarunning. I've gone to places that I never would have gone and met people I never would have met. I never would have gone to Leadville or South Africa or France. I never would have met Nelson Mandela or so many others. The year 2003 will be my sixteenth year running Western States. It is definitely the ultradistance event that I love more than any other. There is not one year at Western States that stands out above the others— it is more the accumulation of all the years. I wouldn't trade them for anything.

I look forward to Western States every year. Carl (my husband) and I usually spend the week before Western States in Squaw Valley. We stay in a cabin that is just about five minutes from the start. We usually spend the day before the event hanging out at the cabin. There is a pre-race meeting, which gives us a chance to see friends we have not seen in a while. And then there is the weigh-in. I don't really like that too much. I guess I'm like a lot of women in that I hate being weighed. It is kind of an anxious period for me anyway. At that point I am getting really focused on what I have to do and I'm usually a little scared because I have no idea what the next day is going to bring. Every year I approach the start line with no idea of what to expect. I've never had an easy Western States. That's one of the great things about it. Some people have come out and run fast and claim they had no problems. Not me. I always have problems. So I'm always nervous the whole day before, worrying about what is going to happen. I don't sleep that well the night before either. I usually watch some bad movie before going to bed, then I just lie there, looking forward to the start.

There is so much energy at the start. Maybe it just seems that way to me because I think it's such a special event. Everyone is so excited, anticipating the adventure to come. I wish I could bottle that energy and take a whiff of it during the year. I mean, it's hard to explain. It's electrifying, that's all I can say. It's more incredibly electrifying than anything I have ever experienced in my life. Everyone is on edge, milling about in the dark. Then all of a sudden, it starts—uphill. We start at about 6,000 feet elevation, and in about 4 miles we are at 9,000 feet. All the while I'm thinking, *Why am I doing this?* or *Can I even do this?* I feel like I'm that 17-year-old kid again, running the first 4.5 miles. I'm impressed, intimidated, breathless, and still wondering if I can possibly run the whole way.

The weather is always unpredictable at Western States. That's part of what makes it so great. Some years it's very cold. Some years it's really warm. Some years it rains. In 1991 there was lightning. There was a lot of snow in 1995, but ironically, it was very hot too. There is a special snow course that runs more on pavement to get around sections that otherwise would be horrific. I've done the snow course twice. In 1995, the irony became obvious about 25 miles into the race. Up until then I was running through snow, and suddenly it was very hot and I was dripping sweat and the snow was melting all around. It was crazy. It got up to 105 degrees that day. It was brutal—impossible to describe. You never know what Western States is going to throw at you, but you can count on it being epic.

Every year I start out very, very conservatively. I don't really plan it that way, it just happens. If you look at the splits, I'll have the 30th or even the 50th fastest split for the first 16 miles. Then after that I kind of get rolling. I really try to take it easy those first few miles because I'm not a morning person. It takes me a while to wake up.

This might seem really silly, but I look at Western States as life in a day. The start is like being born. Then in the first mile I'm one year old and so on. The first 16 miles I run like a child, becoming a teenager. I'm having fun and I think I am going to run a great race. I have this adolescent confidence that I can do anything. I am totally hyper until about mile 20, where, approaching adulthood, I start to worry about what I'm going to do with my life. Then I hit the canyons, and it's like having a midlife crisis. That's where things can start to go wrong. Then I'm 50 years old, cruising along, looking forward to retirement, which is eventually marked by a great downhill section at mile 60. Retirement is followed by a horrid section around mile 78, and I'm forced to remind myself, *Well, Ann, you know you're 78 years old, so you're a little tired now.* And at the end, when I'm 99 and 100 years old, I look really bad. I always look bad when I'm running. Every year brings its own unique ups and downs, but that little mind game helps me get through it year after year.

I've felt like quitting several times. One year I got to mile 55 and it was really hot. I just sat down and said, "I can't go on." One of Carl's friends was there, and he said, "Well, why do you want to quit?" I answered, "Because it's hot." And he just looked at me and said, "You think it's not hot for everyone else?" That changed my perception. So what if I'm not feeling good? Neither is anyone else at that point. I just have to keep marching.

I find myself running alone a lot at Western States. And I really don't like running by myself in the dark. The year 1995 was a particularly bad year. It was earlier that year that Barbara Schoener was killed by a cougar. I dropped my pacer and was running alone when I got to mile 80. It was getting dark, and the next section was going to take me right by where she had been killed. I was so scared, I made some guy at the aid station run with me. He'd just eaten a pastrami sandwich, so it wasn't long before he started throwing up and had to stop. I ended up running about 15 miles by myself. Every time I heard something in the bushes I just knew it was a cougar. And I knew if something did happen to me, no one would find me until the next day. Call me chicken, but I really don't like to be out there alone in the dark.

The second year I ran Western States, they pulled me at mile 92. It was horrible. I was throwing up and dehydrated, so the doctor at the aid station gave me an IV. But they didn't know the rules, and it turned out that since they gave me an IV they had to disqualify me. I was pretty shaken up. I could have walked to the finish. I learned that year that you can't go to the doctors and tell them all your problems. As an ultrarunner, you have to know your limits. The problem is that they have these emergency-room doctors working the aid stations. And anyone who has just run 92 miles is in such bad shape that if they walked into an ER, the doctors would bag them and give them an IV and who knows what else. I've learned to know the difference between being tired, dehydrated, and nauseous and being in real trouble. And if I'm not in real trouble, I keep on running. One foot in front of the other, until I reach the finish.

Ah, the finish. The finish is always special, but until I get to the white bridge, which is less than a quarter mile from the track, I don't even think about it. I just think about getting from one point to the next. One year I was running—it was to be my 10th finish—and this guy I was running with was like, "This is great! Ten years at Western States! This is awesome!" I just had to ignore him and keep pushing on. Until I get to that white bridge, I'm not thinking of winning, placing, or even finishing for that matter. But then when I do get to the white bridge, it is such a relief. Finally, I can relax, and say for the first time that it is all downhill from here. I love that white bridge. In fact, I love it so much that I never cross it during training runs. I always stop before I get there. It's just that special.

Every finish is different and special in its own way. My dad came the first couple of years, and my mother saw me finish in 1989 before she passed away. That was very, very special. For my tenth year, my brother and his family were there with Carl. That was quite nice. One year I was chased by a group of Mexico's Tarahumara Indians and the whole time around the track I was looking over my shoulder. Then another year I was just five minutes behind the overall winner, Tim Twietmeyer. There was a huge crowd at the finish because some people thought I might actually catch him. That was very exciting. But no matter how different the finish, the thrill is always there. Every year I really feel like I've accomplished something—regardless if it was a good or a bad year. I always feel like pinching myself and saying, "Wow, I really did it!" But most years all I can think about at the finish is the massage table. After all, I deserve it. I'm 100 years old!

Fire, Ice, and Competition at the 1995 Western States 100

NAME: TIM TWIETMEYER
AGE: 43
RESIDENCE: AUBURN, CALIFORNIA
YEARS RUNNING: 25
YEARS RUNNING ULTRAS: 23

Photo by Phil Mislinski

While in junior college I worked as a caddy at an exclusive country club in Woodside, California. I started running with my sister as she was starting to run organized races and it looked like fun. At school one day I picked up a copy of *Runner's World* magazine in the library and read about a 24-hour run that was being held at a high school across the street from the country club where I worked. After work that Saturday, I went by and watched the race. Organized by Don Choi, it was the first 24-hour race held in years and there were several famous runners in the field. I watched for hours fascinated by the camaraderie, grit, perseverance, and good-natured competition that was taking place. I watched what people ate, how fast they ran, asked about strategy, and generally marveled at their ability. It looked like fun and the next summer after my junior year of college I ran the exact same race—but it was now a 48-hour run. I ran 83 miles in a total go-as-you-please strategy. I ran for 10 miles then went to a show with my sister! I came back later and ran all night to get my 50 miles in. I added another 33 miles the next afternoon just so I could hang with the legends.

Those track runs were my ultrarunning education. I watched people like Dick Collins and Ruth Anderson for hours. They totally impressed me with their performances. In 1979, Ruth ran 100 miles on the track in less than 19 hours and Dick—well, if there's anyone I've modeled my running career on, it's Dick. He was my idol, friend, and a great all-around guy. There's nobody I'd rather run a race with than Dick. Although you could learn a lot about running from these guys, their best example was how to conduct yourself in the sport. They were great runners, and even better competitors. I've been an ultrarunner now since those college days. It's the one hobby I've done my entire adult life. The thing that I enjoy the most is the other people in the sport. Just about to the person, my ultrarunning friends are the best people I know. There's just an implicit respect that is shared by everyone in the sport. Ultrarunning isn't as much a competition as it is a running celebration. It seems that 10Ks and marathons have certain implied rules like sprinting at the finish, wearing matching tank tops and shorts, no walking, and beeping watches with certified split times. Ultrarunning is a much more casual affair. Since finishing times are much more diverse and conditions are much more severe, there's plenty of room for each runner to find their own particular goal. In ultrarunning, time isn't that important. It's all about personal challenge and exploration. The 1995 Western States 100-Mile Endurance Run taught me more about this than perhaps any ultra I've ever run.

The run in 1995 was special because of the severe conditions. It was the second highest snow total for the last 20 years, and the first 20 miles of the course were covered in snow. On Saturday of the race the temperature in Sacramento topped out at 107 degrees and on Sunday at 109. It doesn't matter how far you're running, that's severe.

We should've known it would be a difficult year when several of us went out the weekend before to mark the first 10 miles of the course and had to abort the effort after 6 miles due to driving snow and poor visibility. If the race had been scheduled for that weekend it probably would've been canceled due to the weather. It would've been very hard to get the aid stations in, even by helicopter and rescuing runners by air would've been equally impossible. It was a good thing that we were marking trail from High Camp at Squaw Valley, as we needed the markings to find our way back to civilization. Fortunately, conditions improved by the time race morning rolled around. But they didn't improve by much.

Evenings before races are always tense, but this one was even more tense thanks to the increasingly alarming weather reports. The weather prediction kept getting hotter and hotter with each subsequent forecast. It finally ended up calling for 107 degrees.

For me, the morning of the race is usually much calmer than the night before. There's no more time to worry or get nervous, just focus and execute. It's like a prelaunch sequence of an orbiter—eat enough food to fill the boiler and top off the tank with water. With that, the engine is stoked to its optimum level, and then it's a matter of refueling the tank along the way and running the race as planned. But this race morning was not your average race morning. It was hot. You didn't need a sweatshirt or sweatpants. Heck, you didn't need anything but a tank top. At 5:00 in the morning at 6,200 feet, that's not a good omen. It was going to be hot *all* day. What made it worse is that we knew we'd have to run through 20 miles of snow before facing the sweltering heat of the river canyons. People were referring to it as Fire and Ice: Ice to represent the 20 miles of snow, and Fire to signify what the canyons would be like in the late afternoon. The conditions were looking so difficult that runners were offered an automatic entry into the 1996 race if they felt they were unprepared to handle the snow and heat. By the start, what is normally a field of 375 had dwindled to 330 as many took the offer.

The start of Western States has the most condensed level of energy of any place on the planet. Over 300 people, all ready to run 100 miles, and when the gun goes off most of them start off by walking. It's almost anticlimactic, but it is a great relief to get going. Now all the anticipation is over, all the preparation complete, and the only task left is to get to Auburn before the time limit. Months, or even years, of preparation are all about to unfold in the next 20 to 30 hours. At the sound of a shotgun blast, the field of over 300 runners ran (and walked) a quarter mile before encountering snow. Over the next 20 miles, maybe a mile would be snow-free, and even that would be mud. But at least we were on our way.

If there was any consolation to the blazing heat we were to face later in the day it was that it softened the snow such that the first 20 miles weren't a total slip-and-slide. The footing was better than what might be expected, but it was strange to be running in the snow, which is normally associated with the cold, and sweating while running before sunrise and at 7,000 feet. I can distinctly remember climbing straight up the Elephant's Trunk, a short steep climb about 15 miles into the race, and watching the sweat drip off the end of my nose. That was my first indication that, although the snow would slow us down, it was the heat that would provide the most difficult obstacle of the day.

It took the leaders five hours to run the first 24 miles. Not exactly a blazing pace for those considered the elite of the sport. It took others 10 hours to cover the same mileage. Not only was the running slow, but the energy expended was well above normal. Once out of the snow at Duncan Canyon, the next 20 miles were on very exposed paved and dirt roads. Although it was nice to have reliable footing, we now started to face the increasing temperatures as the heat radiated from the road.

The heat only became more serious as the hours clicked by. The lead changed hands several times and Scott St. John, a couple of Tarahumara Indians, and I seemed more concerned with just putting miles behind us than worrying about who was in the lead or by how much.

The day was an all-consuming battle with the elements and there wasn't a moment on the course I felt like everything was dialed in. Scott St. John and I had the lead at mile 55 in Michigan Bluff, and we had no idea who was behind us. Scott stopped in the aid station to load up on fluids as his weight had dropped a bit. I continued on, assuming the lead by myself, all the while wondering how hard I could run without self-destructing in the heat. It's an interesting position to be in, leading a race, not knowing who's behind you and how close, and trying to manage running in conditions that practically guarantee dehydration. In the end, I felt the race might boil down to more of a drinking contest than a running contest.

Through Foresthill and down California Street (miles 55 to 78) it just felt good to be one step closer to the finish without having any major complications. As I crossed the river at mile 78 I discovered that there were two runners immediately behind me: Ann Trason and Gabriel Batista. Ann had been third overall in 1992 and 1993, and second in 1994. She was as determined as anyone out there was to win the race. Gabriel is one of the legendary Tarahumara Indian runners who are known for playing running games that cover several days and many miles. He had been invited to the race earlier in the spring to bring more exposure and competition to the event. He was running a great race, stride for stride with Ann.

It was still brutally hot, and the climb out of the river is 30 minutes of steady uphill—and then there is 20 miles of rugged trail left to the finish. Mentally I began to think that maybe third place wasn't so bad. Was it really that important to try to stay in first place? I'd won the race twice before, what more was there to prove? Considering that it was over 100 degrees out, who could possibly try to tell a runner to push harder? I pondered the next 20 miles knowing that neither Ann nor Gabriel would give me a break or expect a break in return. This would turn into a 3-way battle to the finish between the local guy with two wins and 17 WS finishes, the greatest female endurance athlete ever, and the Tarahumara Indian who could reach even higher status by winning the premier event in endurance running.

As I sat in a chair at the Green Gate aid station (80 miles) it all seemed so overwhelming. We'd been running for over 14 hours, through snow for five hours, then in scorching heat for another nine hours. We still had at least another four hours of running left. It's one thing to race someone for one lap around a track or for the last half-mile in a marathon, but for four hours in 100-degree heat?

The turning point for me came at Green Gate when I met up with Ernie Flores, my pacer. Ernie had paced for me several times in the past, and we were old friends. We knew each other well, and he was someone I could always rely on to tell it straight. He was no-nonsense, all business. As I extracted myself from the folding chair and started down the trail Ernie was already talking to me, taking my mind off the heat and turning the entire conversation positive. He told me lies about how good I looked and how fast we were going. He also reminded me that nobody was feeling good out there, it was just not possible given the conditions. These were the most extreme weather conditions of any ultra in history. It would turn out to be the hottest weekend of the entire *year* (Sacramento registered 107 degrees on Saturday and 109 degrees on Sunday). It took every bit of energy just to keep moving.

And we kept moving, one step at a time. We made it to the 85-mile aid station and Ann came in just as I was leaving. She told me that Gabriel was right behind her and that I'd better get moving. The pressure was still on. It was now 8:30 P.M. and the majority of this race would play itself out in the dark. Although the sun was going down, there was no reprieve from the heat, and what little relief the setting sun would provide was offset by the humidity of the forest.

The section between Auburn Lake Trails (85 miles) and Brown's Bar (90 miles) is known as the horizontal canyons. Rather than ascending and descending, the trail winds in and out of ravines and crosses a creek at its midpoint. This stretch of trail is more mentally challenging than physical, as it's generally flat. With 80-plus miles on the body and mind it is hard to continue running when walking seems so appealing. It's also the mental point of contention. With 15 miles and three hours of running left, you're still not within the gravitational pull of the finish line. Pacing is still key, and an eating or drinking mistake could pose huge problems. There was no letup in the competition in this 5-mile stretch of trail. I plowed on with Ernie with the belief that every step behind us got us that much closer to home. Ann and Gabriel were just minutes behind me, and for all I knew they were getting closer.

As darkness took over, the tactics on the trail became interesting. With a race this close no one wanted anyone else to know where he or she was. Ernie and I waited until total darkness to use our flashlights, and then only when we knew the trail was too rocky to run without light. Ann was using the same strategy. This was where knowing the trail became a huge asset, as we were running almost by mental memory and sliding along the trail like an animal with keen night vision patrolling its realm. Even when we reached the aid station at mile 90, we tried to slink in and out without too much noise or cheering.

Every time I thought the race couldn't get any more interesting, it just kept moving up to the next level. After exiting the Brown's Bar aid station, I realized I was running alone. Ernie was unable to keep the pace (I guess we weren't going all that slow after all), and I found myself running alone. Ernie had had the stomach flu the week of the race, so pacing in 100-plus heat probably wasn't the prescribed antidote. Out of the forest and onto the river road, it was now mostly uphill to Highway 49 and the last big aid station. Alone on the trail, I simply had to push on hoping that seeing my crew would lift my spirits and give me the momentum I'd need to carry the lead to the finish.

Being the first runner to Highway 49 (93 miles) was exciting, but it was of little consolation. There was no time to waste in an aid station this close to the finish, especially with two hungry competitors right behind. Of course, everyone wanted to know where the other runners were and also what happened to Ernie. I didn't know the answer to either of those queries and tried to move through the aid station without letting on how hard this race was becoming. It was going to take every ounce of mental and physical energy, and then some, to bring this one home. As I exited the aid station and headed up the trail along the highway, I could hear the cheers as Ann entered the station. My lead was down to three minutes.

Lucky for me I had another pacer waiting for me at Highway 49 to replace Ernie. (Ann also outran her pacer to Highway 49 and had to talk someone into going with her. As it turned out, both of our dropped pacers came into Highway 49 together to the cheers of the crowd—and then had to explain how two runners who had already run 80 miles were able to out-run them). Kurt Fox had paced me for 16 miles earlier in the race, and agreed to return to run the last 7 miles to the finish. This was a great break for me, as Kurt brought some new energy to the task. While Ernie was a no-nonsense pacer, Kurt was all kidding and humor—at least he thought so. I was not able to enjoy any of his jokes at the time.

In the 3 or so miles to No Hands Bridge (97.5 miles) the trail just kept dishing out cruel tricks. It was in the first mile of the rocky, root-strewn sin-gle-track trail that Kurt (running in front of me) stopped dead in his tracks. Without much braking available in my legs, I ran into him. A bit irritable at this point, I asked why he stopped. He pointed out that there was a skunk in the trail just ahead of where we stood. Great, I'm 95 miles into a 100-miler, it's over 100 degrees out, my legs are shot, I'm a few scant minutes ahead of Ann and Gabriel, and my pacer is stopped dead in the trail for fear of a skunk? I let him know in no uncertain terms that I wasn't about to give up my small lead because of a stinking skunk. I also told him that with the running in the heat we'd done, nobody would be able to tell if we'd been skunked because we smelled really bad already. I wasn't about to stand there long, so I walked toward the skunk and threw a few rocks at it. It must've agreed with my assessment, or disagreed with our odor, because it scurried off the trail and allowed us to continue. One more crisis averted; how many more could there be?

With the skunk safely behind us we continued toward the bridge. In the other two years I'd won the race, I had run this section in the light, felt real-ly good, and was able to cruise to the finish line. This year was everything but that. It wasn't another quarter mile past the skunk that I tripped on a tree root. Normally, this is no big deal—you just fall, brush yourself off, then continue. This fall was quite different. My legs had tightened up from all the hills and heat running, and in the attempt to catch myself before I did a face plant in the dirt, both legs cramped and I fell stiff-legged to the ground. I wasn't sure I'd ever get up! But then again, I wasn't sure I even wanted to. What else could go wrong? I could just see myself lying in a bush on the side of the trail, stiff as a corpse, as Ann and Gabriel just rolled by. It took what tiny bit of coordination I had left to bend my legs, and hoist myself up. I must've looked like a foal taking its first steps as I tried to jump-start my legs. Slowly I was able to generate some momentum and continue the downhill to the bridge. I thought that Ann had to be right behind me, as this small leg of the trail was turning into more of a circus with every stride. I also feared that if I fell again, I might not get back up.

We finally made it to the bridge and my crew reminded me of what I already knew—Ann was three minutes behind at the highway. There was only a bit over 3 miles to go and they were mostly uphill. I told my crew to stay behind so when I got to Robie Point (98.5 miles), I would know what the buffer was at the bridge. Now it was a quest for the pavement at Robie Point. Once there, I wouldn't fear tripping on a root or slipping on a rock. Although it wouldn't guarantee victory, being first to Robie Point under these conditions would be a significant advantage.

For as crazy as the 3 miles to the bridge were, the climb to Robie in contrast was rather uneventful. I could see Ann's light well below on the railroad grade and, at times, could hear Gabriel calling at her in an effort to intimidate her. I ran when possible, power-walked on the uphills, and reached the cul-de-sac on the edge of Auburn to find that I'd had an eleven-minute lead at the bridge. It was almost unbelievable considering how slow I thought I was going and the two stoppages. But it was the most relieving news I'd heard all day. Now, barring a catastrophe, I'd be the first to the finish line.

The last few minutes of the race were more about energy conservation than celebratory sprint to the finish. After all I'd been through in the last 18 1/2 hours, there just wasn't any energy left to make a big push. It was one-foot-in-front-of-the-other, trying not to make any sudden movements that would lock everything up. I wanted to make sure that if anyone made a last minute push to catch me, I'd have some tiny bit of strength available to respond. In the end, it wasn't needed.

The finish was more relief than exhilaration. After crossing the finish line it took two people to steady me on the weigh-in scale. I was one giant cramp waiting to happen. I crossed the finish line in 18:35, the slowest winning time by almost an hour since the California Street Trail was added to the course. I'd led the race for over eight hours but it seemed like eight days. I'd never been so exhausted in my life, physically, mentally, and metabolically. I think I lasted the last five hours on M&Ms and Mountain Dew alone. Ann finished five minutes behind in 18:40 and Gabriel six minutes behind Ann. It was the closest 1-2-3 finish in any 100-mile history. Over 100 miles, five minutes is almost insignificant—less than half of 1 percent. The next runner finished an hour behind Gabriel, and only nine others finished in the next three hours. Only 198 runners finished Western States in 1995, compared to 249 finishers the year before.

I've often thought back to that day in 1995 and how anyone in the race ever finished or even found the energy and desire to compete. I often wonder how we were all able to continue under such extreme conditions. I can't even explain it today, except to say that there never came a point where quitting was better than continuing. I know that without my pacers, Ernie and Kurt, I probably wouldn't have come in first. Ernie's positive attitude at 80 miles took me to a level I didn't think I could reach on my own, and Kurt kept me going in the last miles by not letting me think about how bad I felt. I learned that day that there are times when we're limited only by what our minds deem feasible, failing to realize what, through additional focus and effort, can actually be achieved.

A Sunrise (or Two) Worth Falling For

NAME: IAN TORRENCE
AGE: 29
RESIDENCE: MOAB, UTAH
YEARS RUNNING: 17
YEARS RUNNING ULTRAS: 9

© PatitucciPhoto.com

Dawn was just starting to break over the island of Oahu, and I was moving well considering I had already run 96 miles. The end of the 100-mile race was near, and it felt good to see the sun again after a long night of running. Perhaps the first rays of light were what I was looking at when I lost my footing on a rain-soaked rock. My feet left the earth, sliding off the left side of the trail and down the slick slopes below. I don't remember the actual fall, but I did manage to catch myself before sliding too far. My flashlight was somewhere down the slope below, and the mud that had previously covered only my legs now covered my arms, chest, and face. Krissy, my pacer, was amazed by the acrobatic display she had just witnessed. I assured her I was fine but it was just the adrenaline talking. I climbed back onto the trail, borrowed Krissy's extra flashlight, and quickly starting running again, trying to shake out the kinks that had resulted from the fall. It was somewhat reassuring to know that I was following one of the cruelest rules of trail running: If you are going to fall, you will bite it on the smoothest section of trail available. And as if I hadn't learned my lesson, my eyes could not help but drift toward the beautiful sunrise over the ocean below.

I started running in ninth grade after being cut from all of the other team sports I tried out for. I was not an athletic child. In fact, I was what you might call pudgy. Running was different. I steadily improved through my high school and college years, moving from the back of the pack to become a strong "chase-pack" runner. After I graduated from college I needed a break and headed for the Appalachian Trail. I backpacked from Harpers Ferry, West Virginia to the trail's terminus in Maine in two months. I moved quickly and loved being on the trails. I returned to civilization and decided to take my running in a different direction. I headed for the trails instead of the roads, and that is where I discovered ultrarunning. I had come to love the trails and loved training on them, so I assumed racing on them would be good too. I ran my first ultra, the JFK 50-miler, in Maryland in 1994. I did quite well and even seemed to get better as the distance got longer. I soon discovered that there was a culture behind the sport of ultrarunning and I really liked the people I met through training and racing. I'd finally found something I was good at, and I loved it. I was in a trail runner's paradise.

I eagerly accepted an invitation from the HURT (Hawaiian Ultra Running Team) race management to challenge the course of their 2002 HURT 100 Mile Run. I had never visited our fiftieth state before and looked forward to the chance to see the islands up close. Running the second annual HURT 100 also offered a unique opportunity for me to escape Utah's winter weather and run in Hawaii's warm, tropical forests. The mystical 24-hour finishing time has never been broken on this course. This statistic made the race even more attractive. Like several other runners at this year's event, I would attempt the HURT 100 Mile in hopes of being the first runner to break the 24-hour barrier. In preparing for the race, I read all of the reports and trail descriptions from last year's inaugural HURT race. Every report told of rocky, muddy, and root-littered trails. Runners spent more time than they had anticipated between aid stations, as due to the trails' technical terrain, forward progress was very slow for everyone. I accepted the fact that I would be in for a long day, night, and, perhaps, second day of running in order to complete the entire 100 miles. I did, however, come away with the impression that I would be in good hands and well taken care of during the event. Every runner from last year's event complimented the Hawaiian Ultra Running Team for the excellent attention they showed to all entrants. Aid stations were stocked with all essentials, and the course markings were plentiful and well placed. I chose not to scout any of the course beforehand and decided to rely fully on the thoroughness of the race management to see me through the course safely.

Not far from the bright lights, sandy beaches, and busy streets of Waikiki lay the steep, forested slopes of the island of Oahu. The green mountains rise quickly from the flat, densely populated lowlands that encompass the shores. These mountains are often shrouded in clouds and remain hidden from the sunny, warm beaches below. Less than 4 miles from my hotel room was the Hawaii State Division of Forestry's Nature Center, the starting point of the HURT 100. En route to the Nature Center, the tourist shops and rush-hour traffic of Waikiki and Honolulu gave way to an environment of moist, lush greenery. I was surrounded by a myriad of plants, the likes of which I'd never seen before. Huge fronded flora, ferns the size of large bushes and trees that reached high into the skies formed a dense layer that surrounded the Nature Center. My girlfriend Anne Raney and I went to the pre-race briefing, where we greeted fellow runners and listened to the race director's instructions and warnings. We returned to our hotel on Waikiki Beach and later strolled along the beach to a restaurant for dinner. After dinner Anne and I returned to the room and discussed what I would need at the aid stations. We reviewed the maps and I readied my equipment. It was an early night and I slept well.

The next morning I got up at 4:30 A.M. to prepare for the 6:00 start. I had my usual pre-race breakfast of hot chocolate and a peanut butter and jelly bagel. The weather was perfect at the beach, but as we drove closer to the mountains, it took a turn for the worse. It started raining just as we arrived at the starting area. I checked in, made a stop at the rest room, and then returned to the car for a final equipment check. I tested my lights and batteries for the dark start, knowing that I would need them again. I expected to be out there for a long time. Last year's winner completed the course in over 28 hours. I knew even beating his time was going to be quite a challenge, so I just relaxed and accepted the fact that I had a long day ahead of me. One hundred miles is a long, long way in Hawaii's tropical forests.

After an inspirational song and prayer, a blow from a conch shell launched 58 runners into the forest in hopes of completing the 100 miles of HURT before the official 36-hour cutoff. We were instantly thrust upon the first nasty part of the course, the Hogsback, where even the faster front-runners slowed to a walk. The banyan trees' roots were gnarly, eroded, and stretched endlessly in every direction. Footing was difficult, and walking was the only way to sanely negotiate the steep trail in the predawn light. The lead pack consisted of about half a dozen runners, and the pace felt too slow for me, so I took the lead. I led for about a mile and a half, then settled into my groove and stayed there letting some of the runners go ahead. I knew that this run would require lots of patience and persistence, and I had to run my own race.

The HURT 100 course is brutal! And with the rain, it was the most technically difficult race I've ever run. Several sections required runners to use both hands and feet to keep from sliding into the jungle. Some sections were even strung with rope to help runners stay on the trail. These grassy and rocky sections became very slippery, and one wrong step could surely send a runner down steep slopes and into the rocks and trees below, ending their run and sending them to the hospital. The vegetation was thick and damp, and some sections resembled a pigsty: the kind of mud that sucks your shoes right off your feet. And the trail became even muddier as the rain continued to fall. Every lap worsened. The temperature was nice, though, and the tropical trade winds and cloud cover kept the warm sun at bay. The course was a 20-mile loop that we would repeat five times between now and the next sunrise. There were three major climbs per loop that promised to keep things interesting. I found that the same multi-loop course allowed me to learn the terrain quickly. I memorized where I could walk, run, and descend steep sections safely. I was amazed at the diversity of the course. As I passed through bamboo stands that clanked in the wind, along cliffs laden with ferns, and ran under the towering Hawaiian pine forests, I was constantly awe-inspired. The trail passed along several ridgelines that offered sweeping views of beaches, cities, and the ocean below. The HURT 100 course is far from boring.

Two sections of the course double back on themselves, allowing us to see other runners heading the opposite direction on the trail. I particularly enjoyed this, as it allowed us to pass on encouragement to other runners, plus I could keep an eye on my competition. One section of the course was a popular tourist trail leading to Manoa Falls, an incredibly beautiful and noisy waterfall that signaled the upcoming Paradise Park aid station. I found it challenging to pass day hikers on the narrow trails, while at the same time answering their questions about what I was doing, how far I was going, and most poignantly, why I was doing it.

Throughout the day I traded the lead with several other runners. Peter

Bakwin from Boulder, Colorado, would take the lead on the steep down-hill sections, then I would catch and pass him on the climbs. We seesawed back and forth like that for much of the race. Brandon Sybrowsky ran the 100-kilometer version of the event that covers three loops, and we ran together for much of his 62 miles. After 60 miles, I gained the company of my pacer, Krissy Moehl. I felt lucky to have Brandon and Krissy as run-ning partners for the majority of the race. Their companionship and encouragement were priceless. I can't help but recall another event, the 1995 Vermont 100-mile run. I attempted it without crew or a pacer, and felt so totally alone that I dropped from the race at the 63 mile mark. Many runners prefer to run with a pacer for reasons of safety. Others pre-fer the companionship. I like pacers for both reasons.

The three aid stations, spaced 7, 5, and 7 miles apart respectively per 20-mile loop, were well staffed and offered runners all they could ever need in terms of food, liquid, medical aid, and encouragement. The HURT 100 volunteers were the best! Scattered across the aid station tables were Hawaiian delicacies like lau lau, poi, Spam sandwiches, papaya, boiled peanuts, and Kahlua pig. I was, however, lucky enough to be crewed by my girlfriend for the entire race. Anne supplied me with my race favorites: bananas, Coke, peanut butter and jelly sandwiches, Clif Bars, warm soup, and turkey-and-cheese wraps. Her upbeat attitude, smiles, and words of support made all the difference when my energy and enthusiasm waned in the late-night hours. But there are some things that not even warm soup can cure.

I had run for 80 miles in water-soaked socks and shoes, and my feet had become waterlogged. About 300 meters out from the Nature Center aid station which marked the beginning of my final loop, I accidentally stubbed my toe on a rock. Numbing pain shot up my leg, into my spine and into the base of my skull. Without even looking, I knew I had really done a number on my big toe. It was so painful I couldn't even walk. I hobbled into the aid station (which was luckily only 300 meters away) to see Peter, now the leader, heading out for the last 20 miles. With the help of the aid station personnel I took off my shoe and sock to discover that I had dislodged the toenail from the back of its cuticle. The aid station staff cleaned the toe, wrapped it in duct tape and helped me don dry shoes and socks, something I should have done many miles ago. I was back on my feet, but now 20 minutes behind Peter, in severe pain, and very uninspired to say the least. I was down, and I may have just lost the race, but I was not about to quit. I had run 80 miles already; no way I was stopping now! I knew I could keep going, but didn't know how far or quickly I could go, so I just went. The pain slowly subsided with forward motion, and I began to loosen up again. Before I knew it, I was back to a decent pace.

I arrived at the second-to-last aid station, with 13 miles to go, to find Peter still there. The past 87 miles had taken their toll, and his body was shutting down. With some encouragement from his crew he was able to slowly continue on, but his loss was my gain. Just as quickly as I had conceded the race, I had regained the lead.

Krissy and I pushed the pace to the finish. It was a long downhill, and I was running fast. I felt good and was happy and excited to be finishing. It amazed me to see how much zip I still had after having run so many miles on such a rugged course. The last mile before the finish was indescribable. I was elated. Krissy had paced me perfectly for the last 40 miles, and during that time we shared some good conversations and had a blast. I really savored the last mile, and can honestly say I really didn't want it to end. I was so proud of what I had accomplished. This is the best part of an ultra. You know you have finished, but you're still not done. You reflect on a lot of things: the journey to get to this point, all the training, sacrifice, and the last 99 miles you had to traverse to get to this point. It is definitely a catharsis. But then comes the finish line, and you are really done. After 25 hours and 18 minutes and my second Hawaiian sunrise without any sleep, I crossed the finish line. I didn't break the 24-hour barrier, but had an incredible time trying. It is such a beautiful place. I found the HURT 100 Mile Run to be a true trail runner's dream. Over the 100-mile distance, runners climb nearly 24,000 vertical feet. I often forgot that I was only several miles from the busy cities of Waikiki and Honolulu.

After the finish, Anne and I went back to the hotel to shower and rest. I was too excited to sleep, so we returned to the finish line to see others to the end and talk to other runners. That is all part of that culture that I discovered early in my ultra career. Meeting people and socializing at the races is just one of the many benefits of the sport.

I paid the price for this race. Two days later I was in an emergency room on Moloka'i Island getting my infected toenail removed. Even with two shots of Novocain and a shot of morphine, my screams could be heard all over the hospital as the doctor tore the nail off. I don't know if

I'll ever grow another toenail on that toe. However, I gained more from the 2002 HURT 100 than I lost. It taught me that an inspirational crew and pacer who believe in you and care for you are very important. Sure, I probably could have gutted it out alone, but it was much more fun to see familiar faces and to share the journey with others who wanted to be there with me. The stories mean so much more when others are there to share them with you. This was my 93rd ultra finish, and I still take something away from every event I complete. *Wow, I really did this!* I love that feeling.

This essay was adapted with permission from a story previously published in Trail Runner, *the journal of the All American Trail Running Association (http://www.trailrunner.com).*

Running in Circles at Olander Park

NAME: KEVIN SETNES
AGE: 48
RESIDENCE: EAGLE, WISCONSIN
YEARS RUNNING: 34
YEARS RUNNING ULTRAS: 16

I got into running as a high school track and cross-country runner, and enjoyed moderate success with my fastest run being a 9:44 2-mile. After high school I enlisted in the U.S. Navy and reported for two assignments in Europe, where I was fortunate to be able to run with the British. I was sent to a very remote location where there wasn't anything to do but enjoy the beautiful scenery, hang out in the pubs, or run. I hooked up with some local runners who were more advanced than any I'd ever seen before. I was in over my head, but I gradually elevated to their level. The coach trained me very well, the British way: very hard with a lot of quality, fast runs. Running with those guys really helped. This is where I really developed into a better distance runner. I returned to the United States in 1979 during the running boom and became an avid road racer, running anything from the 5K to the marathon. I've run about 60 marathons to date, with my best a 2:23:43 at Milwaukee in 1983. In 1984, as the president of our local Milwaukee running club, I witnessed my first ultra, the Ice Age 50-Mile Run. I was enthralled. These people were running 50 miles on what seemed to me to be pretty rugged terrain. I was impressed by what they were doing, and I decided that if they could do it, surely I could too. So I tried my first Ice Age in 1986, and I failed miserably. I was an experienced, speedy road runner, but I knew nothing about ultra distance running, and it caught up with me after 44 miles. I had a lot of learning to do. I took the failure to heart and applied myself, returning the next year, when I finished fourth, just behind some of the country's best runners. I was very pleased. Since then, I have focused on the ultra distances, primarily the 100K.

Ultrarunning has taken me around the world and taught me that there are no limits to human endurance. The latter became most obvious to me at the 1993 Olander Park National 24-Hour Championships. I'd previously failed at the 24-hour distance, and was challenged by another ultrarunner. He cautioned me to stick to the shorter stuff because, as he put it, "I didn't know how to run the 24-hour." Now, I'm a competitive person and I enjoy a good race, so I took that challenge personally and went to Olander Park in 1993 with one goal: to win.

I trained fairly well for the event and had an average performance at the World Challenge 100K six weeks earlier. I had plenty of speed in my legs, but that also presented a problem: how could I control my speed and maintain it for 24 hours? I developed a 25/5 routine for the race. This routine would have me run 25 minutes at or near my "normal" running pace and then walk comfortably for five minutes. This would accomplish a couple of things. First, it would harness my speed, hopefully allowing me to finish the race at the same pace I started. Second, it would help me keep my body temperature down. My longest training run in preparation for Olander was a 100K run (250 laps) on a quarter-mile track one hot August day. It was just me and my ice chest full of food and drink. Talk about a tough run! It was hot, and learning how to keep my feet and body cool was a real challenge. I thought of that track as a laboratory in which I would hopefully learn how to control my pace and stay healthy. It wasn't a fast run, but I learned a lot. I was ready.

A few people were surprised to see me at the hotel on the Friday before the race. I am known more as an accomplished 100K competitor, not a 24-hour runner. Everyone expected me to run the race like a 100K runner would: to go out fast and burn out after 60 or 70 miles. But I had other plans. I spent a quiet evening with my wife, mostly away from the crowd. I felt pretty calm and collected the night before—which was surprising, knowing that I would spend the entire next day running. I awoke at 7:00 the next morning, as the race did not start until noon. My wife Kris and I went to breakfast and then drove over to the park for the start. I was pretty nervous about the event, but very respectful of what I was about to do. The 160 runners gathered for the event were all fairly subdued and anxious to get going.

The race director played the national anthem and said the usual pre-race remarks. Then the gun went off and 160 runners took off. I ran conservatively from the start, but with the speed I had developed from racing at the

100K distance, it was fairly easy for me to stay at the front for the first few miles. There were five of us in the lead pack, running at a 7-minute pace. I came by my little tent area where my wife was, grabbed something to eat, stepped to the side, and started walking. My 25 minutes of running were up, and it was time to walk for 5. The lead runners didn't really look back, but everyone behind me went by and several turned to look at me. They all had quizzical looks on their faces. That first walking break put me back in about fifteenth place. When I started running again, I caught probably 10 or 12 people, then, after 25 minutes of running, I started walking again. Most of the better-known 24-hour runners ran continuously, pulling farther ahead of me with each walking break I took. Again, my strategy was to put myself well behind the leaders, allowing me to keep a pace I could maintain until noon the next day, and to focus on taking care of myself. If my strategy paid off, I would catch those runners later.

The Olander Park course is a 1.1-mile paved loop around a small lake in an urban park setting. The weather was perfect that day, with the highs in the 70s and the lows in the 50s that night. One of the great things about multi-loop races is the availability of food, drinks, and other aid. At Olander Park there is an aid station every 1.1 miles. And that aid station had just about everything a runner could possibly need. They brought out different items at different times of the day, including pizza at about 10:00 that night. It was a big hit! Every three or four hours Kris fixed me some mashed potatoes and chicken soup—the perfect ultra food.

Other than the usual tiredness and pain with the feet, I had no major problems. After about eight hours I developed a pretty good blister on the ball of my foot. I stopped and took off my shoe, and physically removed the half-dollar-sized blister. I screamed out in pain, then I covered it with tape, put my shoe back on, and resumed running. My foot hurt for about a mile, then just seemed to go numb. That four-minute stop was my only stop during the entire 24 hours.

The pressure from my closest competitor, Tom Possert, was great. But my 25/5 strategy was paying off, and I gradually moved up and was in the lead at 12 hours with a total of 85 miles. Possert was just 3 miles behind. I tried to maintain that 3-lap lead over him for the last 12 hours, but he was gaining on me. I was breaking down; things were really starting to hurt. Sensing my trouble, he surged, throwing in some 8-minute miles in the last hour. He was really making a run at me. He punished me, but I didn't break. At one point

I decided to walk for an extended period. This allowed him to close the lead to about 2 miles, but I was able to hold on from there. I broke the then standing 24-hour American road record during the 23rd hour. There was no way I was going to lose now.

With about eight minutes to go I came through the start/finish area and asked how far I had gone. They told me I had covered 159.3 miles. Even though I had already surpassed the current American record, I still thought that 160 miles sounded a lot better than 159, so I took off quickly to see just how far I could go. Since whatever distance I achieved would be the new 24-hour American road record, two officials had to run with me so they could measure and validate the exact distance of my actual stopping point. High on what I had accomplished and the prospect of finishing, I ran so quickly that I actually made it all the way around the loop before the 24 hours was up! When we finally stopped, one official said (breathing hard), "I could have stayed right here if I knew you were going to make it all the way around!" It was funny to see them breathless and sweating. I really made them work.

It felt simply great to be finished! I found a picnic table and sat down for the second time in 24 hours. It was the greatest thing in the world to finally be able to sit down and just relax after working so hard. Kris was there to take care of me, just like she always does after a big race. It was such a beautiful day; all I wanted to do was sit there and try to enjoy it. I was exhausted and hurting, but it was a very good hurt. The sense of accomplishment was so incredible. I went there to win, and I won. The American record was just icing on the cake.

Later that day I was hurting pretty badly. I tried to nap during the afternoon, but my body was aching so badly, I couldn't sleep. That evening we went out to dinner with a big crowd—about eight of us. By the time we got to dessert I could barely keep my eyes open. I asked to be excused and left the table. They thought I was going to go out and get some fresh air, but instead I went to the next booth, lay down, and started to go to sleep.

I've run Olander several times since 1993. Every year is special, but none have been quite as special as 1993.

Kevin Setnes writes a regular column in UltraRunning Magazine *through which he shares training and racing advice such as his 25/5 strategy with many.*

Adventures in Ultrarunning

NAME: IAN ADAMSON
AGE: 37
RESIDENCE: BOULDER, COLORADO
YEARS RUNNING: 30
YEARS RUNNING ULTRAS: 10
YEARS ADVENTURE RACING: 17

Photo courtesy of Team GoLite

Ian is a well-known, champion adventure racer. It is hard to turn on televised coverage of any adventure race and not see his face. In this story, Ian discusses the important role ultrarunning plays in expedition-length adventure racing.

Ultrarunning is without question the most feared aspect of adventure racing. Athletes learn quickly that their feet are susceptible to being ravaged when hiking and running, and television coverage inevitably includes scenes of blistered, battered, and bloody feet. Many of the lessons I have learned about fast and efficient foot travel over the years have been through ultrarunning. The Collegiate Peaks 50-mile, Colorado's Front Range 100K, Pikes Peak Marathon, and various other events have been indispensable training grounds for my ultra distance multisport racing.

I have considered myself a runner since I was in grade school where I competed in cross-country and track, continuing through high school at the state level and through college in 24-hour orienteering or "Rogaining." As a 20-something student, 24 hours seemed to me the limit of human endurance, and ultrarunners like Yiannis Kouros were of another life-form. How could anyone run 800 miles straight, and do the first and last 26 miles in under three hours? As a student, doing anything other than eating, sleeping, and partying for more than a day or two seemed crazy and pointless, if not simply impossible.

When I was in high school I worked in a hardware store, which required me to spend an eight-hour shift on my feet. It was torture. The idea of running for eight hours was so far beyond my comprehension that it didn't even enter my head until I heard of a guy named Cliff Young who won the Sydney to Melbourne footrace in Australia. Cliff attained national hero status by winning at the unlikely age of 62 on a training regimen that consisted of herding sheep while wearing heavy rubber boots. He further piqued the public's interest by being the oldest competitor and by marrying a woman less than half his age.

I watched the race in awe on national television as Cliff shuffled his way through the pack of elite ultramarathon runners, winning by sheer grit and his ability to go without sleep for a week or so at a time. The main thing I came away with was that ultrarunning was for the lunatic fringe, and I wouldn't be caught dead near such an event. Little did I know that I would not only be running ultras within 15 years, but ultra distance racing would become a passion, a lifestyle, and the basis for 100 percent of my income. Now ultra distance sports are a way of life for me.

My first ultra distance event was a 70-mile overnight kayak race in 1984, quickly followed by a 24-hour Rogaine, which was technically an ultra run since we covered about 60 miles on foot through dense forest. Then in 1985 I participated in my first adventure race, the Subaru Winter Classic. My toughest ultra distance run to date was the 1995 Atlantic City 24-hour race, in an enclosed parking garage on a 0.2 mile square track. At the airport I needed a wheelchair to get to the gate to fly home!

It is extremely difficult to explain to nonrunners why we do this. Most people, understandably, cannot grasp the idea that ultrarunning is in any way enjoyable. Running a few miles is, for the vast majority of Western folk, the limit of their capabilities, and for most, something they would only do under severe duress. The reality is most people would rather spend several extra minutes trying to park a few spaces closer to the supermarket than walk the extra yards in 30 seconds. Why on earth would anyone voluntarily run anywhere, least of all for a full day or more?

Most people can relate more to adventure racing than to ultrarunning. It seems that the team element and exotic locations are easier for the viewing public to understand. Little do most people realize that adventure racing is ultrarunning on steroids and with a few interesting embellishments. There is nothing pure about adventure racing; it is a deliberate mishmash of sports with undefined courses and rules that encourage innovation, decision making, and teamwork. An ultra distance adventure race compresses a year's worth of mental, physical, emotional, spiritual, and cultural experiences into one or two weeks.

Adventure racing and ultrarunning share more than just passing similarities. Both are competitive sports, pastimes, passions and lifestyles. They require exceptional physical endurance, mental fortitude, bombproof lower extremities, nutrition management, some level of sleep management, and more than a dose of intelligence and emotional stability. There are some obvious differences, but one fact is inescapable—ultrarunning is the single largest component of adventure racing. In fact it is typical for more than half of the time spent in an adventure race to be on foot, and this is often where a race is won or lost.

Some of the greatest adventure racing battles I have been involved in have been on foot. In the 1998 Raid Gauloises in Ecuador, we found ourselves in a full-on running race on the sixth day, after summitting 19,700-foot Cotopaxi and crossing the Andes from the headwaters of the Amazon to the Pacific coast. To the surprise and delight of the crowds, we emerged from the jungle after a 3-day absence, running full tilt into the final transition area, neck and neck with our rivals. Three days later we crossed the finish line just a little over an hour ahead of second place. We had spent five out of the previous nine days racing on foot.

Preeminent ultrarunners including Marshal Ulrich, Lisa Smith, Tom Posset, Adrian Crane, and Angelica Castenada have all left their mark on adventure racing, forcing all of us to run when in the past we would have comfortably hiked. In the 1995 ESPN X-Games adventure race, the second-place "Twin Team" of Marshal Ulrich, Tom Posset, Whit Rambache, Angelica Castenada, and Adrian Crane managed to complete the 7-day race on less than three hours of sleep. They ran every foot leg, at least where physically possible, since much of the race was through extreme off-trail forest in Maine. They even ran most of the first canoe leg on a railway track, dragging their canoes behind them and beating the eventual winners through the first water leg (a group of Aussie kayak world champions!).

While ultrarunning does play a major role in adventure racing, there are two distinguishing characteristics that set the two sports apart. Adventure racing is largely off trail and requires teams to carry extraordinary amounts of gear. There are rarely marked trails, and adventure athletes must be completely self-sufficient, carrying all food, fluids, clothing, shelter, and other extraneous equipment. With these impositions, the average speed through a race is painfully slow. Winning teams rarely exceed 2 miles per hour in multiday races, and running takes place with a lumbering gait. It is not uncommon to see athletes lugging large backpacks spilling over with climbing rope, ice ax, crampons, and helmet. Despite this we run everything that is not uphill or over treacherous terrain.

One of my earliest experiences in expedition-length adventure racing was during the 1995 Eco-Challenge in the deserts of southeast Utah. The second leg was a 90-mile foot section traversing the San Rafael Swell. This included wading and swimming in near-freezing water in the Black Box Canyons and enduring 100-degree temperatures through Goblin Valley. Carrying heavy packs on waterlogged feet with sand-filled shoes invariably led to foot problems. My teammates and I were fortunate to have some ultrarunning experience behind us and suffered less than most. Robert Nagle and I had done the Atlantic City 24-hour race, and had learned a thing or two about foot care. Extra-large shoes, spare socks, taking care of hot spots early, and using lubricants helped us build a day-long lead over the rest of the field through the desert.

Going into the leg we had already run 24 miles with three horses in tow (between the five of us). This first leg was a "ride and run" where we traded off riding the horses where possible. Unfortunately one of our teammates was really out of shape and had to ride the entire leg. To top it off one of the horses kicked me in the groin at the start and I ended up peeing blood and sporting a lively horseshoe mark between my legs for about a month. These challenges turned out to be an advantage, as we started quite slowly and moved from 75th to 43rd to 8th place through the first three checkpoints to the start of the canyoneering and desert run. By the end of the day we had pulled into first thanks to some judicious teamwork and a strong resolve to rectify our earlier misfortunes.

Unfortunately our strong resolve also caused us to make a rookie error in team racing, and we paid the price the next day. As dawn broke over the very frosty high-altitude desert landscape, our weaker teammate started to crumble. We were still holding down first place, but in our haste had neglected to pay attention to everyone's state of health. This particular teammate was at the end of her rope, due in part to our negligence and in part to her lack of preparation for the race. By sunup she had achieved a catatonic state, unable to move forward, eat, or even articulate a recognizable sound between her alarmingly shallow breaths.

At this point it looked as if our race was over. We had to finish as a complete team or be relegated to the "unranked" category. After assessing the situation and discussing it for several hours, we decided to allow our ailing teammate to take her leave at the next checkpoint and then continue on as a group of 4. By the time we reached the checkpoint our fourth teammate decided to call it a day as well, preferring to save himself for a race the next month rather than continue on and risk depletion or injury. The desire to quit was extremely powerful now that we had lost some friends and the possibility of a ranked finish. Even stronger was our desire to see what *we* could do, our personal quests for atonement and our curiosity to see what could have been.

By now we were in eighth place and 12 hours behind the leaders, out of the prize money and essentially out of the race, so we just went for it. My other teammates were exceptional runners, so we were in our element. Robert Nagle was a former Irish national cross-country champion and 2:30 marathoner. He won the Atlantic City 24-hour race in 1995 with 130-plus miles, beating the Canadian record holder and the defending champion in the process. Our other teammate, John Howard, had won several of the longest and most difficult adventure races held to date and knew exactly the punishment he could subject himself to.

The course consisted of lots of soft sand and rough dirt roads, but it was mostly flat. About eight hours of the leg had been spent wading through deep canyons full of water. Knowing we had nothing to lose, we really pushed hard. We ran all the downhill portions and speed-hiked the sand and uphills. We were able to "run" about 30 of the next 48 hours. As the mercury increased we shed our hiking boots and opted for sandals to cool our blistering feet. This turned out to be a good move, as we later found out that most of the athletes suffered terrible foot problems.

Mentally it was tough to stay awake, and sleepwalking holding the back of a teammate's pack is a weird and unpleasant experience. On the second night we were hiking through the sand dunes and saw in the distance a small group of lights flashing and probing around in the dark void. Twenty minutes later it became apparent that it was another team stumbling around in small circles in the sand. They seemed barely aware of our fleeting presence; the last we saw of them they were moving in slow motion behind us. Taking a leaf out of their book we decided to avoid the mental fog and confusion of profound sleep deprivation and took a 20-minute power nap. The next morning we shuffled into the transition area after more than 48 hours on our feet, somewhat delirious from dehydration, lack of sleep, and lack of food, but happy to be able to sit down for a few minutes before launching out for the third leg of the race.

In the end, we were faster athletes through the course by nearly two days. Five days and 370 miles after starting, we crossed the finish line knowing our ultrarunning experience had paid off in spades. We paid our dues and would go into the next race with greater confidence and a fire in our bellies.

Tai Chi and Noodles at the
Hong Kong Trailwalker 100K

Photo from Protrek Co., Hong Kong

NAME: MONTRAIL WOMEN: KRISSY MOEHL, JANICE ANDERSON,
    FRANCESCA CONTE, STEPH EHRET
AGE: KRISSY—25, JANICE—36,
    FRANCESCA—30, STEPH—40
YEARS RUNNING: KRISSY—12, JANICE—26,
    FRANCESCA—9, STEPH—26
YEARS RUNNING ULTRAS: KRISSY—2,
    JANICE—13, FRANCESCA—2, STEPH—7

Krissy: I grabbed a pad of paper, a pen, and my water bottle and headed into the meeting. Our Hong Kong distributors, Whelan and Maggie of Protrek, were fresh off the plane for the annual Montrail sales meeting. They had pulled our CEO, president, and international correspondent into the conference room to discuss this year's Hong Kong Trailwalker 100K. Last year we sent a men's team. It was an exciting race and the Montrail men came out victorious and broke the course record. In doing so, they created plenty of publicity and promotions for Montrail and Protrek. This year they wanted to create more of a scene and proposed including a women's team in addition to the men's. Before I could even write the date in my notepad, Scott Tucker, the Montrail president, said to me, "And of course you will be on the team. Do you think you can come up with three others?"

Whatever I was working on before suddenly lost all importance and I got to work contacting some of the best ultrarunning women in the United States.

Steph: In early June 2002 I had a desperate moment. I had just made a commitment to Krissy Moehl, a fast young runner and promotions coordinator for Montrail, to participate on a 4-woman team in the Trailwalker 100K. Nine hundred teams from around the world would take part. We would be expected to put in a top performance—in other words, win and set a course record. I was flattered, I was ecstatic . . . but I was absolutely terrified. Krissy might as well have told me that I would be expected to run on hot coals while carrying a 30-pound load of bricks.

Janice: Last year the men's Montrail team of Scott Jurek, Ian Torrence, Nate McDowell, and Dave Terry experienced great success at the Trailwalker 100K. For several months after reading about their adventures, I wanted to send a note to Montrail with my suggestion that they send a women's team next time. Then, out of the blue, I received an e-mail inquiring about my interest in going to China as part of the Montrail women's team! I was ecstatic to read my name along with Francesca Conte, Stephanie Ehret, and Krissy Moehl.

Steph: I have two overriding fears in life: failure and disappointing others. This opportunity was tailor-made to address my deepest insecurities. Would I be fast enough? Janice Anderson holds five 100-mile course records! Would I be fit enough? Francesca Conte was a contender for first place in the 2002 Montrail Ultra Cup, and Krissy—I've seen her run (from behind)! It was either time to face my fears . . . or bust out the lucky amulets. I did both.

Francesca: They say the best and worst news always comes when you least expect it. Your car never gets stolen when you think it will, and you never think about going to China. So it was that I was reorganizing a drawer full of socks when the call came. All I heard was: "How would you feel about going to China?" The rest was a long litany of: Can I do it? Am I fast enough? Stairs? What do you mean the course has lots of stairs? I was absolutely amazed I had been chosen, and I will forever be grateful to Krissy for thinking about me. Yes, I was worried about my performance, but honestly, I was so excited about running as a team that I never found myself stressing out like I do in other races. It was almost as if the pressure was divided by four, and, somehow, I knew we would do well.

Krissy: Leading up to the race our team started virtual training, or so I called it. Due to the fact that Janice lives in Atlanta, Georgia, Stephanie in Boulder, Colorado, Francesca in Charlottesville, Virginia, and myself in Seattle, Washington, group training runs were not an option. But we weren't total strangers. I had the opportunity to run the Black Canyon 50K in May with Steph, to pace Frannie at Western States in June, and to race with Janice at the White River 50 Mile National Trail Championships in July. I knew a little bit about everyone, but the virtual training really put it all together for me. We talked about our own personal race strategies and how we'd like to apply these to Trailwalker. We discussed eating, hydration, and, most importantly, communication on the course (none of us had ever raced in a group, where it is mandatory that you check in together at nine checkpoints along the way).

For a while it seemed like traveling to Hong Kong for the longest race of my life (thus far) was some far-off fantasy. But after finishing the Mountain Masochist 50-mile race just two weeks before we were to leave, the excitement and reality of the trip really started to set in. A majority of the group flew into San Francisco and then on to Hong Kong. Frannie and Janice met us in Hong Kong, arriving about 30 minutes before us; it worked like clockwork. Whelan and Maggie were there to meet us and help us get settled in. Everyone was tired, and by the time we got to our hotel, we said good night and went to bed in hopes of beating the jet lag.

Steph: I carried the weight of fear on my shoulders until the moment I stepped off the airplane in Hong Kong. I felt better after I got to know the girls in the week preceding the race. One evening as I was relaxing in my hotel room, reading a book on "Personality Types" (the English section at the corner Hong Kong bookstore was pretty limited), Frannie dropped by to say hello. I had already established that my personality is the "Motivator" type (adaptable, ambitious, and focused. Greatest fear: failure). I thought this would be good information for Frannie in dealing with me on the trail, so I read her selected passages. We established that Frannie is a "Loyalist" (engaging, trustworthy, and committed) and Janice is a "Reformer" (principled, orderly, and a perfectionist). Although Krissy missed out on the personality identification evening, after racing with her, I'd give her the "Leader" moniker (self-confident, pragmatic, and decisive). We definitely had quite a mix of personalities.

Francesca: I stepped outside the first morning too early for the city to be busy yet. It was approaching 7:00 A.M., and every park and sidewalk was crowded with people exercising. Runners, joggers, fast walkers, individuals and groups doing Tai Chi, groups of women practicing martial arts with swords: every open space was a fitness arena, and I was amazed by how many people were enjoying the moment. Our hotel was in Sha-Tin, one of the cities in the New Territories, across the bay from Hong Kong, by a large river. The river reminded me of the Seine in Paris, with sidewalks on each side. When I first imagined Hong Kong, I expected a busy city center, but I expected the surrounding areas to be lush and set in the wilderness. There was nothing lush or wild about the area surrounding our hotel. For that, we would have to wait for the race.

Krissy: The next few days were very well thought out, planned, and executed. Whelan had a plan for success. We ran and saw a majority of the course. What we were not able to see in a car or by foot, Whelan had videotaped for us to watch at the pre-race meeting. Personally I have never been so prepared and prepped for a race. But it wasn't all work and no play. We got to swim in the South China Sea and eat many meals, which included lots of noodles.

And we were made out to be stars! Game cards were made with all of our pictures. People could guess the times that they thought we would run, and then once the race was over, the closest guess won a pair of Montrail shoes and other prizes. Whelan took us around to his stores where there were posters of Scott Jurek (from last year's race) and the salespeople all took lots of pictures of everyone. We were getting the whole Hong Kong experience.

Francesca: I soon understood why, in my opinion, so many people in Hong Kong cherish their morning exercise. Between 8:00 and 8:30 A.M. the city becomes a cacophony of cars, buses, trucks, and people: The noise and numbers of people are overwhelming. People living in Hong Kong are used to all of this: It is their life. The malls look like our worst "day after Thanksgiving" nightmare everyday, all of their roads look like Manhattan in rush hour, and this is normal. I believe they need their time alone in the morning, their time to exercise, to somehow purify their minds and souls, to somehow detach themselves and allow them to face another day. As ultrarunners, we hide in the woods for hours, and we need the time away from everything. Some people call it getting in touch with yourself, others call it getting in touch with nature, still others call it having a good time: whatever it is, it's purifying.

Steph: My excitement and confidence in our team grew during a pre-race route-finding run. The four of us found ourselves running stride for stride and it occurred to me that we were running my perfect 100K race pace. I said "So girls, compared to how we're running now, how do you see our pace on race day?" In unison they replied "This pace seems just about right." In that moment I knew we were well matched and poised for a good race.

Krissy: After dinner that night at the Souper Sandwich, we made plans to meet in the hotel lobby at 7:00 A.M. Nerves set in as I lay down in bed that night. Had I done enough training? Had it been the right training? Had we run too much this week? I did not want to let the girls down. Fortunately my fiancé was also running (on the men's team) and was able to help me realize that there was nothing I could do about any of those things now except waste my energy worrying about them.

It's crazy enough trying to get one person and their crew to a race start. Now imagine two teams of four persons each, seven support cars all filled with crew, gear, and enough food and water for everyone. As chaotic as it sounds, the madness was very well orchestrated by Whelan and Maggie. We all made it through registration, interviews with CNN, and so on, and arrived at the start line, ready to go.

Wearing wristbands that we had to scan in at every checkpoint, and Montrail tattoos in at least three different locations on our bodies, we made our way out among the sea of people. We were four women in purple sports bras setting out to run one of the biggest races of our lives.

Janice: The course is along the MacLehose "trail," a combination of dirt trail, asphalt, and concrete, with thousands of stair steps, that winds its way along the ridges of the mountains surrounding Hong Kong. The weather for the 10:00 A.M. start was warm and sunny. The first 10K follows a road that winds and rolls its way along a large reservoir, leading out to a dam overlooking the China Sea. We all ran easily, chatting and laughing. It was a mere warm-up exercise for the rest of the day. As we reached the dam and first aid station, I calculated that we were somewhere in the top 10 overall. As we approached, we could just make out the white shirts of the men's team disappearing around the bend of a distant hill. As always, I was slow filling up my bottles and scrambled to catch up to the other women. We jogged up our first set of concrete steps and then onto a winding trail that had a fabulous view of the beach. Within an hour we had reached a small village, and checkpoint one.

Krissy: Steph said it best in that first 10K, "Ladies, I can't imagine anything I'd rather be doing right now." I think we all felt that way the whole day. In spite of some nausea, getting lost twice, and learning that the second place women's team was closing on us, there was never a moment during that race that I wasn't ecstatic to be enduring this challenge with these three girls.

Janice: By now the sun was full blast and we ran inland away from the cooling breezes of the sea. We still ran together easily, occasionally passing a nonchalant cow or stepping aside to avoid a steer wandering down the concrete path. At checkpoint 2 we all restocked as much as possible to prepare for the next section—a sustained 45-minute climb across bare exposed rock steps. Suddenly I felt overwhelmed by nausea and heat. I jogged but could not keep up with the hiking pace of the rest of the team. When I could no longer jog, I quickly fell well behind the rest of the team. Krissy came back to keep me company and find out what was wrong. Shortly thereafter, Frannie also began to feel ill. With the two of us in the middle, our team trudged along up the mountain.

Steph: The hardest part of the race for me was watching Janice struggle with nausea. Her suffering could be read on her face and in her stride. A couple of years ago while crewing/pacing my husband at Rocky Racoon I watched her run the race of a lifetime. Like a well-oiled, supercharged machine she ran at a quick clip that didn't seem to slow at all over the 100-mile course. Spectators watched in awe as she put in one of the fastest 100-mile performances ever by a woman. At Trailwalker, I knew that if one of us had to be feeling awful, best that it be Janice because, even on a bad day, she has the ability to put in a top time.

Krissy: The heat had set in and done a number on our group between checkpoints 2 and 3. Cold water being poured over my body never felt so good. The Montrail support team had this down to a T, providing us with as many comforts as they could during our brief stops along the trail. I put ice in the back of everyone's sports bras while inhaling a PB&J sandwich.

Janice: Our pacers, Russ Gill (Frannie's boyfriend) and Petra Pirc, joined us at checkpoint 4. We also picked up our lights as it was already late afternoon and it would certainly be dark by the time we saw our crew again at the "monkey area." Nausea and the pressed pace made it impossible for me to eat. I drank water and took electro-tabs, but I had no food for several hours. I despaired that I was slowing the team and concentrated only on forward movement. Steph and Krissy took turns leading our little pack, as Frannie recovered from her sickness and I continued to feel ill and weak. Darkness fell and we seemed to quickly reach our crew in the monkey area, where the men's team had been attacked by monkeys last year. Forewarned not to look into their eyes, we were all prepared for masses of monkeys to approach us as we gathered supplies from our crew. But most had retreated to the trees and other than a few strays and one large male with a wide, gaping red mouth, we could only hear their cries and crashing movements in the trees around us.

Krissy: We were happy to see our crew again and get some more food, water, and encouragement. We were having some good spells (downhill) and bad spells (uphill) but moving along nonetheless. Russ and Petra sure made the difference and stuck the next section out with us as we headed uphill. Personally I was scared entering the monkey area, but also was bummed leaving without sharing an experience like the men had encountered last year. I got over it quickly though, and focused on making time on these uphills.

Janice: A long uphill road led us toward the two most difficult climbs in the course (Needle Hill and Tai Mo Shan). It was here that we learned that the next women's team was only 15 minutes behind. Before the race, we had been assured that (if we ran well) there was no women's team that would even come close, but it was quickly becoming apparent that we were in for a tight race.

The Needle is a sharp incline of rough-hewn steps that lead up a mountain the shape of an upside-down ice cream cone. At night it seemed that the earth dropped away completely just a few feet from the sides of the steps. A view of almost 360 degrees came into sight the farther we climbed. My balance was shot and I listed from side to side, making it hard to go faster than a crawl. I concentrated only on the simple act of one step at a time. Steph led us up the hill and Frannie stuck behind with me (probably to make sure I didn't fall off the mountain). As we topped out, we looked back and could see lights closing in on us. Again our pace picked up as we precariously made our way down the steep steps as quickly as we dared.

Krissy: This last section took a lot of patience and perseverance on all of our parts. Knowing that the Cosmo Girls were closing and that we were having a hard time moving, it took plenty of positive talk from all of us. The singing from our pacers was motivational and added lightness to our demeanor. When we had enough light from the moon, we ran without flashlights to remain more inconspicuous.

Francesca: After the monkey area, we began some of the most difficult climbs. The weather was perfect, I was feeling very good, and it was refreshing to take a break from the sun. Focused on the beam of my light, I could see little or nothing of the surrounding area. Then, I looked up, and Kowloon opened up before me. The view was surreal, because we were in a seemingly desolate wilderness, yet the city seemed less than a mile away. It seemed as if I could almost put my hand out and touch the buildings. There is no place quite like this, I thought, where wilderness and civilization interchange in a second, where skyscrapers rise out of the mountains.

Janice: Tai Mo Shan (the highest peak in Hong Kong) was the final climb followed by 25K of downhill and flat. I still worried that I was about to pass out and ruin everyone's race. Although the climb is longer than the Needle, it is a mix of road and trail and is a little more manageable. The team began to chat again and sing songs to lighten the mood. We turned out our lights in an effort to "hide" from our competition that lurked somewhere behind us. After several false summits we finally reached the "giant golf ball" tower on the pinnacle and began to descend.

Francesca: Running downhill from Tai Mo Shan was effortless. I was worried about the competition, anxious about finishing, but in reality all I could think about was how lucky I was. The view from Tai Mo Shan is spectacular, the city lights melt right into the stars. *No matter what,* I thought, *I am here and this view is all I need.* Victory would be nice, but Russ by my side, sharing this moment, is really what I will remember.

Janice: We rushed through checkpoint 8 upon learning that the Cosmo Girls were less than 10 minutes back. We began to run in earnest, the pace quickened and the mood changed. For a while we all put our heads down and ran as hard as we could. We had been given a pacer who was from Hong Kong and knew the course well. Additionally we met up with a men's team that had a combined 25-plus years of experience on the course. Running down the easy paved streets, most of us with our lights out, we all passed a turn in the course and proceeded to run at least 10 minutes in the wrong direction . . . uphill! Suddenly our pacer came running back toward us shouting, "Wrong way! Wrong way!" Half the team sprinted down the hill along with the pacer. I stopped in my path and listened to the discussion of our pacers and the men's team as they argued over whether or not to believe the Hong Kong pacer. After our pacer, Jenny, checked that there were indeed no course markings in sight, we all began to run as fast as we could back down the hill. I tried not to think about it, but it was very likely that the other women's team had passed us while we were on the wrong road.

Steph: We'd missed a turn! How much time had we lost? Had the Cosmo Girls passed us? To my mind, this would be the only way that the Cosmo Girls could beat us—to pass us without our knowing. I was fully confident that, if they came upon us from behind, we would not let them pass. I was in the company of three of the toughest women in North America. We would pick up our pace, dig deep and, in a worst-case scenario, cross the finish line hand in hand with the Cosmo Girls.

Krissy: Exhaustion set in on the last 10K, but everyone pulled it together and got in a single file line and stayed close. There was a section where the trail curved around, allowing us to see lights coming behind us. Not sure whether it was the men's team or the Cosmo Girls, we kept pushing the pace. We came out on the last canal road hoping to cruise on in; we were all feeling better and I kept looking back to make sure there weren't any lights also popping up on the road. Whelan came into sight and ran with us, telling us how many minutes we had left till the finish. Like a horse for the barn, I tried to pick up the pace with Steph, but realized the pace was great and this group was going to accomplish what we'd set out to do.

Janice: We continued to race downhill and reached the final checkpoint and the bottom. At this point, there was only 10K left to the finish line. The course flattened out and proceeded along a gentle dirt path that ran the length of a reservoir. We didn't talk as much as before. I felt like we were a train, each a car unto itself, but still connected, traveling together at the same speed. We occasionally could hear other voices, but it was hard to determine if they were coming from ahead or behind. We had outrun the men's team that we were with before, so it could just be them again, but we were all afraid that it was the women. Soon enough we came back out onto a road and began running downhill again. Suddenly our wonderful host and sponsor, Whelan, appeared on the side of the road. We all shouted with relief, and with apprehension. Were we still in first? How much farther? How close are they? Indeed, we were still in first and he thought we had a 10-minute lead at the last checkpoint. According to Whelan there was only 20 minutes left to go. I'm not sure if I groaned aloud, but it seemed like we should be so much closer! Luckily, well before 20 minutes were up, we approached an area with lights. Whelan told us that it was just a few more yards to a set of stairs and then we would be able to see the finish line.

Krissy: We finally reached the last set of stairs and I got goose bumps. We joined hands even before we could see the finish line. And then, there it was, right around the corner. We crossed the finish line with our joined hands raised high in the air. As we crossed the line, all of the events of the day flashed through my mind: all the feelings I had, the conversation shared, the helpful faces along the way, and the surreal views throughout the day. And my body hurt. My legs twinged like they've never twinged before. First-place women's team, sixth overall, and a course record. An amazing group of girls and an amazing race.

Steph: Before the race I had bargained with the universe: In exchange for one perfect day I would give up ice cream for six months. On November 10 I had that perfect day: 100 kilometers of great running and hiking on scenic, rugged trails overlooking a neon metropolis and a vast sea in the company of three congenial and talented teammates, three delightful singing pacer-sherpas, and a fantastic crew. Add to that a win, a course record, an unforgettable vacation with my mom, a three-hour massage for under 20 bucks, and dozens of new friends. I might never get to eat ice cream again!

Janice: We had crushed the old record by over two hours, finishing in 15:12. We'd hardly had time to hug each other and begin to celebrate when another team's lights came around the corner. It was the Cosmo Girls, finishing a scant three minutes behind us.

The Ultimate Ultrarunning Adventure

NAME: JÜRGEN ANKENBRAND
AGE: 62
RESIDENCE: HUNTINGTON BEACH,
  CALIFORNIA
YEARS RUNNING: 16
YEARS RUNNING ULTRAS: 15

After 20 years of playing five sets of singles tennis each week with the same partner, a coworker who was a runner asked me, "Why don't you run a marathon?" I thought about it for a moment, and decided that I should give it a try. Thus at age 47, I ran my first marathon in Long Beach, California, finishing in 4:05. A month later I ran my first 50K trail run and have been hooked on trail running ever since. Since 1987 I have run about 25 marathons and over 100 ultras. After running the Mount Everest Marathon, the Comrades in South Africa, and several other adventure events, I ran and finished the inaugural Antarctica Marathon. Experiencing these events caused me to become addicted to adventure running. I am part of an elite group of adventure runners in that I have run ultras on all seven continents.

Ultrarunning differs from shorter running events in several ways. The distance can be anything from 50 kilometers (about 32.5 miles) up to several thousand miles as in the Trans America or Trans Australia race, where runners literally crossed continents on foot in 63 days of continuous running. The terrain can be road, single-track trails, or high alpine mountain treks. But the main difference, I believe, is the endurance and physical and mental toughness required to see you through when things get tough.

Being physically and mentally prepared is everything, which is why I always try to talk to runners who have done the event I am planning. I am not a sports jock—nor do I do any training to speak of by normal runners' standards—but my given natural physical ability and mental toughness have allowed me to do what many would consider impossible, especially at my age of now 62. My motto is, "Do the most with the least effort," which so far has served me well.

The Marathon des Sables is the brainchild of Frenchman Patrick Bauer, who once trekked solo 300 miles through the Sahara and was so spiritually moved that he wanted others to experience it too. The organization is very Spartan and run almost like a former Foreign Legion campaign. This race is not for the weak or fainthearted. When I learned about this race, I knew it was the challenge I needed and it wasn't long before I was on my way. Within an hour of arriving in Casablanca's airport, I sat in a brand-new Volkswagen heading for downtown without a single word of French in my language repertoire. Morocco is an incredible country with exotic cities, people, and customs. After crossing all three Atlas mountain ranges, visiting Fez, Meknes, and Marrakesh, the Red City, I felt that I had really experienced this exotic country to the fullest and was ready for the race to begin.

A 3-hour flight to Quarzazate in southeastern Morocco brought me to my final destination where all the runners assembled for a dinner in the town's finest hotel. It was like a "who's who" of the ultrarunning community. I met at least half a dozen runners from different countries, all of whom I had met before at other races worldwide.

The following day, several air-conditioned buses took us to the middle of the desert near the first camp. From the road, we had to walk about a mile in the sweltering 100-degree desert heat with our 25- to 30-pound backpacks, to a staging area that resembled a tent city. After a good meal of local cuisine we all were ready for a good night's sleep in Morocco-style Berber tents with open sides. Each tent slept up to eight runners. At night, gusty winds constantly threatened to knock over our tent, covering us below.

The next day, our backpacks were inspected to make sure that no one omitted any mandatory item. A medical inspection was also done to assure that everyone was in good shape as required by the medical staff. The entire atmosphere might have been somewhat daunting for a newcomer, but personally I was not intimidated because I was prepared, as I had partaken in other extreme running events. Living in southern California, I have spent much time in the sweltering desert heat, so that, too, was not a problem. About eight months before the race, I severed my hamstring, which would require me to walk the entire distance of this event. However, I was confident that I could make the daily cutoffs, because I am a strong walker, a technique developed on my many trail ultras.

Imagine 225 runners from 20 countries wrapped from head to toe, look-ing more like mummies than runners. Most were impatiently pacing in the sweltering 120-degree heat, which was driven by gusting winds that seemed as if they were straight out of hell. A race official was reading the race rules, first in French, then in English. The French version took about 15 minutes to explain, the English version took only five minutes, leaving me to won-der what they were not telling us. All of a sudden there was dead silence as Patrick Bauer, the race director, stepped up with a pistol in his hand. At the count of three, a gunshot signaled the start of an adventure race so extreme, most people would say it is too crazy to even attempt.

Stage 1 (9 miles)

The faster runners and those having any chance of winning this 6-day adventure race took off like rabbits, while slower runners, myself included, trotted along in the soft sand figuring out how to keep our backpacks from bouncing up and down. The first stage was designed to be an easy day of only 9 miles. It would help give all of us a taste of what to expect over the next week.

Most people believe that the desert is mostly sand, which is incorrect, as many deserts have large areas of rock-hard underground covered with stones and rocks of all shapes and sizes. Walking up a dune in the Sahara, no matter how small, is definitely a challenge. It was like walking in quick-sand. I would take two steps up then slide one step back down. Then there was the powderlike fine sand that got into our shoes and socks, eventually rubbing against the skin. Once I reached the top of the first dune I just dropped to the ground, trying to catch my breath.

The first night at the camp looked more like an open-air first-aid field unit, as many runners were already suffering from rashes, blisters, and other ailments. Bandages of all sizes, ointments, and creams were applied to all parts of runners' bodies.

This is a "self-sufficient" event, meaning runners have to carry every-thing they need, including food, clothing, and anything else deemed neces-sary. Based on the "suggestions" in the race instructions, I brought a good supply of dehydrated food, but after seeing the other runners' packs, I left about half of it behind. I had modified my backpack with extra cushion-ing, wider and padded shoulder straps, waistband, and a sling on both shoulder straps for my hands to hold on to. This would help to distribute the 30-pound weight more evenly. As a way of training, I spent three weeks, four times a week, running and walking on the beach in snowshoes with a 25-pound backpack. Did I look stupid? Several people who saw me thought so, but it gave me an idea what I was in for. Running for an hour on the beach is one thing. Walking/running for six days over sand dunes and rocky terrain with a 30-pound pack is another. Especially in 125-degree temperatures with blistered feet!

It was interesting to see how each runner coped with things like cooking, medical self-treatment, and personal hygiene. All runners got the same amount of bottled water, quantity depending on the distance to be run every day, with the norm being 9 quarts per day per person. This had to be used for cooking, washing, drinking, and so on.

Stage 2 (15 Miles)

After waking up, the Bedouins wanted to break down the tents, and were rushing us to get our stuff off "their" carpets. As soon as I moved my gear off the carpet, I heated a pot of water, part of it for the porridge, the other for two cups of coffee. While the water was getting hot, I got dressed and stuffed my belongings back into my backpack.

Stage 2 started around 9:00 A.M., in 110-degree heat with a barrage of hot sand blowing into our faces. I didn't let this bother me, and instead stayed focused and emotionally immersed into what lay ahead. After a couple of miles I met up with an American runner named Don. We talked for a while, and it turned out that he was a veteran of four previous Marathons des Sables, finishing just one. A few hundred yards behind us we saw a camel driver with his camel on a line, bringing up the rear. It was his job to bring in the stragglers. He asked if we wanted a ride, and we thankfully declined.

That day Don and I walked together and really had a good time exchanging stories about previous races we had run the world over. After 10 miles or so Don got tired and I went on ahead, seeing him later at camp. As it turned out, day 2 was to be Don's last day, but as I learned later he came back the following year and finished.

Arriving at camp after stage 2, I found that there were several casualties already, including Don, and the mood at camp was somber as I made my way from tent to tent, striking up conversations and meeting interesting people.

Stage 3 (18 miles)

During the day we encountered a sandstorm that brought our forward progress to a halt. After the sandstorm, I emerged from under my cover and stripped totally naked, trying to remove as much sand as possible from every crevice of my body. While walking around, trying to get my bearings, I saw none of the yellow plastic course markers. I was totally lost. Soon I saw a form in the sand, which upon closer inspection turned out to be the body of another runner. I approached the body, and attempted to rouse the runner. Initially all I got was an animal-like grunt from a blistered, burned face as he tried to turn his body over. He was totally exhausted, had no water and was near death to the point that he could not talk. I poured a little water into his mouth and covered him with my space blanket, letting him know that I would summon help. I set out for help, not knowing what I would find. After walking for 20 minutes I saw two young Bedouin boys. Not speaking *any* French, I just grabbed their hands and pulled them toward the fallen runner. Once they saw the battered body, they left, presumably to get more help. An hour later I saw a camel on the crest of a sand dune with one of the two boys riding it. We tried to put the runner over the camel's saddle, but he kept falling off. Just then a jeep appeared on the horizon with the other boy and two race officials. After one look they shoved the runner's limp body into the jeep and took off.

Two hours later I arrived at the aid station exhausted and tired. The fallen runner was lying there with an IV in each arm. He had recovered, and thanked me for saving his life. After reaching the next aid station three hours later, exhausted, sweaty, and hurting, I wanted to quit. Every excuse I came up with for quitting was answered with a solution. A race official walked with me to keep me company and told me that I could take all the time necessary to make up for the time lost during the day. When I finally arrived at the camp at about 10:00 P.M., I was greeted with a hero's welcome, causing me to be overcome with emotions. The next morning I thanked those who would not let me quit the night before. I was glad to still be in the race.

Stage 4 (20 miles)

With the third stage behind me, reality was starting to set in. My heavy pack was getting more difficult to carry, making my shoulders sore. And my feet were beginning to get blistered from the fine sand and the rock-strewn hard surface we walked or ran on. Arriving at camp, most runners moved much slower, hobbling around and staying closer to their tent while tending to their injuries. Seeing all those battered bodies, black-and-blue toes, and bloody and blistered feet was *not* a pretty sight, not to mention the foul smell that was getting worse with each day as some opened their blisters. I preferred not to do that. I just added another layer of ointment and bandage, thus adding cushioning as I watched my feet growing. Luckily I brought shoes a size and a half larger that I normally wore allowing for just such an occasion.

As the runners trotted into camp at the end of the fourth stage, hot, exhausted, weary, and in pain, each was handed an ice-cold Coca-Cola, compliments of the Moroccan military, who had flown them in by helicopter. This was a most welcome surprise indeed! The end of the fourth stage also signaled a special point in the race: It was the day before the longest stage, a 50-mile trek. Many looked forward to this with much hesitation, given their physical and mental state with the experience of the first four stages.

I was holding up okay. Each day I covered my shoulders with tape to prevent chafing from the pack, and other than being sore from the weight, they were doing well. The soreness was forcing me to invent new ways to carry a backpack: frontal, over the shoulder, and even on my head. I had developed three blisters, one on the left and two on the right foot. There are as many theories on treating blisters as there are runners. I pricked mine open with a needle, drained them, and covered them with moleskin and a good adhesive bandage. As time went on, the pain became more acute and I added another layer of cushioning over the old one, not wanting to tear away any skin that stuck to all those bandages. Some of the experienced ultrarunners wore shoes up to two sizes larger than normal to allow for swelling feet or bulky bandages.

Stage 5 (50 miles—The Longest Day)

Each morning it got tougher to get out on the course, knowing that my feet were in agony, and only getting worse. It was not even a question whether my feet would hurt, but more a matter of minimizing the pain. Walking with blisters the size of walnuts over terrain that is as hard as cement is pure agony. With each step I could feel the rocks pushing against my sore, blistered feet, but having come that far and with only two stages to go, I wasn't about to quit, which is where mental toughness and maturity came into play.

Stage 5 was by far the toughest. The faster runners came into camp late on the first day and were able to rest, while slower runners like myself did not return till the next day late in the afternoon. After walking for hours, I saw three spots of light in the distance and had to decide which one to head for to reach the next minicamp. Every step in the dry lakebed made crunching sounds, and with a full moon overhead it was eerie, yet gratifying to be one with nature. I walked alone for miles through the wide-open Sahara Desert with only a plastic flag every few miles to mark the way. It was about as far away from civilization as one can get. It left lots of time for reflection, which for me was the essence of this event.

At 11:00 P.M. I arrived at the minicamp and decided to eat and sleep a few hours. The large meal of beef stroganoff with noodles and a cup of coffee was one of the best meals I ever tasted. When I awoke at 5:30 A.M., I shaved and waited for water to heat. Just then a German camera crew came into the tent asking if I was up for an impromptu interview. Are you kidding me? Of course I was!

At 7:00 A.M., five other runners and I, all relegated to walking, decided to join forces and walk together. It was a great idea indeed, as with company it was a little easier to distance our minds from the pain, discomfort, and miles that were still ahead. Eventually the group broke up and I continued solo, finally arriving at camp around 5:00 in the afternoon. I was tired, in pain, hot, and exhausted, and crusty with salt and sweat. My shirt was stiff like a board. We had all been through a very tough stage, and knowing that there was only one more day with only 8 miles to go, certainly gave all of us a spiritual and emotional uplift.

Stage 6 (8 miles)

The last morning greeted us with 100-degree heat, but little wind. The camp looked like a MASH unit full of wounded soldiers. Beat-up and bandaged bodies were everywhere, but all were in high spirits because we were so close to the finish. After a quick breakfast I was ready to hobble the last few miles past date palms, a few fields of wheat, and eventually into the small town of Tazarine. With a couple of miles to go, I hooked up with three Moroccan runners who were singing in French and laughing. Four abreast we linked arms and kind of skipped a few hundred meters in utter elation, singing and happy for having survived.

...tually ran the last mile, not feeling any pain, while locals lined the ...t cheering us on like heroes. Indeed, it was an emotional moment for ...e. It was very gratifying and as I crossed the finish line, Patrick Bauer greeted me with a bear hug and a few friendly words, as he hung a medal around my neck. I am rarely at a loss for words but for a few moments I was overcome with emotions and a few tears of joy and pride rolled down my cheeks. Walking almost the entire race, I came in 175th, dead last. I was very happy to be finishing at all, since 25 others had not. I felt great satisfaction in knowing that I had the guts and determination to hang in there when things got tough. This determination has helped me through other areas of life as well. The Marathon des Sables was more than a sporting event. It was a cultural experience of great proportions, and while out there in the desert, I felt a oneness with nature unlike any I had ever felt before. It further reinforced my image of the desert that it isn't just a dead or desolate place. Rather it can be full of life, if one takes the time to explore it on its own terms. I honestly believe that people that never experience an event like this one are missing an immense spiritual experience. I am not talking about religion here, but a self-awareness and connection with life in general.

Since finishing the Marathon des Sables, I have experienced similar events and know that I will keep seeking out such adventures as long as I can run, have the time and money. Will I do the Marathon des Sables again? No. After finishing this challenging event, there is nothing left to prove. I know what I am capable of and would not have missed this experience for the world, but there are still other races to run.

Hardrock Dreaming

NAME: SUE JOHNSTON
AGE: 37
RESIDENCE: WATERFORD, VERMONT
YEARS RUNNING: 12
YEARS RUNNING ULTRAS: 10

Photo by Cave Dog

Ultrarunning has allowed me to experience a whole new world of adventure, achievement, joy, passion, and pain. It has taken my body and mind to places they never would have gone had I not participated in this great sport. Immeasurable confidence and improved self-esteem are among the many gifts the sport has presented to me. Every event I run helps me find out who the real me is, and what she is made of. But one event, the Hardrock 100-mile, stands out above the rest.

I was a timid, shy child, and though well liked by my peers, suffered from the "kid-who-was-always-picked-last-in-gym-class syndrome." As a teenager, I became pretty rebellious and joined the party crowd. Though I always did well in school and didn't get into too much trouble, I lacked confidence in my physical self. Shortly after turning 20 and graduating from college, I decided I was going to change my lifestyle from one of smoking, partying, and inactivity to a more healthy way of living. Within a couple of months, I quit smoking, stopped drinking, became vegetarian, and started doing aerobics and walking regularly. In the late 1980s I took up road cycling and then hiking, eventually climbing the 100 highest mountains in New England in summer as well as winter.

Sometime in 1991 I decided I wanted to run a marathon. At that time I was running only 3 miles at a time! I remember the first day I ran for an hour straight—I was so proud of myself! I ran the 1992 Boston Marathon and finished in a little over four hours. Later that year some hiking friends, who happened to also run ultras, talked me into running the JFK 50-miler with them. I went down to Maryland with the idea that I'd try to run about

30 miles before quitting, as the thought of running 50 miles was beyond my realm of comprehension. As we ran, my friends taught me how to incorporate walking breaks, what to eat, how much to drink, and so on. I ended up finishing the entire race in just over 10 hours. I was on cloud nine for about a month afterward. I had never been so pleased with myself!

I first became aware of the Hardrock 100 in 1992 thanks to *UltraRunning Magazine*. One of the issues that year had a picture on the cover of a runner descending Virginius Pass with huge mountains looming in the background. Since my background is in hiking and backpacking, I knew then and there that Hardrock was the race for me! Moving swiftly, feeling strong and truly alive in the mountains is what I enjoy over any other kind of physical endeavor. While I longed to run Hardrock, I knew I had to wait until my body was really ready before attempting it.

When I was 28 I through-hiked the Appalachian Trail from Georgia to Maine, which I consider the single best thing I've done in my life so far. During that five-month hike, my self-confidence grew, I became comfortable living outside, and I achieved a lifelong goal. That thru-hike did wonders for my self-esteem, self-confidence, and ability to live with very little. The next year, 1995, I ran my first 100-miler, the Vermont 100, and was very pleased to break 24 hours. In 1996 I ran the Leadville 100. I remember loving the infamous Hope Pass section but found the rest of the course a little boring. Someone later told me if I liked Hope Pass I should do Hardrock because it was basically 10 Hope Passes, one after another! In 1997 I ran the Massanutten Mountain 100-miler and the Western States 100, and in 1998, Massanutten and Vermont again. I also did a bunch of 50-milers during these years. I became a better, more competitive ultrarunner and was able to win a few races and set a few course records. My strength was, and still is, in the longer, tougher "races of attrition," as a friend of mine likes to call them.

By late 1998 I felt like I was finally ready for Hardrock. I entered and was accepted into the race that November. Unfortunately, a few months later I broke an ankle and was unable to run for six weeks. I was very bummed and concerned about how it would impact my run at Hardrock. I spent many, many hours on a stationary bike that winter! In retrospect, the injury turned out to be a positive experience, and I ended up having one of my best running years ever.

My trip to the San Juans was great fun. I arrived in Colorado a couple of

weeks before the race and camped at one of the campgrounds in town, settling into the Avon Hotel just before the race. My husband, Mike, joined me
for the week before the race. We hung out with friends who were also running Hardrock and made lots of new friends there—the camaraderie was
wonderful. We spent many happy days climbing mountains and training on
the Hardrock course. The race itself went well—Mike crewed me to a second place finish. At one point in the race I was climbing Handies Peak, the
highest point in the course at over 14,000 feet, in the middle of the night all
alone. When I got to the top, I looked back and saw about half a dozen
lights slowly moving up the trail below me. Just for fun, I stood up there and
blinked my light off and on just to see if anyone would respond. For a
minute I forgot I was supposed to be running a race; I was having so much
fun! I felt good throughout the entire race and was pleased to have bettered
the previous best women's time by almost five hours. The whole trip was
such a great experience; I even cried when it was time to return home to
Vermont. I knew that I would return to Hardrock the following year.

I returned to Colorado in 2000 with the fantasy goal of finishing as first
woman. Like the previous year, I spent a couple of weeks before the race
camping, climbing mountains, acclimating, and having a great time. I was
a little nervous the night before the race but was generally pretty relaxed
about the whole thing. I do recall a feeling of impending doom the morning of the race. I knew how hard it was going to be, how much it was going
to take out of me physically and mentally, and how much it was going to
hurt—especially if I was going to give it my all, which would be necessary
to win. There was a lot of nervous energy in the air the morning of the start,
but it was a happy nervous energy. It seemed very different from most other
100-milers; but then again, the runners at Hardrock tend to be a little "different"! I was focused, ready to have a good time and do my best.

That year the course was run in the counterclockwise direction, which
seems harder to me because most of the road sections are uphill, so most
people walk them (whereas in the clockwise direction those sections are
pretty easy to run down). The climb up Handies Peak was relentless and
seemed to go on forever! It was over 5,000 feet in a single climb. It began to
rain and got cold as I neared the top, which was a little bit scary. By the
Ouray aid station, about halfway, my feet were pretty beat up and pruned.
I seriously thought about dropping out then and there and didn't think
there was anyway I'd make it past Telluride, the next major aid station. One

of my friends who was helping crew suggested I rub Vaseline all over my feet. It seemed to work, so I repeated it at almost every aid station after that. I had decided to push on because I wanted my pacer, Steve Pero (who was from the East Coast and had never experienced anything like Hardrock), to see Virginius Pass. It is the scariest part of the course because it is very steep, hard-packed snow, and we were to get there in the middle of the night when it would be frozen solid. When we got there, Steve had a few choice things to say about the sanity of what we were doing. His comments and actions had me laughing so hard I was practically in tears. I had all but forgotten about my feet by the time we got to Telluride. Steve was a great pacer!

At Telluride Betsy Kalmayer and I were neck and neck. She had won the women's race the previous year. I saw her go into the aid station and sit down. Knowing this was an opportunity for me to take the lead, I grabbed something quick and kept going. The climb up to Oscar's Pass was interminable, but at the top we were treated to a beautiful sunrise. At the next aid station, mile 82 or so, Betsy ran in just as I was leaving—too close for comfort! On the tough climb up Grant Swamp Pass I was finally able to pull away and put some distance between us.

Unfortunately, I started to develop pulmonary edema at about mile 90. My lungs were filling with fluid, and I couldn't push as hard as I wanted in the last few miles because I was having trouble breathing very deeply. When I got to the last aid station at about mile 93, they told me how far back Betsy was. I was so excited I forgot about my feet and my lungs, and just started flying down the trail. I ran pretty hard the last few miles (or at least it seemed hard to me at the time). It felt great to cross the finish line, but I was too physically spent to really comprehend being first woman. After returning to the hotel room, my lungs really started to fill up, and for a while I thought that I might have to go to the hospital. Instead I took a long bath and tried to sleep. I was pretty scared for a few hours, wondering if I could actually die from the degree of pulmonary edema I was experiencing; on the other hand, I was too exhausted to really care or make the effort to go to the hospital! I coughed up green sputum for about 24 hours after the race and had a lingering cough for about three weeks after the race.

Looking back on that win two years later, it actually means more to me now. I can't believe that I, living at an elevation of 1,500 feet in northern Vermont, was able to win the Hardrock 100 after two weeks' acclimatization. I am very proud of that win. When I look back on my life and consider how far I've come—from the teenage girl with low self-esteem to an ultrarunner who's been fortunate enough to race in, and win, one of the sport's toughest races—I feel blessed and empowered.

I returned to Hardrock again in 2001 with the hope of not only being first woman but with the fantasy goal of breaking the course record. I felt I was in the best shape of my life. Unfortunately, I developed bronchitis shortly after arriving in Colorado and went on a 10-day course of antibiotics. During the early part of the race I pushed too hard—I was running with the lead men!—and felt awful on every climb. A little over halfway through the race I started vomiting, something that had never, ever happened to me in over 50 ultras. Then hypothermia set in, and I was unable to get warm even though I was wearing every item of clothing I had, including a hat and mittens. I decided to call it quits at Grouse Gulch— very disappointing, to say the least—but it was the right decision. Some may say I ran a stupid race, and that may be; however, I am proud that I had the guts to go out hard.

I want to go back and run Hardrock again one of these years because I know I can do better on the course. We've even considered moving to Colorado; not because of my desire to do well at Hardrock per se, but rather for our love of the mountains and the lifestyle that area has to offer. It would be cool, though, to see what it feels like to run Hardrock fully acclimatized!

The Mountains Win Again, and Again

NAME: WILL BROWN
AGE: 56
RESIDENCE: RALEIGH, NORTH CAROLINA
YEARS RUNNING: 35
YEARS RUNNING ULTRAS: 7

Massanutten Mountain rises majestically from the Shenandoah Valley. It sits among strong and proud mountains that shine like emeralds in the springtime. They look serene from a distance, but as runners of the Massanutten Mountain Trail 100-mile run can tell you, those looks are deceiving.

I weighed just over 200 pounds when I dropped out of college in 1967 to enlist in the marines. There was a three-month waiting period to get to Parris Island because of the Vietnam buildup, and my friendly recruiter suggested that I use that time to lose some weight or "they would lose it for me." I stopped on the way home and bought my first pair of running shoes: white leather Adidas with three red stripes. I lost 50 pounds in three months and running became a habit. My first marathon was in 1976. In 1996, after two failed attempts at qualifying for the 100th Boston Marathon sent me into a deep snit, I decided to forget about Boston and instead set my sights on a loftier goal. Later that year I finished my first ultra, the Bull Run Run 50-miler, and was hooked.

The Umstead 100-Mile Endurance Run takes place in my hometown, and I've finished it three times in three attempts. The first was the most memorable, naturally. The second, in 1998, was the race of my life. I finished in 24:08 and didn't want it to end. Seeking out more 100-milers, I ventured out west, and after three DNFs at the Angeles Crest 100 and one at Western States, my wife made the pithy observation that if I wanted to DNF a tough race, I could at least find one closer to home. She had a good point, and the Massanutten Mountain Trail 100, just a few hours' drive from my home, was the obvious choice. My problems at Angeles Crest and

Western States were the cutoffs, and the 36-hour time limit at Massanutten Mountain seemed like it would be more than enough.

An anxious group of 128 runners gathered at the Skyline Ranch Resort at 5:00 A.M. on a Saturday in May for the start of the 2000 Massanutten Mountain Trail 100-miler. The loop course would take us south on the Massanutten Mountain East Trail, then bring us back on the west side of the mountain. The first 2 miles were on rolling asphalt road. I knew I was in a 100-miler when almost everyone began walking even the slightest uphill. Within minutes I felt the sweat begin. It wasn't the free-flowing sweat of midsummer heat, it was the greasy, sticky sweat of high humidity.

We reached the trailhead and began to climb. The trail was full of rocks: small rocks, middle-sized, rocks and big rocks. I've heard that the course is beautiful, but I don't recall. My eyes were always on the trail, not on the scenery. We continued to climb, and the air was still. The sun came up, and the greasy feeling on my body intensified. There wasn't any breeze, even after we reached the ridgeline. No one was looking very happy. I refilled my bottles at the early aid stations, and finally the early morning humidity broke and a slight breeze sprung up. Ahhh. By midafternoon, things were going well. I was staying about 30 minutes ahead of the cutoffs, which are tight in the first 50 miles, and I was probably about two-thirds of the way back in the pack. I was climbing well, passing people, and even getting used to the rocks.

The first storm hit late in the afternoon. Luckily, I was only a few minutes from an aid station, and I got my drop bag poncho on before I had a chance to get hypothermic. I cinched my pack up tight, covered my head, and ran out of the aid station into pounding, marble-sized hail. The trail had become a stream, and there was no option but to slog through it. After about 30 minutes the rain slowed down and finally stopped. The skies cleared and a brilliant late-afternoon sun warmed me. Thinking that the weather front had passed, I put my poncho in the next drop bag. Wrong. It stormed again with a vengeance sometime around 6:00 P.M. I was without a poncho and there was nothing to do but keep going and hope the hail didn't crack open my head. At least I had a hat that offered some protection. This storm lasted about 45 minutes, and I was able to maintain enough forward motion to keep from going badly hypothermic. I warmed rapidly when it stopped, and before long I was happy again.

I got to the Visitor Center aid station (48 miles) at about 7:00 P.M. after a difficult climb up Waterfall Mountain. I picked up my flashlights and spare batteries and began a particularly vicious climb to Bird Knob, the halfway point in the race. That climb went well, and the aid station personnel told me I was in 82nd place of 128 starters. Not bad, and I was still passing people regularly. The downhill from Bird Knob was too rocky to run, and I could feel the effects on my feet and legs from all the rocking and rolling.

Darkness fell on the way down from Bird Knob. I caught up with my ultrarunning heroine, Suzi Cope, in the early evening, and we ran together with her pacer for about an hour. My morale was high. I like running at night, and on this occasion I was running with my ultra heartthrob while being serenaded by piercingly loud whippoorwills. Who could ask for more?

After the aid station at Route 730 (66 miles), I began a climb up steep switchbacks. The cutoff times allow four hours to cover 8 miles at this stage. There is a reason for this liberal offering. It's called Short Mountain. It's not short. In fact, it is the worst trail I've ever tried to run on in my life. The rocks can't be described in words. I begged for mercy and for it to end. At times the trail dropped off the ridgeline and the terrain got better, and I would begin to think I was done. Then the trail would begin to ascend again and I would be forced to climb back up for more of the same fun. That cruel trick happened half a dozen times. The whippoorwills were taunting me, and I screamed for them to shut up. *Get me off this mountain!*

Finally, with the sun coming up and Short Mountain nothing but a painful memory, I headed into the Edinburg Gap aid station at 75 miles. I deposited my night gear there, including the poncho I had carried all night in case of another storm. I was 45 minutes ahead of the cutoff. Things were still going well.

Then something happened to me for the first time in a 100-miler. I began having hallucinations. Tree stumps looked like bears. One of them looked like my dog. I saw a runner standing off the trail taking a leak, but it was just a tree. The hallucinations bothered me a little, but I shrugged them off and they soon abated. I got to Woodstock Tower (83 miles) still 45 minutes to the good, and my morale skyrocketed. I warned myself not to think about the finish yet, but I couldn't help it. The aid station folks described the next stretch as a nice, generally downhill 6 miles. Worried about my caloric intake, I tried to cram down some aid station food before leaving. Some of it stayed down, but I had no desire for food. That worried me.

Deterioration began to set in on that nice, easy downhill stretch. I tried to push some, but couldn't. I knew I was starting to lose time to the cutoff, and the aid station was nowhere in sight as I ran down the switchbacks. Worry swept over me and I looked at my watch every minute. Finally I got to Powell's Fort Spring at 88 miles, having lost 10 minutes. I was now down to a 35-minute cushion.

I charged into the aid station, and for the first time noticed the heat of the new day. It was just after noon on Sunday and I had been going for 33 hours. The volunteers there had a full spread and urged me to eat. I grabbed a couple of brownies and said I had to get going. I was worried about getting dehydrated, about not having another real hot-weather hat or any sunscreen, and about not having eaten enough. I stumbled out of the aid station carrying all that baggage with me. I still had 12 miles to go.

The next stretch was 2 miles down a hot, dusty, dirt and gravel road to get to the trailhead for the first climb to Elizabeth Furnace, the final aid station. I tried to run part of it, but couldn't. That caused me some real concern. When I began to climb I had 10 miles left. Then about 10 minutes later my entire world suddenly collapsed without warning. I looked up at the crest of the hill I was climbing and felt a sudden, overwhelming despair wash over me. Without any conscious thought I stopped where I was and gave up. I abandoned my quest. There was no decision-making process—it just happened. I didn't cuss or beat my fists against my head—I calmly turned my back on a dream and walked off the mountain. I had reached a point of complete emotional and spiritual breakdown, and there was not a thing I could do about it but turn and walk away.

To make a long story short, I wandered around for the better part of three hours trying to find my way out. I couldn't find the previous aid station and my brain was in near-total shutdown. I drank untreated water from a stream and found myself walking in a huge 2-mile circle trying to find anything or anyone. It dawned on me that the aid station must have shut down, and I was getting ready to take the nearest dirt road off the mountain when a guy and his wife in a pickup magically appeared. They took pity on me and hauled me all the way back to the start/finish area, about a 30-minute trip. I got there as the awards ceremony was under way. Ed Demoney, the race director, had said at the race briefing that it can be quicker to finish MMT than to DNF. He was right.

I know now that I could have finished. My mind and spirit were broken, but my body was still able. The splits show that I was doing far better than I thought in the late stages of the race. I was catching people who went on to finish. From mile 74 to 82 I had the 20th best split time in the entire field. From 82 to 88 I was the 40th fastest out of 61 finishers. I was doing fine, but I didn't know it. If I had just rested for a couple of minutes when those feelings of despair washed over me, it might have been enough to allow me to get my head back into the race and push on.

In spite of the outcome, a lot of things went right during the race. I climbed very well and did make it to 90 miles in a difficult race where fewer than half the field finished. My appetite for mountainous 100-milers had not been diminished, but only whetted for the next one. I remember driving away from the start/finish and looking back at the mountains with a mixture of fear and affection. The love/hate relationship had begun. I would be back.

I did several things different in training for my second Massanutten Mountain attempt. I ran all of my long runs on single-track instead of a mixture of road and trails. I extended those trail runs past five hours every week. I intensified a weekly treadmill climb workout and included a long tempo run. The idea was to add strength and speed. I also decided to use the Umstead 100 as the last long run before MMT. The previous year I had done just the 50. Part of that was mental—I needed a 100 finish after a string of DNFs.

Better prepared, I came back to Massanutten Mountain expecting to finish. I've never entered a 100 with the idea of doing anything else. I heard someone say that he'd see how he felt at the Visitor Center, and decide whether or not to go on from there. Sure enough, that's where he DNF'd. The 2001 MMT started out very well for me. I was pleased with my early splits, and found myself running safely ahead of the cutoffs. However, it soon became evident that I should not have run 100 at Umstead. I began to deteriorate much sooner this year. My Visitor Center time was 10 minutes slower, and I didn't feel as good. As I moved on, I began to slow and eventually found myself right on the cutoff bubble at Moreland Gap (65 miles). As I hurried to get out of the aid station, an old East Coast ultra friend, James Moore, tried to get me fired up for the trip across Short Mountain. James had missed an earlier cutoff and was helping out at Moreland. The aid station captain walked with me to the trailhead and asked me how I felt.

I told him I was fine, but I wasn't. I felt like I was on a fool's errand. The previous year it had taken me well over four hours to get across Short Mountain, and I was in far better condition at Moreland that year. The urge to quit right there was overwhelming, but I was still in the race. Perhaps a miracle would happen and I could get in under the four hours it would take to make the next cutoff. I thanked the aid station captain and plunged into the darkness.

It took me almost five hours to cover the 8 miles between Moreland Gap and Edinburg Gap. I had lost leg control and kept losing my balance. Once I stopped and just fell over backward. I went down hard on my right side, and my flashlight spun off about 20 feet and crashed into the rocks. I got my light back and continued. None of the flat trail was runnable, and it was all I could do to pick my way very carefully on the downhills, grabbing rocks and trees for balance. The sun came up and I felt a little better. It had been cold and windy, so that was welcome. The Edinburg cutoff time had come and gone. I was out of the race, but still on the mountain. The end of the Short Mountain leg is regular single-track that winds down the side of the mountain. I could still run, but there was no need to push. My race was over. I was deeply disappointed, but at least I hadn't quit. This time I had been forced out, but just like last time, I would return again.

I looked at the splits of the finishers for 2001 and realized that I wasn't losing ground on the climbs, but on the runnable sections. Unlike 2000, when I suffered a mental breakdown, my mind was fine in 2001. My problem was that the pace that I call my "ultra slog" just wasn't fast enough. To improve my leg speed for 2002, I added speedwork to all of my training runs, including the long runs and the recovery days. The idea was to imprint a faster "ultra slog" in my mind and my legs. I also swore off doing 100 at Umstead, settling instead for the 50-mile option. A moderate effort there produced a 10:36, not far off my 50-mile PR. Recovery was rapid, and I did a last long run of five hours two weeks out from MMT. I felt I was in the best shape of my three MMT attempts. I was quicker and ready to make better time on the runnable sections. My biggest fear was that Short Mountain would eat me alive the way it did the previous years, but I felt confident in my training and preparation and was anxious to take the test once again.

The atmosphere before the start of a 100-miler is unique. Everyone is outwardly calm and smiling, but on the inside you know they are churning.

They want the race to start, but then again, they don't want it to start. I think it was Ted Corbitt who said at the starting line before his first 100, "I've been looking forward to this race for months, and now that it's here I don't want to do it." I started off at what I thought was a conservative pace, but the weather was perfect early on and I found myself with some people who are much faster than I. I pulled back some and felt good about my pace when we hit the trailhead. I felt strong both physically and mentally for the first few sections, but then things took a turn for the worse. Somewhere after Camp Roosevelt (33 miles) I went down hard while moving at a good clip. I landed on my elbows, thighs, and knees and howled in pain for about 10 seconds. There was plenty of blood, but none of it was gushing. I bandaged the worst of the wounds and decided nothing was race threatening, so I kept running. Everything had clotted up by the next aid station. When I left the Visitor Center aid station, I had two hours on the cutoff and was high as a kite. I was almost halfway done and it looked like I finally had MMT figured out.

The climb to Bird Knob seemed to go slowly, but I still picked up a few minutes on the cutoff. I started slowing on the climb back down Bird Knob. Not much of it was runnable, and I felt out of control. I lost 30 minutes to the cutoff on the Bird Knob to Route 211 segment and another 40 minutes between there and Gap 2.

The section after Gap 2 went better, and I hadn't lost any more to the cutoffs when I met my pacer at Moreland Gap (63 miles). I was glad to see him and was in good spirits when we left with a solid 45 minutes on the cutoff. For the first time ever, the trip over Short Mountain went well and my time of four hours was the fastest I'd ever run it. We ran the downhill hard to Edinburg Gap and got there with 30 minutes on the cutoff. I was still high from the Short Mountain section when we left the aid station, but I was starting to feel the effects of over 70 miles and 24 hours of running.

Suzi Cope, who was running her last 100, passed me on the way to Woodstock and said, "C'mon, Will. We've got to finish this thing." She was walking at a good pace, and I tried to match it. I couldn't, so I tried to shuffle a bit. That didn't work either. I resumed my snail-like pace and watched her disappear ahead of me. At that moment I had a pretty good feeling my race was over. It wasn't a question of putting out more effort. I was giving it all I had, which was a pitiful shuffle of a walk. Fighting the desire to quit, I decided to push on until the next aid station and see how I was doing on the cutoff there. I did not want to drop knowing I still had time to spare. But my body was failing me, and I knew that at the rate I was slowing, I would never make it to the aid station after Woodstock in time.

There would be no finish line in this race, just another heartbreaking DNF after 29 hours of effort.

The mountains have won three times now, and my spirit is a little bent. But it's not broken. I'm not done with Massanutten Mountain. I've got a stubborn streak, and giving up on anything isn't in my nature. I've grown to love the sport of ultrarunning, and the Massanutten Mountain Trail 100 has become the ultimate challenge for me. It has made me really appreciate the other successes I've had in running and in the rest of my life. Life has always been fairly easy for me. I was a natural athlete and played many sports well. I hold degrees from two Ivy League schools and have become financially comfortable without working 80-hour weeks. I did well in the military, retiring from the marine corps reserve as a colonel after beginning as a private at Parris Island. However, Massanutten Mountain doesn't know or care anything about that. In order to be successful there, I have to keep trying. And keep trying I will, as long as the race director keeps letting me back on the course.

Running on Sacred Ground

NAME: JASON HODDE
AGE: 33
RESIDENCE: WEST LAFAYETTE, INDIANA
YEARS RUNNING: 11
YEARS RUNNING ULTRAS: 10

Photo by Tesh Teshima

Flying over the lush, green valley on our approach to Honolulu, I saw the steep hills that I would be climbing less than 48 hours later. The hills dominated the landscape with their steep, green facade. It was the perfect backdrop for a running vacation, for running through America's rain forest, and for experiencing the "Aloha" of the islands. Even though this wasn't my first attempt at the Hawaii Ultra Running Team's HURT 100—I'd tried the year before, and failed—I knew and realized that my body and mind were not ready again this year.

I came back for a single reason: I realized during my attempt last year that ultrarunners in Hawaii run on sacred ground. They run through a place full of security, a place of healing. That's what I came here for.

I got into the sport in 1993, deep into denial. I was struggling with anorexia nervosa and used ultrarunning to perpetuate my disease. Ironically, not only did the ultrarunning serve to feed my negative psychological condition, it later saved me from it. The heart of the story begins my sophomore year in college, at the end of my "rookie" year in the athletic training program. Up to that point, I hadn't given my weight (232 pounds) much thought. But I found myself in the athletic trainer's office with the head of the program telling me that I was fat and out of shape—it wasn't phrased exactly that way, but that's what my mind heard. I knew I had to change.

Initially, the process of weight loss was not all success after success. I avoided many of the foods that I used to eat, but I wasn't always happy doing it. At times I would struggle with food and begin to lose hope, only to end up crying in a corner. By the start of the fall semester in 1990, I weighed around 206 pounds. But as I changed my lifestyle back into student mode, I found that my weight stabilized. By the middle of the semester I was frustrated, unable to lose any more weight. I decided to remedy that situation by picking up racquetball and cutting red meat out of my diet. With the combination of diet and exercise, the weight again began to come off.

I dropped to 180 by the end of the semester—26 pounds in about nine weeks. I had begun to exercise more, was able to control my food intake, and was feeling much better about where I was heading in life. But what was lacking in all of the process was any guidance or direction from the person who made those comments earlier in the year, those comments that set off the obsessed exerciser within me and made me realize that I was not happy with who I was. I interpreted the lack of positive reinforcement as negative reinforcement and vowed to be better, to be more fit, to get thinner.

Thinner I got. When the 1991 spring semester began, I decided that even though I liked racquetball, it wasn't giving me the amount of physical activity I needed. My weight had stabilized at 180 over the holidays and I was again becoming frustrated. Already avoiding red meats, I cut out poultry and fish, and began to work out on the StairMaster every day. I began running around the block to supplement my stair climbing, running my first mile in March 1991.

I still don't understand how I was able to generate the energy I needed to exercise when I wasn't fueling my body with anything. But I did, and the weight continued to fall. I used exercise to make up for eating, as if eating that single yogurt was going to make me fat again. To justify the caloric intake, a mere 110 calories per yogurt, I would hit the StairMaster immediately after eating, for an hour, or roughly 900 calories, at a time. By the beginning of the summer, I was 150 pounds, over 80 pounds lighter than I was 52 weeks before. I was very thin. But in my mind, I was still not thin enough.

My first road race was the 1991 Old Kent River Bank Run, a 25K adventure that I registered for the night before on a challenge from my brother, a seasoned runner. I still remember the excitement and the joy that I felt when I finished ahead of him. I had beaten him in spite of my emaciated state. In my mind, that proved that my eating habits were yielding positive results. I continued to race that summer, and continued to train vigorously—running up to two hours a day while skipping as many meals as I could.

It took ultrarunning, the support of friends, and a loving relationship to eventually change my self-destructive attitude. I ran my first 50-miler in November 1993 weighing around 138. I did it while drinking only water, and taking in no calories in the process. I enjoyed the run and the distance, as well as the emaciated feeling I experienced for the few days after the event. I was hooked, and I continued to seek out more opportunities to do longer and longer runs. In 1995, I met another ultrarunner who was also struggling with anorexia. We leaned on each other for support, and I was eventually able to gain some weight, stabilizing myself at a healthy 155 pounds.

Like any addiction that comes under control, it never really goes away. There is no "cure," only remission. And that's what I was able to accomplish in 1995. I was able, with ultrarunning as the backdrop, to put my disease into remission and to continue my life down a healthier pathway. Ultrarunning made me feel special and helped me see the positives in myself and in my body. It gave me confidence. It offered me serenity and peace. In a nutshell, ultrarunning helped change me from being a person with a negative body image to one who could be secure in himself—happy with who he is and what he looks like.

It was the eventual establishment of a relationship, in 1997, that provided the final stability in my life that I needed to overcome the day-to-day turmoil of the disease. Ultrarunning certainly deserves much of the credit for putting me on the right track, but it was really my partner, Corey, who looked past my outer shell and instilled in me the confidence I needed to put the disordered eating patterns behind me.

As I realized that weight (actually, a bit *more* of it) was important to a successful running career, my body healed and I became a stronger and more dedicated ultrarunner. I was passionate about the sport, and was even able to complete the Grand Slam of ultrarunning in 1997. Since I had run most of the "local" races, it became a goal of mine to run more exotic races. This led me to Hawaii in February 2001, for my first attempt at the HURT 100-miler. Even though I decided to stop after finishing 100K (62 miles), I left with quite a story to tell, a story of running through the rain forest on Oahu. On the trail, you get the feeling that the tourists are missing out on god's perfection. In the backcountry, creation is defined. So is the ultrarunner. The mountains are so steep that they hurt to climb. They hurt even more to descend. The forest canopy is so thick that the other competitors disappear and you are alone with god, the trail, and yourself. It is the runner against nature. It is the runner against himself. It is the will to continue against the will to stop. As you run the trail, you are treated to pristine beauty. You are forced to walk and listen to nature around you. You are forced to listen to the beating of your heart. Nature, within and without. It is eerily peaceful. You work so hard that in the serenity of the rainforest, your mind struggles with every step. You are brought to your knees as the course wins. And you become whole. That is a story that most island vacationers will never be able to tell, and the reason that I needed to go back. My story still needed the final 38 miles.

As I prepared for the 2002 HURT 100, several things happened that threw my training off course. I was traveling extensively for work at the time, which made training difficult, and was ending the toughest part of the journey on September 9 when Corey called to tell me that my dad had suddenly and unexpectedly died earlier in the evening. Thus started one of the longest days of my life, one of the longest plane rides of my career, and just the beginning of a wave of emotions that continue to this day. Then came the tragic events of September 11. Although I recognize that day as horrific, it's different for me. I feel only bitterness. Bitterness because I couldn't fully concentrate on my dad that week. Bitterness because nobody understands the range of emotions that I was feeling. Bitterness because the terrorists didn't allow me to heal from the trauma of losing my father.

Everyone carries stress in a different location—most people carry it in their shoulders, but when I get stressed, my lower back feels the brunt of the pain and absolutely every activity becomes unbearable. I was emotionally devastated from my dad's death, and I was resentful that I couldn't mourn as a result of the attacks on the World Trade Center and Pentagon. My back hurt terribly and I just had no desire to run. But I really needed to get away. I needed to think. I needed to be alone. And I knew that there was no other place that I could get that type of serenity—that type of peace and quiet— than on the sacred trails overlooking Honolulu. I would go back to participate, to feel the warmth, to pray, to be healed. And four months later, as I looked down from the jet at the forest below, I knew that I had made the right decision, that healing was not too far away.

There is always a certain degree of anxiety when you are getting ready to run for a day and a half. My greatest fear was that I wouldn't make it to the starting line in time. That I would have car trouble. That I would miss the start and have to play catch-up from the very beginning. Once I awoke for the race, I put on my running clothes right away. There was no reason to take a shower since I was going to get hot and sweaty, so my morning time was minimal. I left the room without checking the weather forecast. I knew that in the rain forest there would be rain. As I left the parking garage, the rain was already falling. A large, fallen tree, a victim of the rain, temporarily blocked my path as I drove to the start in the mountains on the edge of Honolulu. I helped a couple of other runners pull it aside so everyone could get to the start, a quarter mile farther into the forest. It began to rain harder as I pulled into the parking area. So much for staying dry. I grabbed a bagel from the aid station table and sat down to readjust my shoes, and wait.

Away from the check-in area, it was pitch black. At least it was warm, about 70 degrees. Locals tell us that the rain can be small and warm or big and cold. For me, however, everything was warm and extremely humid. I was uncomfortable, but there was nothing I could do but sit and wait and hope and pray that things would be better this year.

The unrelenting rain broke through the branches of the trees and showered us with water from the heavens. Even though I knew that I would end up sweating myself wet in the first 15 minutes of the race, I couldn't help but feel frustrated. It was a fitting beginning to 100 miles of rugged trail and mountains that never let man call the shots.

The group of runners walked from the start/finish shelter to a bridge crossing a small creek that bellows forcefully from the rain forest to the ocean. Once the runners were all on the bridge, we were told to pause for a moment of silent reflection to concentrate on the task set before us. Burning tiki torches lined the first few yards of the trail, glowing brightly in the dark and rainy morning air. As we paused, a native Hawaiian woman opened her arms and, in her native island tongue, began to pray a hallowed prayer for our strength and safety. I didn't understand any of the words, but I knew they were being said in the true spirit of the islands, and I felt like I belonged. The ritual prayer (called a pule) was followed by three long blasts on a conch shell. We headed off into the dark forest amid the burning torches, up the ridge of the Maunalaha Trail, and into the enchanted world of the Hawaiian rain forest.

The format for the course was five 20-mile loops over almost 100% rocky, rooty trail. The first climb was characterized by twisted roots and gigantic rocks that had to be traversed. Locals call this trail Hogsback because the roots twist and turn and intertwine between each other, making the trail look like the spine of a wild pig. The ridge climbs almost 2,000 feet in just under a mile; by the time I reached the top, my lungs were burning, sweat was dripping into my eyes, and I'd only been working for 15 minutes! The humidity was 100 percent, it was about 75 degrees, and I hopelessly realized that the sun had yet to rise. It was going to be a grueling day.

The next section of trail was less steep but the footing was uneven and rocky, and finding a comfortable place to plant my feet was impossible. After the brief reprieve from the climb, the trail turned upward once again, through vegetation that towered above me. The rocks were gone for the next few miles, but overgrown vegetation replaced them, making progress difficult. The rain was coming sideways, whipping my face with the large, cold drops that the locals warned us about. The distant buildings of Honolulu reflected the sunlight (at least the sun was shining somewhere), forming multiple rainbows, reminding me that nature was watching over my every move. I splashed through the next few miles and arrived at an area of the course known as Pauoa Flats. Here, the rain had turned the trail to mud, which stuck to the bottom of my shoes as I made my way through. Even the best-lugged shoes refused to grasp the earth securely. The trail descended steeply through this section. When at last I finally reached a flat area, the slippery roots of banyan and other trees returned, spreading out across the trail like black, slithering snakes.

My early mood was playful. I was in one of the most beautiful places on earth, experiencing nirvana, running a steady, even pace. My level of exertion was tempered by the serenity that I felt, and although the rain was somewhat frustrating, it was enjoyable. But things would get worse.

The climb down, and then up Nu'uanu was the steepest part of the trail. Here the trail followed narrow ridges that fell off steeply on either side. The trail was a mud bath, and a rope had been placed to help the runners slowly and safely descend—and to assist us in pulling ourselves back up. The spine of the ridge was covered in green rain forest trees that moaned in the wind. I descended on a narrow, muddy trail littered with loose rocks that rolled under my feet. As I descended, the trees changed from short, thick rain forest foliage to tall, stately Cooke pines that were arranged in rows. I was now in the area known as the Enchanted Forest. The wind howled far above, but down here there was a stillness in the air that gave the area a regal feel and a sense of security. In the Enchanted Forest, the trail was soft and groomed—very different terrain from the majority of the course. It was fun to run.

Another part of the trail passed through forests of bamboo. The clacking of the reeds in the strong wind was deafening and eerie, especially in the dark. The noise consumed all of my senses, including the pain in my legs and the soreness in my knees. I closed my eyes for a minute and I could see, feel, and hear the clacking of the bamboo. I could feel the rain on my face and hear the wind whistle through the Enchanted Forest. For a minute I felt as if I could touch the lights of Waikiki in the distance. I felt so real. I felt so safe. The sound woke me up and told me it was okay to continue to run.

I think I quit about 20 times during the race, mostly between the time the sun went down and the time that I finally walked away. Reality sets in when it gets dark. The trail gets lonely. At this HURT 100, the wind and the rain never stopped. My feet hurt, but so did the little muscles between my vertebrae and the muscles that hold up my head. My shoulders were sore, and the muscles that help my chest expand with each breath were sending S.O.S. messages to my brain. The rational part of my brain responded by telling me that three loops would be enough. Wouldn't 100K be enough again? Hadn't I had enough? The mind has an uncanny ability to block out pain and discomfort, but there comes a time when the overriding desire becomes the desire to save itself for another day and time. We all need to pick our fights carefully, and in the case of the HURT, to continue would have meant sacrificing much more than I was ready to sacrifice at the time. I don't know if others feel like I do when I make the decision to quit. My brain fights against itself and against my body, weighing the good and the bad, coming to a conclusion of whether or not to keep it up or pack it in. Once that decision to stop is made, serenity ensues. The final few miles of the event—after the voluntary decision to quit—are very enjoyable.

I said I was coming back to Hawaii for healing, security. I came back to pray. And pray I did. I prayed, and I cried. The mountains worked their magic, stripping away several layers of protective covering that I'd placed on myself since September. The bamboo clacked, the wind howled, and the rain battered my face. In the middle of the night, in spite of the darkness, in spite of the elements, I felt secure. I felt alive. And for a few minutes at least, I felt healed. As far as I know, I may never be able to beat the HURT 100. I guess maybe we're not meant to finish everything we start. Maybe we all need to live with things that we continually struggle with. Like the death of a family member. Like an eating disorder. Or like a persistent DNF.

A Dream Fulfilled

NAME: REBEKAH TRITTIPOE
AGE: 46
RESIDENCE: LYNCHBURG, VIRGINIA
YEARS RUNNING: 9
YEARS RUNNING ULTRAS: 9

Photo by Rick Meagher

I can't believe it's been a week. Seems like a dream. It's Saturday morning and I'm doing the cardiovascular perfusion for an emergency cardiac surgery. I glance at the clock. 6:40 A.M. I suddenly feel transported back in time. Last week this time I was just coming into the first crew point of the Old Dominion 100-Mile Endurance Run. Nineteen down, 81 to go. David Horton, one of my crew, asked me if I was having fun. I said, "Yes, and I'll take that blueberry muffin—please! It's breakfast time." I ran on down the road with a goofy grin on my face. A beautiful horse farm on the left came into view. I took in the serenity of the expansive green pastures, the grazing horses, the impressive home and barns. I took another bite of muffin and gulped down some fluid. I told myself to be patient. Run when I'm supposed to run, walk when I'm supposed to walk. Go aid station to aid station. Don't worry. Be happy. I am.

The day was gorgeous. Perfect temperature and low humidity. I was running by myself. I liked it that way—at least for the time being. *Run relaxed, run smooth,* I whisper. I'd never attempted a 100-miler before but I knew I needed to conserve my running resources. I'd love to be able to run later in the race but there's no telling what my legs would do. Having suffered another stress fracture in February, the last 17 weeks benefited from a lowly running average of 19 miles per week, with five weeks seeing zero mileage. Not exactly a traditional approach in preparation for my first or any 100-miler! I cross-trained for countless hours in the pool and on the skier and elliptical trainer, doing my best to prepare for this race. I was determined to get to the start line. Three times before I had entered a century run, only having to withdraw due to other ill-timed stress fractures. God help me, if a bone wasn't sticking out of my foot, I was running this one! Sure enough, here I was. I was actually doing it!

Looking back, this ultrarunning thing all started in the summer of 1993 when I was playing USTA tennis at a very competitive level. I was feeling reasonably confident with my game, but the hot and humid days of summer about killed me during some of the matches. I could almost handle being beaten by someone with higher skills, but I certainly had no intention of getting beat on the basis of conditioning. So I started to "run" on a regular basis. I was only putting in 20 to 25 miles a week for the first month and those who saw me on the roads might have described me as that awful J word: *jogger*. Then our family's friendship with David Horton and his family soon put a strange twist on things. I got to work aid station 10 and the finish line of the 1993 Mountain Masochist Trail Run with Nancy, David's wife. I was impressed—perhaps even inspired—by what I saw. David knew I had always been an athlete but never a distance runner. However, I guess he figured I would be a sucker for a challenge. After that, David's flippant comments like "Bet you can't run fifty miles" got under my skin enough to make me resolve to do his 50-mile race. What I did not count on was that I would soon become obsessed with this running stuff.

By December, I did my first 20-mile mountain run with Horton and loved it! Several more "fun-run adventures" in the ice and snow actually added to my enthusiasm. However, in January 1994 I suffered a metatarsal fracture in my right foot and mentally hit bottom with disappointment. I did lots of deep-water running and stair-stepping in the next four weeks and traveled to Maryland in March to run the Catoctin Trail Race 50K. Because of severe conditions (ice, snow, and lots of deep, swift streams), my first ultra of 50K was shortened into a "not quite an ultra" of 35K. Although I led the women (much to my surprise!), I was again in despair when I broke another metatarsal just over a mile from the finish line. It made that last climb to the end rather painful!

So back I went into the pool and onto the stepper. What a pain—literally and figuratively—to try to come back from injury! It was a good six weeks this time before I could do anything beyond very light running. And, just when I thought I was running well again, my foot broke for the third time. Talk about frustration! My husband should get a medal for having to play counselor through all those setbacks.

From those first months of successes and setbacks until this day in early June five years later, I dealt with six more metatarsal fractures, a femoral neck fracture, multiple torn ligaments, and other soft-tissue injuries. Lots of people told me I was crazy to continue in my ultrarunning pursuits. However, perhaps the single thing that captured my imagination and served as a tremendous encouragement to me stemmed from a school assignment of Caleb, my then kindergarten-aged son. Instructed by the teacher to finish and illustrate two sentences, my son penned:

The turtle will not run.

The Mommy will run.

Out of the mouths of babes. . . . Those words stayed plastered to my refrigerator.

So there I was, running down a country road on a summer morning in my first 100-miler. But soon all my rambling philosophical musings were temporarily tucked away as I began to feel a couple of hot spots on my feet. I had heard how blisters had been the undoing of many a runner. Although it would mean an extra minute or two, I decided to have my crew moleskin those spots at mile 32. As they worked on my feet, I downed a can of Ensure and guzzled some fluid. Then, after putting my socks and shoes back on, I grabbed a sandwich to go and continued on my journey. I would not see my crew for another 15 miles but I was looking forward to those miles, 10 of them run on trail. I feel so free when I run trails. Roads, even remote country roads, pale in comparison to these narrow ribbons woven intricately through the forest.

I made good progress and was quite content when a runner came flying by on a particularly rocky section. Using his most concerned voice, he asked, "Are you okay?" I didn't think I looked quite as bad as his tone implied. Nevertheless, I assured him that all was fine as I watched him bound out of sight. Talking later with other runners I learned that he did the same thing with them. None of us ever did figure out if he was a racer or just an annoying show-off. Peculiar. Anyway, the last downhill portion of this section would not prove to be one of my favorites. With the blisters worsening and a few of my toenails lifting off their beds, I knew I would have to deal with my feet again as soon as I saw my crew. Considering the circumstances, the trail portion fortunately gave way to a smooth gravel road, leading back to the crews.

Retaping the expanding blistered areas, I decided to change into my worn, but tried-and-true trail shoes. As I left the aid station, I prayed that my blistering would be put on hold—especially since there was another 53 miles to go. As I made my way over the next 9 miles, I had plenty of time to walk, as the course was predominantly uphill. Some runners passed me going up the grades, but I really didn't care. Eventually, I would catch then again on the flat or any slight downhill section. It was like a big game of cat and mouse—which I thoroughly enjoyed. I did get some good conversations going with the guys who were running around me. It's amazing what you can learn about someone in the span of a few minutes. I was also quite willing to talk as it took my mind off my feet.

By the time I saw my crew again at 57 miles, my blisters had cooled off and I was still in a very good mood. I joked with Horton about now having run as far as the Mountain Masochist race; a "50-miler" with the reputation for being just a tad bit longer. My crew handed me food and drink, which I dutifully downed. I did not stay long. I had places to go. People to see. I was on a mission.

With each passing aid station, the miles seemed to mount quickly. It was so exciting to get into the 60-mile range. Then, the 70s. I was looking forward to mile 74, where I would pick up my pacer for the next 13 miles. Four years prior, I had served as David Horton's pacer at this very spot. Now it was his turn. Since the Elizabeth Furnace aid station was the last medical checkpoint, I hopped on the scale to find that I was still six pounds heavier than my pre-race weight. I was third-spacing volume (swelling up like a toad) but still urinating frequently. I got released to my handlers, who once again handed me food and drink. Okay. That was enough. Let's go, Horton!

The climb over Sherman's Gap was rockier and steeper than I had remembered. But when I served as a pacer, I was trying to figure out how to get Horton to drink something and stop heaving. That was an impossible job! Thankfully, I experienced only a slight nauseous feeling after eating so quickly but had no problems keeping my food on the inside. With the summit conquered, it was down the other side, up the gravel road, and up Veach Gap. I had caught up with a number of runners at this point and spent only a few seconds at this aid station. I seemed to have a burst of energy and climbed strongly up the mountain. We distanced ourselves from the rest and soon found ourselves turning on our flashlights as the sun finally set on the day. Nevertheless, the descent proved trying. Very rough and rocky, I stumbled a lot and failed to get into a rhythm. My feet shifted in my shoes, displacing even more skin. I was surprised at my keen anticipation for more gravel road.

Now just 13 miles remained. I was back on solid surface and put my light into the pouch of my fanny pack. I love running in the dark! And besides, a bright moon, though sometimes obscured by drifting clouds, provided enough light to run. I was again by myself, running through the shadows, in awe that I had come so far with relative ease. The day had gone by quickly and except for one statement, I may not have even realized the time. Horton, however, had done his homework. Before leaving for the race, he had investigated how many women across the nation had run under 23, 22, 21, 20, and 19 hours in 100-milers over the preceding two years. He eloquently stated the facts to me at 87 miles. My first response was, "It doesn't matter! I'm doing all I can!" However, perhaps those raw statistics were the impetus I needed to pass a few more runners and keep from being passed by others. When my crew saw me at 93 miles, Horton told me breaking 21 hours was within reach. Okay. Okay. I'll push it more. I really did not want to blow an opportunity for breaking a significant time barrier.

On paper, there remained only 2 miles of road before hitting the big descent down the switchbacks of Woodstock Mountain leading to the final miles through town. Though I was moving quickly, it seemed as though I ran forever to get to the top of that mountain. Then it was down, down, down. It was only now I realized my quads were weary. I was surprised to see three runners in front of me. Running without a light, I startled two of the men as they descended together. "Hey," they called, "are you in the race?" "Yeah," was my response. "Well, why don't you have a flashlight?" they blurted, as though it was a race rule. "I don't like flashlights. See ya." I was inwardly amused by this exchange and ran on, trying to catch the runner yet in front of me.

Finally, the switchbacks ended and I crossed over the river on the bridge. The road rose in front of me, for which I was grateful. I was able to walk quickly up the hill, a welcome break from the pounding of the downhill. Though tired, I enjoyed the stillness of the night. I even said hello to a few grazing cattle. I ran on, pushing as hard as I could until I came to the last aid station. My crew was happy, glad the day was coming to a close. A couple of them were even teasing, asking why it had taken me so long. Big mistake! After 20 hours of running, my fun meter had run dry. I was in no mood to joke.

My feet now felt as if they would explode. There was not an absence of pain. I scowled as Horton lay in the middle of the road to take my picture. I ran down Water Street to the right-hand turn. Then up the incline, I tried not to walk, but had to take an occasional step. Then I heard the sound of footsteps behind me. Oh, no! Try as I might to kick it into a higher gear, a single runner quickly came up behind me, overtaking me with about a mile and a half to go. Watching him disappear in the darkness, I refocused on getting myself to the fair grounds for the final lap around the horse track.

Finally, there it was. I entered the gates to see my crew waiting for me. They cheered me on. Horton looked at his watch and urged me to push. In my physical and mental state, I took it as undue pressure; a gesture that I wasn't doing well enough for his standards. *I am pushing!* I screamed silently. Outwardly, I snapped, "I'm doing the best I can!" Immediately, I felt bad that I lost my humor so close to the end. As I ran around the back side of the track, out of view, I wanted to walk. But, no. I couldn't. Not this close. I ran on, albeit slowly, finally crossing the finish line in 20:54:27. I fell into the arms of my husband, who politely informed me that I could now stop running. Thank the Lord! Hugs were given and received and I was pleasantly surprised when informed I had finished 13th overall. However, Pam Reed, a great runner who PR'd at this race, had finished about an hour ahead of me and in eighth place overall. A twinge of disappointment welled up momentarily for having finished behind her, but faded when I reflected on the fact I had run well, finished, and with nary a broken bone! Besides, all I wanted now was a shower and a cup of coffee.

My crew and I went back to the hotel, eager for sleep. I rested on the bed as they quickly took showers. I was never so glad to get the bathroom to myself. But the thought of a gloriously warm shower lasted only until the water and soap caused my blisters to scream out in agony. Then the nausea, light headedness, spinning room, and collapse on the floor put things into perspective. My husband burst into the room to rescue me, thinking I was dying on the spot. After a number of tense minutes, he managed to get me dressed and helped me to the bed. Everyone else in the room was asleep in about 10 seconds. Ironically, I was now wide awake. I doubt I slept more than an hour for the duration of the night. Besides, my raw feet against the sheets were reason enough to stay awake.

As the sun rose and the day's light filtered into the room, we made our way to the awards ceremony. The greatest challenge was not in making my legs move, but in putting shoes on my feet. However, nothing could dampen my spirit. I looked toward those mountains that served as the battleground for the challenge of the previous day. Despite numerous setbacks and meager mileage, I had conquered the course and lived to tell the story!

I was back in surgery at 6:30 Monday morning and have worked a lot throughout the week. I have no idea where the time has gone. The race of last weekend seems surreal, dreamlike, a very hazy piece of history. I have become more aware of all the people who actively prayed for me during the race. My mother, for one, had recruited many of her prayer partners to the cause. But right now, it's almost depressing. It's like Christmas: You anticipate and wait for the day and then it's over before you know it. I am fearful I will forget the details of this first 100. I want to hold on to every memory of this race: the high points and the low, the good running and the bad. I am eternally grateful for having the opportunity to run and to finish. I do not take lightly the privilege of running at all, given my extensive injury history. Whatever happens in future races, this first one will always be special.

Now the chill of the operating room and the music from the radio slowly and subtly return me to the present. I put my reminiscing on hold and turn my attention back to my patient and the logistics of this surgery. Life goes on.

The Last 100

NAME: SUZI COPE
AGE: 54
RESIDENCE: SOUTHLAKE, TEXAS
YEARS RUNNING: 23
YEARS RUNNING ULTRAS: 18

Virginia Happy Trails Running Club

My husband dares to say I'm a control freak. I'm sure he means it in a loving way, but that doesn't change the fact that he's right. Throw in *obsessive-compulsive* and the description is even more accurate. Running a 100-mile trail event would seem perfectly normal for a sick mind like mine. I have run many 100s in the last 18 years, but I ran the last one in Virginia's George Washington National Forest in May of 2002.

The northern California jogging craze of 1979 was too much to resist, and a permanently "disabled" left knee from a motorcycle accident posed only a brief setback. I ran my first 100-miler at Western States in 1985. The run was as exciting, challenging, and rewarding as expected but it took more than I had to offer. And it made a lasting impression. It was years later before I better understood the post-100 depression, which is similar to postpartum depression, with only a finisher's award to show for it. My parents crewed for me, and I had four friends pacing different sections. Even using some veterinary-source electrolyte powder, I still suffered from stomach problems and dehydration, as expected. During the night near the river I saw a possum with babies on her back, which my pacer explained was actually a rock.

Sunrise caught me sitting on a rock letting the clock run out. Another runner walked by and said he was just doing the best he could, even if we were out of time. I realized I was *not* doing the best I could. So I got up and started running. At Auburn Lake Trails I was within five minutes of the cutoff. Marty Liquori announced on ABC's *Wide World of Sports* that no runner in that aid station at that moment would make it to the finish in time.

I ran the next section faster than I thought I ever could. My pacer was absolutely stunned. I finished with just minutes to spare, and had no interest in running for about three months after the event. But time heals all wounds, and before long I was back for more.

The ultrarunning community was so small at that time, that I knew the names of all 23 women who had completed a 100-mile trail run. In this small pond I became a big fish by completing the Grand Slam of ultrarunning during the summer of 1989, finishing first of the four women to do so. Three of us managed to complete Angeles Crest 100 that summer, making it five trail 100s in 16 weeks. I became a trail 100 junkie, and would enter every new event on the calendar. The thrill of the unknown added excitement to the distance challenge. Some of the races were only run once or twice, and are now just part of ultra history. Then came the Hardrock 100 in the San Juan Mountains of Colorado. We became adversaries for six years, until I finally completed the event in what was probably the pinnacle of my trail-running lifetime.

Over three dozen 100-miler starts and two dozen finishes later, it was time to step back. I thoroughly enjoyed controlling my destiny by announcing that the 2002 Massanutten Mountain Trail 100 would be my last 100-miler. MMT 100 is a worthy opponent. It had beaten me in 2000 just short of the infamous Short Mountain. To return was a great challenge and calculated risk, but this time I was ready. In my corner was Keith Dunn as crew and Jay Freeman as pacer. Both were seasoned veterans who deeply cared about my run and were fully committed to helping me finish.

Once the entry was in and the travel plans set, the pre-race emotions gradually flooded my consciousness. With the decision that this would be my last, the MMT 100 became more like a date with an old friend or lover. We had so much ground to cover and catching up to do. I began the immersion ritual of packing for a 100-mile trip for the last time. So many fond memories came rushing back as I worked my way through filling the fanny pack and choosing the clothing. Just once more to wear my favorite lucky bandanna from the Arkansas Traveller 100. I have about 100 bandannas, including one I designed for Hardrock with the directions printed on it. The AT 100 bandanna is just one of my favorites that I've worn many times. It's not that I'm superstitious—I believe in making my own luck, good or bad. But wearing a favorite bandanna can't hurt.

The morning of the MMT 100 was special, as are most race mornings.

Many of my friends from over the years were at the start, making this one even more special. I savored every moment, reminding myself constantly that *this is the last one*. So many moments became mental postcards to take home. Then, just like I'd done on so many early Saturday mornings in the past 18 years, I hit the trail with 100 miles to go.

During the early hours of a perfect Saturday I worked my way among the back of the pack, covering ground and storing memories. I was very confident of a finish and found the first few miles calming, overwhelmingly peaceful. Before long I came across a couple of my old California ultra buddies. We did what I have always done in these events, caught up on each other's lives. It took miles to swap stories and share encouragement before we separated. I also met new people along the way. The weather was delightful and I was on my schedule comfortably. I came upon a guy who knew something about endurance riding, and we spent about 5 miles talking about horses. Another runner recognized my name and started asking history questions. We talked at length about the stories that make up ultra history. Brags about my own Grand Slam, Barkley, and Hardrock were mixed in with gossip and history of the "names" in our sport. The miles rolled by and the conversation was good.

Aid stations were welcome and generous, and when accessible, my crew was there with a smile. I mentally went over the usual checklist: Feet are completely taped, and happy in dry socks and new shoes, chafing is managed with Bag Balm and bike-length shorts, I'm staying hydrated and well fed. What could possibly go wrong?

I wrote an ultrarunning newsletter in the late 1980s, and a quote of mine from one issue reads, "The one thing you can depend on in a 100-mile trail event, is that there will be a surprise." I was still waiting for the surprise when Jay joined me at the halfway mark to pace me through the night and to the finish. Neither of us had ever experienced the dreaded Short Mountain section, and all of our joint effort went toward looking forward to, and then surviving, that horrid piece of trail. Our goal was to move through the Gap Creek aid station and start climbing in earnest. That lasted for about 2 uphill miles in the middle of the night before my systems redlined. Jay didn't see it coming, and exclaimed in amazement that I could actually vomit and run at the same time. There was my first surprise. The last 100 would not have been official without a performance by the original Barf Queen.

Short Mountain is dark, and anything but short. It takes a lifetime to traverse that twilight zone. I just focused on my blue light and the moon rocks in its glow. With the muscle fatigue of almost 20 hours on the go, foot lift often falls ¼ inch short—causing a trip, followed by a grunt, *ouch,* and a swear word or two. Repeat as needed. I was really sliding into the grips of sleep deprivation, and at one point dozed off on my feet. I stopped and shined my flashlight directly in my own eyes, which Jay thought was not a good sign. We laughed and stumbled on. It was between rock-related expletives and route finding that we met Phil Hesser. Phil was just what I needed. He was running at my pace, and was fresh conversation material. Nothing makes the miles pass with greater pleasure or speed than a good conversation. Phil, a local, was loaded with just the details Jay wanted about distance, cutoff times, and pace. He was also possessed with a dedication to finish. Jay encouraged our teamwork.

Daylight found us "moving past trees and rocks as though they were standing still," to quote Red Fisher. Sunrise is always redemption for me. My sense of humor returns, and with it comes some unexpected strength. With Phil and Jay there for conversation, the miles just rolled along in relentless forward motion. The second surprise had come during the night and manifested itself in swelling of both my ankles. I'm sure it was just overuse injury from repeatedly stepping over the rocks that carpet Short Mountain. I added baggies of ice to the front of each ankle, secured with my gaiters. The pain and swelling would diminish for about 2 miles following each ice treatment, but then they would return. Jay was beginning to worry about cutoff times and suggested I waste less time at the aid stations. So I brushed my teeth while walking the trail, and tried not to let him catch me combing my hair or applying Chapstick.

My first sixteen 100-mile trail attempts resulted in completion. I felt invincible until the 92-mile mark of the inaugural Hardrock Hundred. It was at that time that I coined the definition of *DNF*. "Did Nothing Fatal." Once I discovered that there was life after a DNF, I looked at completion in a different light. I know now that running 100 miles is a greater percentage mental than physical. If I choose an event that I believe I can safely accomplish physically, then there is little to keep me from the finish line. Only my mind can change the outcome. I had chosen and prepared for the MMT 100 well, and the finish was never in doubt. Missing a cutoff was the only danger, and we worked hard to ensure that did not happen.

When the cutoff did get a little close for comfort, we just made a game plan to put some time in the bank. Phil told us the last couple of miles before Elizabeth Furnace (mile 95.9) was all downhill, and he led our charge. I am not exaggerating when I say we ran that downhill at a 7:30 pace. It felt like magic. The three of us had been discussing how very strange it was to have hallucinations in the light of day. But we were, and they were frequent and vivid. As we ran the 2 miles down in a hard running form, I jumped over a full 3-pound box of individually wrapped fine chocolates. Honest! Jay was so surprised by our quickened pace, he was sure it was just another halluci-nation. He kept saying, "I don't believe this!" There was strength and rhythm again in the Sunday-afternoon sunshine and we negotiated the rocky descent with style. I took the lead and arrived in the last aid station before the guys. I dropped my fanny pack and grabbed a bottle to head out for the final 5 miles. As soon as I was around a bend and out of sight, I jumped into the river for a quick "personal hygiene" moment.

Let me be perfectly honest here. It isn't about swollen achy ankles and knees, although the cold water does help. It's more about chafe, stink, and dirt. No kidding, it's the little things that count. The uplifting feel of fresh water inside shorts I had been with for 34 hours was heavenly. And rinsing the sweat from my hair was priceless. Who cares about wet shoes? As I hauled myself up the riverbank and onto the trail, cool water puddled in my wake. What a luxurious feeling! It took Jay and Phil a half-mile to catch my refreshed and rejuvenated self. I even had time to comb my hair in private! I knew nothing could stop me now as I practically floated the remaining 4 miles to the finish.

The emotional tidal wave of a 100-mile finish is a memory to treasure, and I'll certainly miss that ultimate high. I wonder if I will still be an ultra-runner when I drop my distance below 26.2 miles. I already miss the spot-light reserved for entrants during a 100, but many of the experiences can be shared by pacing, crewing, and race directing. Just as I did before my first 100-mile trail race, I plan to assist fellow ultrarunners who have the heart to reach for the century-mark finish line. The last 18 years and 110 ultra events have given me an inner strength that warms my self-esteem and guides me through periods of uncertainty in all areas of my life. Each 100-mile finish just reinforces that again and again. Nothing compares to the extended concentration of effort, or the reward. I finished my last 100 just like my first: with a smile on my face, and 20 minutes to spare.

His Heart Is Still In It

NAME: GENE THIBEAULT
AGE: 57
RESIDENCE: COLFAX, CALIFORNIA
YEARS RUNNING: 31
YEARS RUNNING ULTRAS: 20

Ultrarunning plays a large role in my life, although I am no longer able to run. I enjoyed a 30-year running career that began in high school, progressed to the marathon, and finally to ultras. My best years were in my late 30s and early 40s when I was able to run in the top 5 percent of most non-ultra road events. I moved on to ultras because I enjoyed the trails more than the roads and I was getting beat up from the speed work necessary to compete at that level. Ultrarunning gave me a new confidence and actually allowed me to change my job from a classroom teacher to a physical education teacher. It was more than just physical exercise for me. It was my social group as well. We ran every Wednesday and Saturday. It also provided an emotional release when stress came bearing down.

In the pursuit of my passion I had several injuries that required surgery. My back also became problematic, but I ignored the warnings and kept at it for several years. Finally after limping off a 100K racecourse after just 5 miles, I hauled my aching back and numbing leg to the spine specialists. I was given three different opinions, but they all pointed to the end of the trail for me. I would never run another ultra again.

I lived in Auburn, California, during the ultrarunning boom. That area truly was the hotbed of ultrarunning. I was a runner before I moved to Auburn, but could not fathom running ultra distances. I heard that there was a 100-mile race and I thought that was completely ridiculous. With curiosity piqued, I volunteered to work one of the aid stations at the Western States 100 in 1979. This was the second or third year that there was an actual race. Western States had a relatively small field of about

200 runners that year, and they literally came from all over the world. It was the only 100-mile race there was other than the Old Dominion 100, in its first year in Virginia. Working that aid station and watching those runners come through on their way to accomplishing such a goal really meant something to me. The next year I paced a man named Bill Weigle. He was such a great walker. I asked him where he'd learned to walk so strongly, and he said, "Munich in 1972." It turned out he was an Olympic race walker. He finished very well that year, mostly on the strength of his walking. The next year I paced Bruce LaBell, who ended up running fifth. He beat me to the finish line by over two minutes. By this time, I was hooked.

My first ultrarunning experience was the High Sierra Three-Step. This 3-day run covered about 80 miles of the Western States course. Prior to the Three-Step, I had never run any distance longer than the marathon. We did 35 miles the first day. We didn't know anything about drinking or proper nutrition. I carried only one water bottle, which didn't last long. There was one guy with us who had run Western States before. He carried water in an old Mrs. Butterworth's bottle. The rest of us were not that smart. We had horses carrying additional water but they stirred up so much dust that someone told them to ride on. Well, they did—all the way to the finish. It was so hot. After about 15 miles without water we drank out of Duncan Creek. Even with the creek water, we were very dehydrated long before reaching Robinson's Flat. We knew nothing about the physiology of ultra distance running.

My first official ultra was the American River 50 in 1982. I dropped out at about 41 miles due to swelling in my foot. I believe it was anterior tibialis, although I never would have known that at the time. I probably tied my shoes too tight and didn't know enough to stop and loosen them. I had that marathon mentality to "push on" no matter what. The next year I entered the AR 50 again, and the second time was a charm. High on that finish, I entered Western States in 1984. I had trained hard for the Boston Marathon, where I ran a 2:50. I tackled Western States with the same mentality that I had at Boston, which is no way to run a 100-miler. Despite cramping, I just kept pushing, running until I couldn't run anymore, then walking until I couldn't walk anymore. After 75 miles I was completely hammered.

I didn't finish a 100-miler until Wasatch Front in 1987. I managed to run about 75 ultras over my ultrarunning career, finishing 11 out of fourteen 100-mile events. I enjoyed running in inaugural 100s. I ran the first Vermont 100 finishing sixteenth, the first Kettle Moraine finishing eleventh, and the first Eagle 100 in British Columbia finishing tied for third. I also ran the first 10 Cool Canyon Crawl races and 9 American River 50s. My best race ever was the 1990 Leadville 100 where I tied for ninth. It was one of those races where everything happened right.

I got a lot out of ultrarunning, but it was at a high cost. I had three foot surgeries, and one knee surgery as my running career progressed, so things were obviously not good with my biomechanics. But it was eventually my back that got me out of it in the late 1990s. Because racing wasn't going well for me, I was doing some long adventure runs like running around Mount Ranier, and a double crossing of the Grand Canyon. I was having problems, but trying my best to run through them.

I knew things were pretty bad going into MiWok, but I thought it was just a hamstring pull. I wanted to do well because I'd finished strong there a couple of years before when I ran a sub-11-hour 100K as a 50-year-old. But my injury started getting to me. I had not been able to train very well going into the race due to the hamstring. Things got really bad on one particular uphill section. By the time I got to 5 miles I was limping. I just knew it was over. I walked 2 miles downhill to the nearest bailout point.

Desperate to find out what was wrong, I finally went to San Francisco to see the doctors who put Joe Montana together. They told me my discs were getting hard. They called it degeneration of the spine: wear and tear of the discs. Although they believed that my running exacerbated the condition, they told me that I might have been genetically predisposed to it as well. The doctors equated the degeneration to wrinkles: Everyone gets them, but some have more than others do. I do believe that running for 30 years contributed to my problems.

The first doctor looked at me and told me I would not run anymore. He recommended I take up swimming. I asked about surgery and he told me not to consider that option until I could no longer walk. He was totally dismissive.

The second doctor came very highly recommended. He told me he could perform surgery, but that there was no guarantee it would not get worse. I was still able to do a lot of things, so I wasn't willing to take that risk.

The third doctor was more conservative. He mentioned surgery, but again there was the risk.

I can put up with the pain and discomfort with the help of some medication. It is better than the risk of having surgery and ending up unable to do anything at all. My condition has stabilized, and possibly even improved a little. I consider myself lucky. I have another friend who was a runner and now spends much of his time lying flat on his back, in too much pain even to walk.

I have discovered that there is life after running. Do I miss it? Hell yes! I miss being able to run with my wife Deborah Askew, and my friends, and I miss the trails and sense of freedom that ultradistance running gave me. If I had to do it again, would I? Hell yes! But if I did, I would listen to my body more and not be so hard on myself. I would also put less focus on racing and concentrate more on the enjoyment of being with friends on the trails.

So what does an old injured runner do—curl up and die? Hell no! I lift weights at a local gym three times each week to strengthen my body. I also spend lots of time on the bike. I rode the California Death Ride (5 mountain passes in 129 miles) the last two years and finished the Leadville 100 bicycle ride this year with less than three minutes to go. It is on a parallel course to the famous Leadville 100 run. I got to ride the lead bicycle in the Way Too Cool 50K. I still help out at aid stations when I can, and I still read about ultras and get out on the trails as often as I can, hiking or biking. I paced a friend for the last 7 miles at Western States this year. I joined Deborah for the last two days (60 miles) of her 7-day John Muir Trail fastpack, and I have hiked numerous 14,000-foot peaks. Deborah still runs ultras and recently had a PR of 23:04 at Leadville. She trains with all my friends who are still able to run that kind of distance. She's happy, fit, and has had very few injuries. Some people can go on. More power to them. I'm able to go out and run short distances just to stay in that kind of shape. But that's it. I am still enjoying life, traveling, hiking, and biking; it's just a life in which I can no longer run ultras.

All runners have to stop sometime. Take my advice: Enjoy it while you have it, but realize that it will end. Ultra distance running can lead to chronic aliments that may lead to the end of your running career. A large group of friends from the Sierra Express Running Club have grown into our 50s together. Only a few are still actively running in races, and most of us run less than 10 miles at a time. Ending your ultrarunning career is just another part of your ultrarunning career. So take it easy, have fun, and make it last. And when it does end? It will be okay. There are other things in life. Trust me.

Joel's Story
BY ROBERT B. BOEDER

On July 7, 1999, eighty people gathered in the Silverton, Colorado, high school gym to attend a memorial service to celebrate the life of Joel Zucker. Joel, a 3-time finisher of the Hardrock 100-Mile Endurance Run, died the day after completing the 1998 Hardrock. Since the invention of 100-mile trail running by Gordy Ainsleigh and Cowman Shirk in the High Sierras of California in the mid-1970s, no other runner has died during or immediately following one of these events. At 44 and in great physical condition, Joel seemed an unlikely candidate for the Grim Reaper. Most ultrarunners, especially the people who do Hardrock, feel invincible. What went wrong?

Joel described himself succinctly as a member of a small select group of "short, ultrarunning, tattooed, Jewish librarians." With his penetrating blue eyes, he reminded Silverton dwellers of a Tommyknocker. Tommyknockers are the spirits of men who have been killed working in the gold and silver mines of the San Juan Mountains in southwestern Colorado. Like the 5-foot, 3-inch Joel, Tommyknockers have big heads, big feet, and short legs and bodies. They can be evil, but mostly they are friendly and mischievous.

Tommyknockers live underground in the cold damp mine world of utter darkness. The comparison ends there. Born in New York City, Joel lived joyously and gregariously aboveground. He graduated Phi Beta Kappa in mathematics and economics from SUNY at Albany; earned two Masters degrees; served as an officer in the U.S. Navy; and was a dedicated Popeye fan who enjoyed announcing "I am what I am." A computer geek, Joel co-founded the Internet Ultra List. Although he made friends easily Joel could be brutally frank. He angered a lot of people, especially with the way he managed the Ultra List. Like a good librarian, Joel proclaimed rules about what subjects he would allow to be discussed on the list. When a list member transgressed the rules he let them know about it in no uncertain terms. Eventually, his insistence on strict adherence to his rules led to the creation of an alternative list for ultrarunners that was more flexible in its subject matter.

An average athlete but tenacious competitor, Joel played tennis and other sports in high school and college and began running to relieve stress in his early 20s. He started with the usual short-distance races, then graduated to marathons. By 1993 when he entered his first ultra, the Elkhorn 100K in Montana, he had completed 85 marathons.

Obsessive-compulsive behavior characterized Joel's daily life. Everywhere he lived he needed to keep one place immaculately clean. He would scrub that area—a kitchen counter, table, or room—many times every day. He couldn't bear to have dishes pile up in the sink. He insisted on having all his clothes facing the same direction in the closet. A trip to the mall to buy running shoes turned into a major all-day event with Joel ceaselessly turning the decision over in his mind and discussing it with anyone who would listen. He hated loud noise and background sounds, would complain about a clock ticking and turn radios down so low they couldn't be heard. It's no wonder he never married and refused to consider having children. His aversion to noise was also one of the reasons he became a college librarian.

Joel's obstinacy resulted in a less-than-successful library career. No one questioned his ability to do his job. He was very good at it, but his passionate defense of his principles and lack of diplomacy made him a difficult person to work with. He never lasted very long at any one school. At the time of his death, his contract with SUNY College at Cortland had not been renewed. Job interviewers were put off by Joel's "New Yorker" abrasiveness. Usually he was either unemployed or underemployed, but he lived frugally and didn't care if he had a job or not. Dogs and running, especially the Hardrock 100, occupied Joel's thoughts.

Actually, the two dogs, a black Lab named Congo and Bob, a golden retriever/shepherd mix, belonged to Joel's partner, Gail Wood. She fed them, cleaned them, took them to the vet, and saw to it that they had their shots, but Joel took them out running. And they went out every day, rain or shine, even once in two feet of snow when the three of them ran around Gail's backyard for an hour. Joel had an intimate way of making friends with dogs. At the memorial service Chuck Haraway demonstrated Joel's technique of kneeling down on all fours and exchanging licks with his new canine pal. Most people keep their mouths shut tight when licked in the face by a dog, but Joel enthusiastically licked back in a deep-throat saliva swap that was one of his signature acts.

In March 1998, while chasing after one of the dogs, Joel fell and hit his head. He telephoned Gail to tell her that he had a gash on his head, and probably had a concussion because he was dizzy and couldn't focus his eyes. She asked him if he wanted her to drive him to the hospital and he replied no, he wanted her to find the dog. The concussion was only one of a long list of injuries and medical problems Joel faced. He suffered six stress fractures of his left tibia, chronic right hamstring tightness, runner's knee in the left leg, and scoliosis—curvature of the spine that resulted in foot and knee difficulties and made him tilt when he ran. As a teenager, doctors told Joel he had high blood pressure, which later resulted in periodic kidney failure that occasionally forced him to drop out of an ultra.

For years after he was diagnosed with high blood pressure Joel took medicine when it was convenient, but in 1995 he stopped. It may have been that he wanted to avoid impotence, one of the side effects of some blood pressure medicines. Nothing could make him visit a doctor or go near a hospital. His exact reason for refusing medical treatment couldn't be pinned down. He would just say, "What do they know and what can they tell me that I don't already know?"

The difficulty of the "wild and tough" Hardrock 100 appealed to Joel. The most challenging of all the 100-mile trail races, Hardrock advertises itself as a "post graduate" trail run consisting of 33,000 feet of climb and descent including 11 climbs over 12,000 feet of altitude. The high point of the race is Handies Peak (14,048 feet) in the rugged San Juans. Most 100-mile races have a 30-hour limit. The cutoff time for Hardrock is 48 hours. Novice runners are not accepted. Those who choose Hardrock for their first 100-miler are discouraged. Qualifying standards are strict.

When Joel applied for the 1995 Hardrock 100 he had finished the Arkansas Traveller, Mohican Trail, and Vermont 100-milers, but none of the more difficult trail 100s. Despite his stutter, Joel could speak clearly and be very persuasive when necessary and apparently he talked the Run Committee into approving him as a participant in the 1995 race that eventually was canceled due to deep snow on the course.

Even successful 100-mile trail runners fear the Hardrock race. Most of those who complete the event live at altitude in Colorado, New Mexico or Utah and specialize in running rocky trails on severe terrain in difficult weather. Hardrock is a strength race, and ultrarunners seeking fast times on the "easy" 100-mile courses stay away. Looking like a "scrawny elf," as Gail Woods described him, living and training in central New York State, afflicted with all kinds of physical problems, Joel was a poor candidate to enter the Hardrock 100, much less finish it.

He signed up for the 1996 race anyway, flew to Denver in late June, then took the long bus ride to the quaint but grubby ex-mining town of Silverton. Arriving eight days before the race, Joel helped Charlie Thorn, one of the race organizers, mark part of the course, thereby learning some of the route he would be taking on race weekend. Joel obsessed about the race, fretting endlessly about what he should put in his drop bags, how he was going to eat enough food to generate the energy he would need to conquer the long climbs, what the weather would be like, how to survive if he got lost, and how he could keep his wet feet from blistering and being too sore to finish the race.

Somehow he made it all the way around with 10 minutes to spare. Cannoning down the final descent in what became his trademark finishing style, yelling and screaming, laughing and crying, hugging everyone in sight, he completed the grueling event in 47:50, good for next-to-last place. The qualities that made Joel a washout in the eight-to-five business world—his stubbornness, refusal to compromise, and a certain meanness—gave him the ideal mental attitude to join a small elite group of Hardmen and Hardwomen, the Hardrock finishers.

After the 1996 race he had the Hardrock ram's head logo tattooed on his right bicep. He spent the next 12 months thinking and talking about the race every day and exchanging hundreds of e-mail messages analyzing the fine points with his pacer, Carolyn Erdman, and with fellow finishers Dana Roueche and Blake Wood. Joel was hooked. No other race mattered. Everything he did, whether it was mowing the lawn or finishing the Umstead 100-miler, was training for Hardrock.

The Hardrock course changes direction every year. In 1996 it followed the counterclockwise direction, deemed by race aficionados the more difficult of the two because the hardest climbs come late in the race. In 1997 it was the "easy" way around from Silverton to Telluride to Ouray then back to Silverton, but the course contained more snow than usual.

The Hardrock application form requests medical information including a list of regular medications that should be noted by the medical director, Dr. Lou Winkler. The Hardrock Runners Manual suggests medical hints for runners and crew members about what to do in case of injury or loss of consciousness. This advice boils down to keeping the person warm and informing the nearest aid station. Each aid station is equipped with a first-aid kit and is supposed to be in touch with race headquarters in Silverton via ham radio.

At the runner check-in on Wednesday and Thursday before the 6:00 A.M. Friday race start, runners collect their Colorado Hiking Certificates. The equivalent of a search and rescue insurance policy, the certificate entitles the holder to be rescued at no charge by the county search and rescue team. Also, at the check-in runners undergo rudimentary medical exams by an EMT or a physician limited to measurement of their pulse and blood pressure rates. Along with the runner's name and pulse rate, any allergies or medicines being taken are written on a hospital bracelet that is attached to the runner's arm.

At the 1996 race Joel's blood pressure was high. Kris Maxfield, who is an EMT and was co-race director along with Dale Garland at the time, questioned Joel about his medical history. Joel told her that pre-race anxiety always raised his blood pressure. No pulse or blood pressure measurements are taken during the race. Race organizers were concerned about Joel's health, but at Hardrock the emphasis is on personal responsibility. Runners are expected to be fit and acclimatized. They must carry their own food and water since they are on their own between the 12 aid stations, 6 of which are located in remote areas inaccessible to crews.

At the 1997 race check-in Joel's blood pressure measured 240/160, twice the normal rate. Medical personnel asked that he be tested again to make sure the first measurement was correct. It was. Since Joel had proven the previous year that his body could withstand the rigors of extended exercise at high altitude he was allowed to compete. Again, he finished yelling and screaming in 47:50, exactly the same time as in 1996, but in last place—which qualified him for the coveted Caboose award.

After each race Joel wrote a story about his adventure that he posted to the Ultra List. He tended to romanticize the actual events. In recounting a three-pitch glissade off the top of St. Sophia Ridge, Joel wrote that he "squealed with delight" during the 1,000-foot descent, referred to by runners as "the rocket." Dana Roueche, who was with Joel at the time, later commented that in truth Joel was screaming his head off in a total panic as he plummeted down the slope completely out of control. He also enjoyed describing his hallucinations during 100-milers and saw things appropriate to each race locale. At Umstead in North Carolina it was pirates and pirate ships; at Hardrock the rocks metamorphosed into animals and Native Americans as if the spirit of the land was calling to him.

In 1998, Joel returned to the San Juans a seasoned, hardcore Hardrocker. As usual, he stayed at Charlie Thorn's house in Silverton. Every day, like a marathon monk, he ran the same 13-mile training course up and down Kendall Mountain. Afterward he enjoyed hanging out on Silverton street corners joking with the other runners who were drifting into town. At the pre-race medical check the top number of Joel's blood pressure was 160—nearly normal.

The 1998 race was won in 30:12 by Ricky Denesik of Telluride, the former holder of the speed record for ascending all of Colorado's 14ers. Joel was 17 hours behind Ricky at the 70-mile point in the race, starting the climb up to Virginius Pass, when he was struck by a severe headache. The pain ebbed on his final ascent to the top of Virginius, but came back so strong on the descent into Telluride that he had to stop.

Once Joel reached the Telluride aid station he took some aspirin, and his pacer, Brian Scott, and course director, John Cappis, tried to convince him to lie down to rest in order to get the headache under control. Lying down was not part of Joel's race plan. He knew that taking any extra time at the aid stations would ruin his chance of finishing the race in under 48 hours. He refused to rest and somehow endured the last 30 miles of the Hardrock course to complete the race in 47:37, the fastest of his three finishes, in 37th place out of 38 (82 started).

At the awards ceremony on Sunday morning Joel was on top of the world, high as a kite, basking in the warm congratulations of well-wishers, telling Steve Pattillo, "S-S-S-Steve, I can't believe I'm th-th-three for th-th-three at Hardrock."

On Monday morning at Charlie's house Joel looked tired, but otherwise appeared completely normal. In a discussion with two other runners, the only health problem he mentioned was having diarrhea late in the race. When Brian Scott, his wife Sara, and their two children Luke and Anna, collected Joel for the ride to the Albuquerque airport Joel told them he was "fully recovered from the race." Joel rode in the backseat of Brian's truck goofing around with the kids who called him "Uncle Joel." They drove through Durango and stopped for lunch in Pagosa Springs, where Joel ate three enchiladas and half of Anna's burrito. After lunch he fell asleep.

On a remote stretch of New Mexico Route 84 between Chama and Abiquiu at around 2:00 P.M. Joel took two sharp breaths in his sleep. The Scotts knew something was wrong and yelled at Joel to wake up but received no response. Brian pulled his vehicle over to the side of the road and checked Joel's neck for a pulse. There was none. He hauled Joel out of the truck onto the dirt shoulder and began CPR. Brian's wife was waving down passing cars, and a state trooper stopped. After five minutes Joel's pulse came back. The trooper told Brian to start talking to Joel about something he had done recently, so he told Joel that he needed to finish Hardrock. Upon hearing this news Joel opened his eyes and tried to sit up. Brian asked Joel if he had ever had a seizure before. Joel looked Brian in the eye and whispered "no." Joel was able to move both his arms, but he started to fade so Brian asked him to repeat the names of the Hardrock aid stations back to him as he said them. Joel did this with slurred speech.

The state trooper had radioed for an ambulance. Just as it arrived from Espanola, Joel lost his pulse and stopped breathing. The EMT crew took over, restored his pulse and loaded him into the ambulance. Two people worked on Joel during the 30-minute drive to the hospital at Espanola. He was unresponsive. Riding in the front seat, Brian yelled at Joel trying to reach him but to no avail. Joel was gone, but efforts to revive him continued.

At the Espanola hospital, arrangements were made to airlift him to Albuquerque. Joel's mother, Lynn, in New Paltz, New York, was informed of the situation, as were Carolyn Erdman in Silverton and Charlie Thorn and Charlie's wife Andi Kron, in Los Alamos, New Mexico. As Joel's helicopter lifted off, a rainbow appeared in the sky. Brian and Luke drove to the hospital in Albuquerque where Joel was lying in a bed hooked up to a life support system. His strong heart was beating on its own, but he needed a ventilator to breathe for him. Brian spent some time alone with Joel, talking to him and touching him, but there was no response.

On Tuesday morning Brian was in Joel's room with him when the doctor told him Joel was not going to wake up. Brian brought Luke in to say good-bye to Joel. The doctors performed their final series of neurological tests. Joel was confirmed brain dead. Andi, Charlie, Steve Pattillo, and his wife Peg arrived at the hospital in time to say their good-byes. The cause of Joel's death was brain bleed, cerebral hemorrhage. His high blood pressure caused a stroke that killed him. His mother asked that his organs be donated; then his body was cremated.

The wind moans through Grant Swamp Pass, at 12,920 feet—Joel's favorite spot on the Hardrock course. It's a wild and desolate place. Forbiddingly steep scree slopes plunge down both sides of the mountain. At the top of the pass, a plaque decorated with a mountain range, a runner, and two dogs is attached to a rock. It reads:

> JOEL ZUCKER, October 6, 1953—July 14, 1998
> An inspired ultrarunner who loved dogs, the mountains and trails. A beloved companion, son and friend. He always had a word, a joke and a dog biscuit for everyone. Arf, Arf!
> Joel died shortly after completing his third Hardrock Hundred race. For him it was the ultimate challenge and his greatest achievement. May he run in peace.
> "Whatever you think you can do or believe you can do, begin it. Action has magic, grace and power in it." Goethe.

Following Joel's memorial service, a group of Hardrock runners climbed Grant Swamp Pass. At the top, each of them touched the plaque and said, "Hey man"—Joel's favorite form of greeting. Each carried a rock that was placed below the plaque, the beginning of a cairn that would contain Joel's ashes.

Could Hardrock medical personnel have done anything to prevent Joel's death? Difficult to say. Their duty was to monitor his progress as he passed through the three aid stations in the final stages of the race. Joel made his own decisions about his health. A severe headache should be a red flag to anyone with high blood pressure, but finishing the race meant everything to Joel and once he crossed the finish line, no one could force him to go to a hospital.

Joel's favorite lines of poetry were from Robert Frost: "The woods are lovely, dark and deep, but I have promises to keep, and miles to go before I sleep, and miles to go before I sleep." For Joel the promises were kept, the journey ended, sleep has come.

Bob Boeder is the author of several books, including Hardrock Fever: Running 100 Miles in Colorado's San Juan Mountains, *and* Beyond the Marathon: The Grand Slam of Trail Ultrarunning.

The Finish Line

Your alarm clock screams. It's still dark, and you just fell asleep two hours ago. You stumble around a dark hotel room (or campsite) looking for your favorite shorts, a bandanna, and the race number that was given to you along with that heaping plate of pasta the night before. As hard as you try, you can't go to the bathroom—which means that pasta will be with you for a few more hours. You walk out into the brisk early-morning air and look for the crowd. The crowd means comfort. And if you are lucky, it might mean a cup of coffee or a bagel as well.

The front-runners begin to gather over on the edge of the parking lot, and the race director has found his bullhorn. You are summoned over to hear the pre-race instructions. A prayer is recited, followed by some muffled cheers from the runners around you. Then it happens. You didn't hear any-one say "go," but the crowd is going, and you are going with them. You run ahead a few feet to get beside a stranger, who, unlike you, has not forgotten his flashlight. You follow the shaky beam of his light along the edge of the parking lot, onto the road, and after 100 yards or so, you turn onto the trail.

You are running an ultramarathon, and no matter how many you've run before, the rest of the day holds for you unknown adventures. At some point you might feel bad. Real bad. But you will not be alone. Your fellow runner may feel worse then you, but she will help you anyway. So will the volun-teers, the race officials, the crew members and spectators. Before you know it you will be feeling good again and having fun. You will make friends. You will laugh. You will cry. In the end if everything works out, you will cross the finish line with your arms raised high, and for the first time since your alarm clock went off many hours before, you will be able to stop and relax, and be proud. You are an ultrarunner.

I hope you all—seasoned ultrarunners to those who do not run at all— enjoyed these stories. Nothing would please me more than to have some-one tell me that this book got them into ultrarunning. So for any of you non-ultrarunners who are feeling inspired, motivated, or even tempted, please visit some of the following Internet sites, find a race that is right for you, and make it official.

UltraRunning Magazine: http://www.ultrarunning.com/
Stan Jensen's Run100s Web Site: http://www.run100s.com/
David Horton's Extreme Ultrarunning:
                         http://www.extremeultrarunning.com/

See you out there . . .